*Journal of a Georgia Woman*

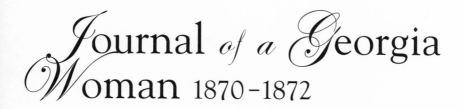

# Journal of a Georgia Woman 1870–1872

## Eliza Frances Andrews

Edited, with an Introduction,

by S. Kittrell Rushing

THE UNIVERSITY OF TENNESSEE PRESS

KNOXVILLE

Frontispiece: Fanny Andrews about the time of the trip to Newark, New Jersey. She wrote on the reverse of this photograph that her hair was much lighter than pictured. From the *Frances Andrews photograph album*, Mss004, Lupton Library Special Collections, University of Tennessee at Chattanooga.

Library of Congress Cataloging-in-Publication Data

Andrews, Eliza Frances, b. 1840.
   Journal of a Georgia woman, 1870–1872 / Eliza Frances Andrews; edited, with an introduction, by S. Kittrell Rushing.— 1st ed.
      p. cm.
Includes bibliographical references (p. ) and index.
   ISBN 1-57233-171-2 (cl.: alk. paper)
   1. Andrews, Eliza Frances, b. 1840—Diaries. 2. Women—Georgia—Wilkes County—Diaries. 3. Reconstruction—Georgia—Wilkes County. 4. Wilkes County (Ga.)—Social life and customs—19th century. 5. Wilkes County (Ga.)—Social conditions—19th century. 6. Upper class—Georgia—Wilkes County—Social life and customs—19th century. 7. Wilkes County (Ga.)—Biography. I. Rushing, S. Kittrell. II. Title.

F292.W7 .A52 2002
975.8'172061'092—dc21                                                    2001004329

*for my*
*Frances*

# Contents

Preface                                                                    xi
Acknowledgments                                                          xvii
Introduction                                                              xix

## *Journal of a Georgia Woman, 1870–1872*

1870                                                                         1
1871                                                                        35
1872                                                                        55

## *Articles by Eliza Frances Andrew*

Romance of Robbery                                                         61
Georgia: The Elections, A Peep Behind the Scenes                           68
Dress Under Difficulties; or, Passages from the
Blockade Experience of Rebel Women                                         74
Professions and Employments Open to Women                                  84
Southland Writers                                                          98
A Plea for Red Hair                                                       100
Paper-Collar Gentility                                                    104

Notes                                                                     107
Bibliography                                                              129
Index                                                                     133

# Illustrations

*Following Page 60*

Metta Andrews, Fanny's Younger Sister
Park Place, Fronting Military Park, Newark, New Jersey, c. 1875
Broadway from the Footbridge, New York City, c. 1870–75
Bennett Monument, Greenwood Cemetery
Tourists at Niagara, c. 1872
Annulet Ball Andrews
Judge Garnett Andrews
Marshall Andrews, c. 1864
Wilkes County Courthouse, c. 1855
Haywood's Front Gate, Summer 1867
Site of Haywood's Front Gate, Summer 1999
Col. Garnett Andrews
Frederick Andrews
Rosalie Beirne Andrews
Julia Butler Toombs
Cora Andrews Butler
Troup Butler
Arnold "Touch" Elzey Jr.
General Arnold Elzey
Maude Andrews
Fanny, c. 1879
Cousin Lucy Pope
Cousin Will Pope
Aunt Cornelia
Sophia
Hobbs
General DuBose
Andrews Family Servants, 1906
Andrews Family Plot, Resthaven Cemetery, Washington, Georgia
Fanny's Grave

# Preface

Fanny Andrews came into my life quite by accident in the fall of 1998, as I worked on an unrelated research project. I was searching through archival material—journals, letters, and documents—trying to find evidence of how people used mass media during the mid-nineteenth century. While examining the contents of a folio in the archives and special collections section of the University of Tennessee at Chattanooga Lupton Library, I found an old ledger tucked away among the papers of former Chattanooga mayor Garnett Andrews.[1] I opened the book and discovered neat, clear, woman's handwriting on page after page of what appeared to be a diary. The first pages had been torn from the ledger, but from what remained, I began to read: "number of pleasant acquaintances, and made as many more. Our special escorts, besides old brother Knowles, were Dr. Ford of Augusta, Mr. Phelps of Warrenton, a perfectly charming fellow, an educated Irishman named Walter Scott, and Captain Francis, the dearest man that ever lived. We arrived in Charleston by six A.M. had an elegant room and breakfast at the Charleston hotel, and then rode about the noble old city till noon."

I was holding the 1870 journal of a young southern woman describing a summertime visit to Yankee cousins in Newark, New Jersey. Here was a 130-year-old voice reaching across the years from 1870 to 1998. I could not stop reading. The diary's author was obviously well educated. She was also opinionated. She was intelligent, sharp-witted, and a skilled observer. I sat enthralled for more than three hours—reading the story of a southern woman's six-week trip during Reconstruction to visit her "Yankee kin." It was also a commentary on the victorious society of the northern manufacturing elite seen from the vantage of the vanquished southern aristocracy. The writer's observations continued page after page, presenting 1870 Newark through the eyes of an educated, upper-class southern woman. The diary fascinated me, too, because of its historical value. A number of wartime diaries written by Confederate women exist, but I was unaware of any significant Reconstruction-era journals.

Upon investigation, I discovered that this 1870 diary was the work of Eliza Frances Andrews, a woman recognized for an earlier work, *The Wartime Journal of a Georgia Girl: 1864–1865*, a diary that chronicled the last years of the Civil War.[2] Here was a continuation of that journal, written five years after the surrender, in a time of dramatic social and cultural transition. When Fanny Andrews visited Newark, the victorious Union general Ulysses S. Grant was in the White House. Former Confederate president Jefferson Davis, released from federal prison only two years before, was living in Memphis, trying to support his family as an insurance executive. The defeated Confederate general Robert E. Lee had recently assumed the presidency of the college now known as Washington and Lee. Radical Republicans controlled the United States Congress. The Haymarket bombing was about ten years away. The Gilded Age was beginning, and the United States was on the verge of financial recession. The country and its people were changing.

The diary covers only two years, but it reveals clearly the social and cultural attitudes of aristocratic southerners of the period. It also reveals the beginnings of change in some of those attitudes and beliefs. The diary shows the contrast between the hard-driving, profit-oriented merchant aristocracy of the North and the South's easier, low-key, class-sensitive elite. The cultural differences Fanny Andrews recognized, the conflicts she described, and the changes that began with her generation were to continue into the twentieth century. Andrews's 1870 diary hints at the beginnings of a changing role for women, and the diary demonstrates signs of change in the belief among the southern aristocracy that industry and manufacturing were pursuits only for the lower classes. Andrews wrote on September 12, 1870, after a visit to a factory owned by a neighbor of her wealthy New Jersey cousins: "It was a very interesting visit—and heavens! how it opened my eyes! I will never turn up my nose again at a manufacturing of spool thread. Cotton planting is nothing to it. . . . What a fool I have been! I know now that cotton planting and soldiering are not the only occupations for gentlemen, and I have found out that rich manufacturers are not necessarily shoppies and upstarts. . . ."

Fanny's changing vision was prophetic for her family, for within the next generation her nephews would become leaders of manufacturing in East Tennessee and North Georgia. Fifty years after their aunt's comments about manufacturing not necessarily being for "upstarts," her nephews, Champ, Oliver, and Garnett, would be running one of the largest folding box companies in the world. These nephews would be instrumental in founding the hosiery industry that became a significant element in the economies of North Georgia and Southeast Tennessee.

Fanny's diary gives evidence of the impact of the male-dominated culture, in both the North and the South, on talented nineteenth-century women. Fanny's diary, like her earlier *Wartime Journal* and several other war diaries—including Mary Boykin Chesnut's *A Diary from Dixie*—reveal women chafing at their tightly-defined antebellum roles.[3] Fanny's diary voices her awareness of those limits and her resolve for independence. She reveals in her diary on September 3, 1871, a determination to see that her young niece had options unavailable to many women of their social position: "I have taken Maude[4] in, and think she is going to be bright about her books. I shall do my best to give her a good education, for it is all I shall ever be able to give her, I expect, and it will make her independent. What would become of me now, if I were like Mattie Morgan, and most other girls of my class in society, who were educated only for show?"[5]

At about the same time she was recording her experiences in the diary, Fanny Andrews was sharing her observations and beliefs in articles she was writing for national publication. She probably was voicing the concerns and frustrations of many women of her generation, as her work was receiving national attention. Her reputation as a writer grew through the 1870s and 1880s. Years later, her earlier diary chronicling the last year-and-a-half of the War Between the States, *The Wartime Journal of a Georgia Girl: 1864–1865*, would also be acclaimed. The *Wartime Journal* is a classic in the genre of non-combatant Civil War era diaries. With its most recent release in 1997, the diary has been republished twice since the original 1908 edition. Andrews's *Wartime Journal* is important for two primary reasons. It is a graphic, first-person portrayal of the turmoil and tragedy of the Southern secession. The diary was written as a personal record, not intended for eyes other than those of its author. Its tone is honest, sometimes brutally so; and Fanny's observations reflect the social and cultural realities of the time in which it was written.

The second major importance of the *Wartime Journal* is the journal's prologue and epilogue. Andrews added these elements in 1908, forty years after the events and reactions chronicled in the 1864–65 diary. They represent the wisdom gained through maturity and experience. Andrews was twenty-five when she wrote the *Wartime Journal*. She was a matron of sixty-eight when the diary and her commentary were published.

Now, with the discovery of the 1870–72 diary, we are able to look at the beginnings of the transitional Frances Andrews. The diary reveals the genesis of change that would eventually give us the mature Fanny Andrews, who emerged in 1908. In her 1908 commentary, Fanny would then describe the two different realities as the contrast between "Philip drunk and Philip sober."[6] Her 1870–72 journal is evidence of the beginning of the sobering.

Andrews's attitudes, values, and beliefs recorded in the diaries are those of the nineteenth century; and that view, combined with her honesty of opinion, makes the diary valuable. The Andrews diaries provide a window into the culture, the politics, and the society of the period. Together with the 1908 material, the view is tempered with the reflection and wisdom of time.

I edited Fanny's diary sparingly. For example, in the diary she often writes "atall" for "at all." I left it that way. Fanny rarely inserted an apostrophe in contractions like "can't," "won't," and "didn't." I inserted those apostrophes for the sake of readability. Andrews also used the dash liberally. Those dashes remain as she wrote them. I used brackets [ ] to indicate major changes, corrections, or explanations; but for the most part, the writing remains as it appears in the original. Fanny numbered each page in the diary, and I indicate her original page numbers, which appeared at the top of diary pages, by enclosing them in parentheses, for example (115). The hand-penned numbers appear at the top outside corner of each of the original pages. I include notations to indicate missing or torn pages. Apparently, the primary editing technique Fanny described in her introduction to the *Wartime Journal*, she also used for the later diary entries—that is, she simply tore from the ledger those passages and pages she found objectionable.

Andrews's handwriting in the diary is clear and easy to read. There are, however, a few words that proved difficult to decipher. In the two or three instances where neither I nor my expert in nineteenth-century penmanship was able to make out a letter or a word, I included a question mark enclosed in brackets [?].

Fanny's writing began to develop a national reputation during the years just after the war and through the 1870s. The articles and this diary provide a window into the attitudes and values of the era. Taken with her private diary, her public writing gives insight into the challenges faced by Fanny and other women of her class. Fanny's public and private writing reflects the conflict she felt in wrestling with nineteenth-century constraints on women while recognizing the special place and considerations accorded to her gender. She was a female on the pedestal of southern chivalry. On the one hand, Fanny appreciated and apparently enjoyed the role. On the other hand, she chafed at the strict limits it placed on her. Andrews envied the freedom of men, and she promised herself that she would not become dependent on a man.

I have included six of Fanny's pieces that received wide exposure in the years around the time she was keeping the journal. The first of the articles, "Romance of Robbery," appeared in the *New York World*; and, as far as can now be determined, it was her first work to appear in a national publication. The second, "Georgia: The Elections, A Peep Behind the Scenes," was also published by the *World*. The piece expresses Fanny's views on race and politics during early Reconstruction. The third item, "Dress Under Difficulties," appeared in the premier women's magazine of the nineteenth century, *Godey's Lady's Book*.

Also included is an article written in 1869, "Professions and Employments Open to Women," in which Fanny expresses her distress with the limitations and restrictions placed on women while, paradoxically, applauding their benefits. The conflict is one with which she wrestled in several of her articles and novels during the next ten or more years—an independent, intelligent woman dealing with the restrictions of a male-dominated culture. Fanny shared this dilemma with many other southern women; it was in many ways the "distinctive burden" described by historian Drew Faust as one consequence of the South's defeat.[7]

The two following essays were written about the time of or just a little before Andrews's Newark visit. The two articles, as they were reprinted in 1870 in *Southland Writers*, revealed to the world the true identity of "Elzey Hay." Taken together, the six pieces and the 1870–72 diary demonstrate a maturing nineteenth-century woman dealing, often humorously, with the tragedy and the conflicts of a society and culture turned upside down. Fanny's writing provides first-person nineteenth-century testimony to twentieth- and twenty-first-century questions and observations about the socialization of nineteenth-century women and the world of separate spheres in which they lived.

In Spencer Bidwell King's 1960 edition of *The Wartime Journal of a Georgia Girl*, he observes that the journal really had two authors.[8] Both were Fanny Andrews. One was the young Frances—the twenty-four-year-old—who saw the collapse of the Southern Confederacy and recorded her experiences and her feelings in the journal. The second author, King wrote, was the mature Frances—the "gray-haired editor"—who, in 1908, at age sixty-eight, reflected soberly on the young rebel she had been a half-century before. Now, with the discovery of the 1870–72 diary, we have the privilege of knowing a third Fanny Andrews, the woman in transition. This Frances is verging on middle age. She is developing from the youthful rebel into the mature adult who, in transition with her native South, is surviving Reconstruction. She is developing and adapting with a new culture, a new reality. She is moving from the sheltered life of a privileged female of the antebellum southern aristocracy into the world of the transitional South. This Fanny Andrews represents women negotiating the transition from the tightly-structured, linear, patriarchal society of the nineteenth-century South to the more equal-gender or "degenderized" culture of the late twentieth and early twenty-first centuries.

Bell Irvin Wiley wrote in the introduction to *Confederate Women* that his interest in the women of the South came from the influence of his grandmother.[9] Like Professor Wiley, I am a child of the South, of mid-twentieth-century southern culture; and through the old diaries of the women of the nineteenth century, I hear my grandmother's voice, as did Wiley. I hear, too, the voices of other southern women of my youth—strong women, cultured women, women not afraid to take a position on what they believed; but women still limited by their culture to only a few roles. My Aunt Virginia, who devoted more than forty years of her life to teaching, influenced me as she guided and influenced hundreds of other young people. My tenth grade English teacher, Mrs. Doris Davie, was a woman who took gentle but firm control of her students and their lives. I remember Miss Martha Lou Jones, a sixty-year-old-plus American history teacher, sharing with her students the story from her own youth of a visit to her Yankee relatives, in many respects similar to the New Jersey visit chronicled in Fanny Andrews's diary. I still carry the influence of Miss Faith Stewart, who shared with my sixth-grade classmates in 1956 her then radical view that the 1954 Supreme Court decision in Brown v. Topeka Board of Education would have long-term positive effects for the South.[10] The women I mention are all long dead; but these women, in a way, were all resurrected in memory by the 130-year-old voice of Fanny Andrews's diary. These southern women—all intelligent, all educated, all influential in the lives of those they touched—were strong in their beliefs. They excelled in their world. They influenced positively the young people who came under their tutelage, and they were a part of the huge social changes that began with the South's defeat in the Civil War. Their students have continued the changes that began with Fanny Andrews's generation.

I believe that Andrews is too valuable to be lost in the dustbin of history, and I trust that this new material will provide additional insights into what Andrews and women like her contributed to our history and to our culture. In her 1984 *Making the Invisible Woman Visible*, historian Anne Firor Scott observes that Fanny Andrews, because of her time, place, culture, and education, was destined to be a leader—a "notable" of her civilization.[11] Scott analyzes the backgrounds of the twenty-three women from Georgia, including Frances Andrews, who were included in the 1971 *Notable American Women*.[12] In her evaluation of Frances Andrews, Scott concludes simply with, "She was, in the vernacular, quite a gal."[13] Using Scott's assessment of those variables that are shared by notable women, Fanny Andrews could have been nothing else.

# Acknowledgments

Recovering the life of Frances Andrews would not have been possible without the support, work, and advice of University of Tennessee at Chattanooga librarians Holly Hodges and Neal Coulter. Ms. Hodges's assistance in searching through old documents and photographs, coupled with her deep love and respect for the traditions of southern history, greatly supported the project. The librarians of the Floyd County Library in Rome, Georgia, provided access to archival material; and the assistance of Ms. Glenda Billingsley during the first stages of the research was vital. New Jersey archivist and historian Deborah Hall provided material and advice in developing information on Fanny's New Jersey connections. Rutgers University's Bernadette Boucher devoted a great deal of time to the project, asking in return only the satisfaction of her good work.

Elizabeth Dunn of Duke University's Perkins Library gave several hours of one of her busy mornings searching for Andrews related documents in her Rare Books and Manuscripts Collection. Shayera Tangri and Rachel Canada of the Southern Historical Collection at North Carolina, Chapel Hill, provided assistance in navigating Chapel Hill's famous and priceless collection of materials.

I appreciate, too, the encouragement and support of my colleagues at the University of Tennessee at Chattanooga. Dr. Felicia Sturzer's French translations and Dr. Verbie Prevost's insights into nineteenth-century southern literature deserve special mention. The University of Tennessee at Chattanooga and the University of Chattanooga Foundation provided a sabbatical and a small stipend to support the research on which this project rests. Jennifer Siler and Scot Danforth of the University of Tennessee Press, copyeditor Joanna Juzwik McDonald, and the reviewers Jennifer recruited provided invaluable criticism.

Much can be said about the generous people of Washington, Georgia, who helped so much in developing the explanatory notes that accompany Fanny's diary. Wilkes County librarians Celeste Stover and Charles Irvin, and historian "Skeet" Willingham gave generously of their time and their knowledge. In fact, many of the notes concerning Fanny Andrews's Washington, Georgia, family and friends are the result of the willingness of Celeste, Charles, and Skeet to share their time and expertise. Charles Irvin's memories of the families and the community are a treasure. Irvin volunteered hours to this project, checking facts and offering invaluable comments and corrections.

Washington native and Andrews family connection David Harris provided information, documents, books, and Metta Andrews's family photograph album, all of which came to him through the son of Fanny's sister. Harris's very special support for the project was generated only by his desire to help preserve Andrews family history.

Betty Slaton and her parents not only opened their beautiful antebellum home and guesthouse to my wife and me; they shared their extensive knowledge of the history of Washington and Wilkes County. Louise and Ross Maynard provide a special experience for visitors to modern Washington, Georgia, in their bed and breakfast. Maynards' Manor maintains a nineteenth-century ambiance for twenty-first-century visitors.

Everywhere I traveled in the quest to discover Fanny Andrews, I found the footprints of Charlotte Ford. In the 1980s Professor Ford began the work of rediscovering Andrews and Andrews's place in our history. I hope this work carries forward the beginnings made by Professor Ford.

The work of Corlyn Adams provided important genealogical information at a crucial time in the research.

I appreciate the support and encouragement of another "iron magnolia" of the South, appropriately also a Frances—Frances Alexander. "Miss Frances" can easily be recognized as a twentieth-century incarnation of the nineteenth-century Frances, with that same self-determined, "never give up" attitude.

Acknowledgment must also be made of the strong southern women who molded me, as well as to the dear ones who continue to provide their support. Most significantly, I thank my own Frances, a woman who smiles politely at my escapes into a world long lost but through diaries and my attempts at scholarship. My children, Sam, Callie, and Annie, tolerate their father; and their toleration means so much.

Any success or value in this work is due to the support and encouragement of those mentioned and to many others unmentioned. The weaknesses and failings of this effort are mine alone.

# Introduction

## The Balls and the Andrewses

Few, if any, of those who watched Frances Andrews's casket lowered into the ground that January day in 1931 remembered a similar scene sixty years before when Frances had stood in the same family plot and watched the burial of her mother. Almost sixty years, actually fifty-nine years to the week, separated the two burials. But, in a way, the mother had never left the daughter. Both women were exceptional. Both were intelligent. Both were strong-willed. Both were contributors to their worlds. The mother was described by those who knew her as one of the best-informed women of Georgia and arguably, at the time of her death, the most knowledgeable expert on Georgia history in the state. However, the mother's options were limited by the narrow range of acceptable roles for women in her antebellum culture. She was, as her culture expected, the benevolent wife and mother. The daughter's life marked the beginning of what would evolve over the next century into the unprecedented expansion of opportunities and redefinition of roles for women.

Fanny Andrews is a case study for Anne Firor Scott's argument that the Civil War was the catalyst that opened doors for southern women. Had it not been for the huge cultural changes that began with the crashing defeat of the antebellum culture of the South, Fanny, like other women of her class, would have remained locked into a role similar to her mother's— dependent and domestic.[1] The daughter's life was different. Because of the cultural and economic devastation following the defeat of the southern aristocracy, Fanny was forced to make decisions unknown to a woman of her class prior to Appomattox. The few women of the mid-nineteenth-century South who were prepared and willing, as was Fanny Andrews, began a cultural and social revolution of historic proportions and consequence. According to Fanny's diaries and novels, a large number of women of her class, including her sister-in-law Mattie Morgan, were neither prepared nor willing. However, Fanny's diary and her life attest to her place in the vanguard of the changes that began with Andrews's generation and continue into the present. Eliza Frances Andrews became a journalist, a teacher, an author, and an internationally recognized scientist. Her life spanned and reflected the sweeping cultural changes that occurred in the years from her birth in 1840 to her death in 1931.

Andrews was born into the genteel culture of the antebellum South's social elite. She was raised and educated to be the epitome of what Christie Anne Farnham describes as the "Southern Belle."[2] Andrews may have been raised as a southern belle, but she refused to be constrained by the role.

Eliza Frances Andrews, called Fanny by her family and friends, was born on August 10, 1840, the sixth of the eight children of Judge Garnett Andrews and Annulet Ball Andrews. There were three girls and five boys, one of whom died in infancy.[3] The Andrewses were lively, well-read, educated members of Georgia's upper-class antebellum society. The family certainly was not among Georgia's wealthiest, but as Fanny recalled years later, the family moved easily among the best people. Her father served for more than thirty years as a judge in the state's superior court. He owned land and slaves, and he was active in politics. Judge Andrews ran unsuccessfully for governor as a Know-Nothing candidate in 1855, and he served for a short time in the state legislature during the secession crisis. He was strongly pro-slavery; but he was just as strongly against Georgia's secession, correctly believing that leaving the union would be more destructive of the South's way of life than remaining. The judge's children did not share his unionist sentiments. Three of his sons joined the revolution as Confederate officers; and his daughters, without the Judge's knowledge, sewed together their hometown's first Confederate flag while hiding in a bedroom.

Both Judge Andrews and his wife, Annulet, traced their family ancestries to colonial America and to the patriots of 1776. Annulet Ball's family was among the first to settle in New Jersey. Her grandfather, Dr. Stephen Ball, served with George Washington at Valley Forge; and, according to family tradition, the old Ball home, Tuscan Hall near Newark, New Jersey, served as a meeting place for patriots during the Revolution.[4] Some evidence exists that the Ball family was related to the first Episcopal Bishop in the United States, Samuel Seabury; and the Seabury name continued to appear down through several generations of Balls and into the Andrews family after the marriage of Garnett Andrews and Annulet Ball.

Long before Annulet's birth, her architect father, Frederick Ball, moved from New Jersey to Savannah, Georgia, to make his fortune. Frederick apparently believed the new state would have need of architects, and he established himself quickly in the busy seaport's professional community. He married a Savannah belle, Elza Hoxey, in the early 1790s, and the couple settled in to the late eighteenth and early nineteenth-century life that was fueled by Georgia's booming cotton economy. Frederick became one of Savannah's leading architects during the first decades of the nineteenth century. He appears to have been proud of his profession if for no other reason than he named each of his children after an architectural style or motif. Annulet's eldest brother, Tuscan, was born in 1795. The older sister, Corinthia, was born in 1799. Doric Seabury came a year later in 1800. Ionic followed the next year. Annulet was the fifth child, arriving in 1803. Frederick's next son, Frederick, was born in 1809; and a daughter, Cornelia, in 1814.

Frederick was responsible for a number of buildings in Savannah, and he also accepted commissions outside of the city. One of those commissions was to design and build the first brick Wilkes County Courthouse in Washington in 1817. Frederick was attracted to the little town and its active society, and he bought property on the outskirts of the village, upon which he built a summer home. For several years before his death, the architect and his family spent their summers in Washington. It was during these visits that young Annulet Ball came to know Garnett Andrews—he, a young man aspiring to the law; she, a member of Savannah's social elite.

Garnett Andrews descended from Virginia colonists. Garnett's father, John Andrews, was a Revolutionary War veteran, who, according to family stories, took part in the siege at Yorktown. John was described years after his death as a "solid and substantial" man who moved from Virginia to Georgia sometime in the late 1770s or early 1780s. To John, as to many other young men in the years just after the Revolution, the new state probably seemed a good place to make a fortune. When he died in 1816, the estate that was divided among the eight children named in the will included a plantation, livestock, furniture, and slaves.[5]

John Andrews's wife and Garnett's mother, Nancy Goode, was also a descendant of early English colonists. Family records indicate that the Goodes arrived in Virginia from England sometime in the 1650s, and they traced their lineage to a Richard Goode who lived during the reign of Edward III in the 1300s.[6]

Garnett was born on the Andrews plantation in Oglethorpe County, Georgia, in 1799. He moved to Washington about 1820 and studied law with one of the community's early lawyers, Duncan Campbell. Garnett was twenty-nine in 1828; eight years after the death of her father, he married the twenty-six-year-old Annulet Ball. She was quite a catch for the young lawyer. Noted for her beauty, Annulet was well read, articulate, and not hesitant to share her opinions. In 1835 the young lawyer purchased a large, rambling plantation home for his growing family. The home was located on the outskirts of Washington, but within earshot of the town square. Dr. Gilbert Hay had built the house in the late 1700s; and the name of the house, Haywood, was a combination of its builder's name and the woodland in which the home was built. Years later, as a result of the Andrews family's financial crisis following the Civil War, Haywood and its surrounding property was sold. It returned to a descendent of the Judge and Mrs. Andrews when their youngest daughter, Metta, married Washington merchant Theodrick Green. Metta was the last owner of the old Haywood. In the 1890s, Theodrick and Metta had the house torn down, and they built near its site a Victorian-styled "New Haywood." A hundred years later, New Haywood still stands at the intersection of Greens Grove and Robert Toombs Avenue in Washington. Little evidence remains of the old home, although the modern Greens Grove is said to follow the old wide drive that once led from the main road to the front door of the mansion.

Fanny was born at Haywood, and the rambling house provided ample room for her large family. By all accounts, growing up in the Andrews home was a pleasant experience. Judge Andrews and Annulet were well connected politically and socially, and they enjoyed company. Guests were many and frequent. Mealtimes were affairs of good food and lively conversation about politics, law, arts and literature, society, and other topics of interest to the family and their guests.

Among the aristocracy of nineteenth-century Georgia, tiny Washington was a fashionable place to have a residence. In antebellum days, Washington counted among its citizens some of the leaders of Georgia's political and social elite. A number of wealthy families, including the Toombses, the Stephenses, the DuBoses, the Irvins, and the Mercers, built and maintained homes in the town, far from the plantations on which their wealth depended. The Andrewses moved easily among the planters, politicians, and warriors of their pre-war world. Years later Fanny described that upper level of southern culture as "the 4,000"—the four thousand aristocratic ruling families of the South's antebellum society.[7] It was within this social circle that Fanny and her brothers and sisters grew up.

Judge Andrews owned cotton lands in Georgia and Mississippi. The precise number of slaves the Judge owned is now hard to determine, but the number was sufficient to maintain the work of his plantations and to serve the family's personal needs. Servants filled the Andrewses' home. The girls had personal maids. There were cooks, housemaids, a coachman, a delivery boy, and a butler.[8] Fanny's social life before the war was one of attending balls and parties, making and receiving calls, and engaging in the other social activities that characterized her class. Young women of her time and position were trained to be accessories to the privileged young men. To fulfill their role, men were expected to be planters, military officers, or both.

Antebellum life was good for the Andrewses, but the fabric of the Andrews family was severely tested with the upheaval of the Civil War.

## Fanny before the War

Fanny was a precocious child, and for a youngster with her wide-ranging interests, Haywood was a stimulating place in which to live. The Andrews family library filled a room in the old house from floor to ceiling. The table in Haywood's entryway was always overflowing with newspapers and magazines. Fanny's earliest memories were of books, literature, and family discussions about current events. The hospitality of the Andrews plantation was legendary, and during Fanny's youth, mealtimes without guests were the exception.

As a girl, Fanny spent hours roaming the woods and the parkland surrounding Haywood, developing an interest in nature that became a lifetime passion. She brought home to her tolerant family and servants leaves, plants, rocks, and creatures she found attractive. Fanny told an interviewer years later that, during her childhood, nature was her only teacher. It had to be. Fanny was raised in a time and culture in which science was not always part of a young lady's education.[9] The wealthy families of Wilkes County provided two schools for their children—the Washington Female Seminary for the girls and the Washington Academy for the boys. Teachers were hired from the North, and the schools provided the best education money could buy for the community's elite.[10] Very little was provided for the education of children from lower-class families. A few plantations supported one-room schoolhouses for white children, but for Wilkes County children who could not afford school tuition, there existed no formal education during much of the nineteenth century. Public schools were not available in Wilkes County until the late 1870s.[11]

Fanny, like most of Wilkes County's upper-class young women, attended the seminary. From all indications Fanny was an outstanding scholar. She was ranked among the seminary's top students in 1856. However, because of an incident with one of her teachers, she was withdrawn from the school before her final year. The episode resulted when one of the teachers accused Fanny and a friend of some indiscretion. Fanny responded to the accusation by writing a poem poking fun at the idiosyncrasies of the accusing teacher. The teacher interpreted the characterization as mocking and disrespectful, and she demanded that Fanny either be expelled or write a letter of apology. Fanny refused. The incident became the talk of the village, and people began to take sides. Some of the young men from the boys' academy expressed their support for the young poet by parading, beating pots and pans, in front of the home in which the offended teacher lived. Fanny later referred to the event as a "tin pan serenade.[12]

Neither the teacher nor Fanny would back down. Judge Andrews determined the best way to handle the controversy was to withdraw Fanny from school. The judge then enrolled his unrepentant daughter in the senior class of LaGrange College, a new college for women about two hundred miles from Washington by railroad. The next year Fanny was graduated with LaGrange's first class, the class of 1857, although she was a member of the class for only one session. Fanny returned to Haywood, continuing her life as one of Washington's eligible belles.[13]

## The War

Washington, Georgia, reflected the South's turmoil during the political upheaval that led to secession, war, invasion, and defeat; and the Andrews family was a microcosm of the catastrophe. As Fanny described in her wartime journal, the family split over secession. Her father and mother were on one side, the children on the other. Judge Andrews was a staunch unionist. His children were secessionists. The father argued that the South had the law, the Constitution, on its side and should remain and defend its legal rights. Fanny and her brothers argued that the South was being forced out of the union, and if the South did not leave, then their way of life was doomed. The Judge countered—correctly, as time would prove—that, for their world, secession was a direct path to disaster.[14]

Georgia voted itself out of the union on January 19, 1861. The night the news reached Washington, citizens celebrated the new Confederacy with a bonfire and torch parade in the town square. There were speeches, songs, and ringing church bells. Judge Andrews refused to give his daughters permission to observe the celebration; and while he paced behind closed shutters in one part of Haywood, his rebellious daughters—Cora, Fanny, and Metta—hid in a bedroom piecing together Washington's first Confederate flag from material provided by their physician brother, Henry. Memories of that night lived with Fanny until she died: the town's jubilation, her secret work on the flag, her father's agitation and prophetic words of warning: "Poor fools! They may ring their bells now, but they will wring their hands—yes, and their hearts, too—before they are done with it."[15]

The next month, elder brother Garnett, with a three-year-old law degree and just recently admitted to the state bar, joined the Georgia Regulars of the new Confederate States Army. Garnett was the first Wilkes County man to go off to the army—a fact in which he took pride for the rest of his life. He was commissioned a second lieutenant, and within a year he was chosen by Gen. H. R. Jackson to be Jackson's adjutant and chief of staff in the Army of Northwestern Virginia. Garnett was seriously wounded in the last days of the war, as his unit attempted to assist President Jefferson Davis's escape from federal troops.

Fanny's brother Henry was a physician; and shortly after Garnett left for the army, Henry, too, offered his services to the Confederacy. He served as a surgeon in several units. Thirty-year-old Frederick went off to war as an artillery officer. He saw a great deal of action, and achieved the rank of major. Of the three Andrews brothers, Frederick had the most difficulty in dealing with his wartime experiences and the South's defeat. Family records hint that he returned from the war with a serious drinking problem. In a family characterized by success, Frederick never was able to find his place in the world of post-war Georgia. Frederick attempted a number of jobs, but he was unsuccessful in all. He never married, and died in 1890.

The first years of the war were bittersweet for the three Andrews children who remained at Haywood. Fanny, her teenage sister Metta, and their young brother Daniel Marshall were euphoric with the initial successes of the Confederate armies, but their joy was tempered by their father's refusal to embrace the rebellion.

Fanny's older sister, Cora, was married to Troup Butler, a planter who owned a cotton plantation between Albany and Thomasville in the southwest part of the state. Butler received a commission in the army, and after he left home, Cora took care of their two young children and managed the plantation. Because of its remoteness, the plantation came to be seen by the family as a place of safety and sanctuary as Georgia became a major battleground. So, in the last year of the war, when General Sherman's Union invaders turned east from Atlanta toward Washington, the seacoast, and Savannah, Judge Andrews sent his young daughters to the safety of the Butler plantation. Fanny chronicled the nightmarish travel adventure in her diary.[16]

As described in Fanny's diary, she and Metta were able to reach Cora, after a long adventurous trip. For Fanny and Metta, the several months spent with their sister was an exciting time of war, gallant soldiers, frightening rumors, parties, social calls, worry about their brothers, and worry about the approaching Yankees. Fanny's diary reveals her distress at the conditions she observed when her travels took her past the notorious Andersonville prisoner-of-war camp. The diary also chronicles their odyssey back to Washington and to Haywood.

The sisters returned to their home to find a community in turmoil, retreating Confederates, and the specter of invading Yankees. Fanny was witness to the last official action of the Confederate administration, when President Jefferson Davis and his cavalry escort, trying to escape capture by pursuant federal troops, stopped in Washington to eat and to issue the Confederacy's final orders. Union troops were not far behind, and within a short time, occupation soldiers became a daily affront to Fanny. She vented her anger and frustrations in her diary and increasingly in newspaper and magazine articles.

## Reconstruction and Newspapering

Not many issues of Fanny's hometown newspaper, the *Washington Gazette*, remain from the end of the war and the years immediately after, but from those that do remain, it is evident that Fanny's writing and the work of her cousin, Eliza Bowen, received a great deal of exposure in the paper. However, because Fanny and Eliza followed the custom of the time that the name of a lady should not appear in the newspaper, few of their articles are signed. Those articles directly attributable to Fanny carry the initials "E. H." for Elzey Hay. Fanny's selection of a pen name came from the family name of Confederate general Arnold Elzey. The Elzeys were close friends of the Andrewses; and General and Mrs. Elzey are mentioned by Fanny a number of times in her journal from the war years. General Elzey's son, Touch, was the one who brought word to the Andrews family that Colonel Garnett Andrews, Fanny's brother, had been wounded. At the close of the war, General Elzey's family lived for some time in Washington, or as some accounts relate, "refugeed" in the community. The second part of Fanny's pen name was taken from the name of the family home, Haywood.

Fanny's cousin wrote at times using the initials "E. A. B." or the pen names of Betsy Trotwood[17] or "Antiquarian." Fanny's surviving scrapbook of clippings gives evidence that many of her articles and editorials were unsigned in any way, but the scrapbook makes possible a fairly accurate attribution of authorship for many of the articles.[18]

Fanny's talent as a writer first gained national exposure when her description of a robbery and the subsequent heavy-handed investigation by occupation authorities appeared in the *New York World*. Apparently emboldened by the acceptance of the article, the young writer began offering other material to national media, and Fanny's southern perspective on the impact of Reconstruction began appearing in the *World* and other publications. Her views were expressed with humor and irony; but her writing is racist, patronizing, and—read from the perspective of more than a century —arrogant. Andrews's views probably accurately reflect the then prevailing attitudes and beliefs of her class. In a November 1865 *World* article Fanny gave northern readers her view of voting in post-war Georgia. The report, "Georgia: The Elections, A Peep Behind the Scenes," indicated that white people were not participating in the election, that rampant corruption characterized the Radical politicians, and that emancipated slaves were overwhelmingly ignorant and easily manipulated.[19]

A year after the *World* article appeared, Fanny described the plight of southern women as they attempted to maintain feminine wardrobes during the recent war. Continuing to write under the name Elzey Hay, "Dress Under Difficulties" appeared in *Godey's Lady's Book*, the most popular women's magazine of the time. Two satiric essays followed. Both were written in the late 1860s: one is on society's prejudice against red-haired women; the second is a none-too-gentle commentary on the popularity of paper collars and the degradation of the culture they represented. Fanny's opinions and her humor attracted national attention. About the time of her visit to Newark, New Jersey, "A Plea for Red Hair" and "Paper Collar Gentility" had been reprinted in a collection of the works of rising southern authors.

Fanny wrote frequently about race. She expressed repeatedly, both in her private and public writing, her opinion that the "race problem" was the major issue facing society. Her publicly expressed opinions seen from the twenty-first century are racist and patronizing. However, in the privacy of her diary, Andrews's observations seem less condescending. She wrote in her diary that, in her view, part of the South's problem was that Reconstruction-era white southerners saw the emancipated negro as a reminder of their own defeat. Writing on September 7, 1870, Fanny said she did not object to social equality "at the North," because "it is not a symbol of my country's degradation, and besides, there are not enough negroes (in the North) to make the question one of any practical importance." "At the South," however, the issue was of grave and long-term importance. Her opinion became stronger over time. She wrote in 1908, for example, that the Civil War and Reconstruction "brought forth as its monstrous offspring a race problem in comparison with which the Cretan Minotaur was a suckling calf."[20]

At home, the *Washington Gazette* provided a platform for Fanny's as well as her older cousin Eliza's political and social views. Fanny used her platform to defend the old regime and the class system it represented; and as she pointed out in 1908, her views in the 1860s were intensely class oriented.[21] She did not recognize—at least she did not recognize in her writings of the late 1860s and 1870s—what now, in the early twenty-first century, seem to be contradictions in her views on gender roles. In Fanny's private writings she said that she could not accept the role for which women of her class were trained; yet in her newspaper articles, she argued against women's suffrage. She wrote that women had more important responsibilities to the society than devoting time and energy to the political process. Fanny's public expressions indicated she believed strongly that men and women had different talents and were destined for different roles. A woman's place, wrote Fanny, was to protect society's morals and to advance the culture.[22] In an unsigned article that appeared in the *Washington Gazette* sometime in 1869, Fanny expressed delight with a group of New England women who apparently agreed with her views on woman's suffrage.

> We learn from a Northern exchange that some of the ladies of New Hampshire have held a meeting to protest against female suffrage. They declare it to be their opinion that the character and position of women both in social and domestic life—that their usefulness as wives and mothers, would be greatly impaired by the extension of the franchise to their sex, and therefore protest against having it forced upon them. We confess that we would hardly have looked for such an appeal from such a quarter, and are agreeably surprised to find that even in fanatical New England, there are left some women of sense and character—a chosen few who have not bowed the knee to Baal.

> The protest of these ladies is just and reasonable, nor are we included to think it premature. When we consider what rapid strikes the doctrine of female suffrage has made within the last ten years, and how the advocates have increased from a few contemptible fanatics to a very respectable minority (respectable as to numbers, we mean) of the politicians and writers of the day. When we consider that it is advocated by the ablest organ in the English language, the *Westminster Review*, it is but reasonable to suppose that the day is not far distant, when a practical experiment will be made of the political capacities of women. A people that have swallowed the camel of negro suffrage will not strain long at the gnat of woman's rights.

Whether women have the mental and physical qualifications for the exercise of political powers are questions not material to the point, so long as it is certain that the majority of women do not want them, that they are better satisfied without them, and are fully convinced that their extension would be a positive injury to the sex. It would certainly be a gross injustice if the men were to combine with a few fanatical women, and force female suffrage upon the whole sex, the great majority of whom do not want it any more than a majority of the Southern people wanted negro suffrage. If the question is ever brought before the public, we contend that it ought to be decided by women alone. We are so far an advocate of women's rights, as that we do not believe the male sex entitled to a voice in forcing upon them a responsibility that the best of them do not wish to accept. We say forcing upon them, because, if the elective franchise were once conferred upon the sex, the better class of women would be compelled to make use of it, in self-defense. It would not be optional with them to suffer the right to lie dormant, because all the bad and ignorant women would vote anyhow; and the others would have to do so whether they liked it or not, in order to counteract, if possible the pernicious influence of their unworthy sisters, and thus we should see many a gentle, timid creature, who merited better things, trudging her way to the polls along with rowdies and blackguards, and dragged through all the indignities and obscenities of a political campaign. The picture is a very revolting one to Southern minds, and there are surely very few of us who wish to see our wives and mothers dragged into an arena where we loathe to venture ourselves. If the thing is ever brought about in this country, it can only be done by a combination of the fanatics of both sexes. If left entirely to the women, as in justice it ought to be, we may confidently assert that female suffrage will never be a *fait accompli*. The responsibilities of social and private life rest almost entirely upon women, and the sensible ones know that they have enough to do without assuming the additional burden of public cares. One who discharges properly her duties as mother of a family, will not have much ambition to figure as the mother of her country. With regard to the women of the South, at least, we make bold to assert they will never accept women's suffrage, unless it is forced upon the country, as negro suffrage had been, and in that case, of course, Bridget and Dinah will have it, as well as your wife or my sister. Charming picture of equality for Southern ladies to contemplate![23]

Even as Fanny was supporting in her public writing traditional roles for women, in private she was crediting her pen and her education for giving her options unavailable to most women. She confided to her journal: "I am afraid my pen has spoilt me: it has opened such a world to me, and I shudder at any kind of a marriage, as a divorce from it."[24] Her aversion to marriage, expressed in an 1871 diary entry, echoes sentiments she expressed six years earlier in an 1865 entry when she wrote, "I am never going to marry anybody. Marriage is incompatible with the career I have marked out for myself. . . ."[25]

In addition to her newspaper editing and writing, Andrews began work on a novel sometime in the late 1860s. She was working on the project during the trip to New Jersey and during her mother's final illness, which is chronicled in the 1870–72 diary. The novel, *A Family Secret*, appeared to positive reviews in 1876.[26] In 1877 a serialized novel, "How He Was Tempted, A Story of the South," was published in the *Detroit Free Press* and was reprinted a year later in the *Washington Gazette*. The *Gazette* also carried on its front pages reprints of the positive reviews of *A Family Secret* from northern newspapers.[27]

By this time, Fanny's physician brother Henry was listed on the mast of the *Gazette* as editor and publisher. He may have been editor and publisher in name only. Some of the surviving evidence indicates that Fanny and her cousin Eliza were the people actually overseeing the day-to-day editorial content of the newspaper, a conclusion that could be reasonable in view of Henry's responsibilities as a physician with a fulltime practice.

"Cousin Liza" is now, more than a hundred years after her death, a shadowy figure in the Andrews family history. She was the daughter of Judge Andrews's sister, Sara Martha Andrews Bowen. Eliza's father, Isaac Bowen, practiced medicine in Augusta, Georgia, until his death in the yellow fever epidemic of 1839. Eliza was eleven years old at the time. For several years after Dr. Bowen's death, Eliza's mother operated what members of the family later described as "a fashionable boarding school." The school's French teacher lived with the Bowens for several years after the doctor's death, and it was during that time that Eliza became fluent in French. Her mother died while Eliza was still in her teens, and she was taken into the family of Judge and Mrs. Andrews. With the exception of several years in the late 1860s and 1870s when she taught school in Atlanta and Kentucky, Eliza lived in Washington. Like her younger cousin Fanny, she had both scientific and writing talents. Eliza authored an astronomy textbook that was published in the 1880s by the same company that later handled Fanny's botany texts. Eliza was a major contributor to the *Washington Gazette* and to other periodicals, and her example probably encouraged Fanny into newspaper writing. Fanny mentioned "Cousin Liza" often in her wartime journal. The older woman may have been a role model to the younger. However, the actual relationship between their orphaned relative and the Andrews children may have been strained at times. Fanny wrote that her cousin was a woman of unusual intelligence, but that Eliza was "full of amusing eccentricities that were a constant source of temptation to us fun-loving young people, and often got us into trouble with our elders."[28] Fanny's sister Metta wrote a curious tribute to the older woman when Eliza died in 1898. In the tribute, Metta revealed her opinion of her cousin's weaknesses as well as her strengths. According to Metta, Eliza's major "weakness of character" was a "lack of stability of purpose." Metta said that Eliza was unable to stick with any project until the end. Metta also wrote that Eliza had no practical sense. "She was incompetent in practical affairs of this world."[29]

Like Fanny, Eliza never married. She taught for several years in the Washington Female Seminary under the principalship of her cousin Fanny; and like her cousin, Eliza authored a number of magazine and journal articles, as well as the astronomy textbook. She continued to contribute regularly to the *Washington Gazette* until her death in 1898. At the time of her death she was working on a history of Wilkes County taken primarily from the material she had written over the years for the county newspapers.[30]

## Fanny's Fiction

Fanny followed her first novel with *A Mere Adventurer* in 1879; and then, in 1882, with a third, *Prince Hal; or, The Romance of a Rich Young Man.*[31] Andrews's fiction reflected public tastes of the late nineteenth century. It also voiced Fanny's views on the political and social realities of the era. According to Ida Raymond, a woman who reviewed Fanny's work at the time it was published, the Andrews novels were a favorite with women because they dealt effective blows to men, "the lords of creation."[32] On the other hand, a modern biographer, Barbara Reitt of Emory University, has written that Andrews's novels would probably seem overly sentimental to modern readers. Even so, Reitt maintains that Andrews's novels reveal ideas unorthodox for the period in which they were written. Fanny's heroines sought independence and fulfillment in artistic or literary pursuits, even though the women eventually abandoned such "strongmindedness" in favor of marriage, as Reitt observes.

Fanny's personal life did not follow her fiction, although her fiction certainly reflected her attitudes and beliefs. In one of her early articles,

"Professions and Employments Open to Women," that appeared in *Scott's Monthly Magazine* (Atlanta), in January of 1869, Andrews wrote of the difficulties that faced women who refused to "sponge" or "impose" on family or friends.[33] The article was prophetic. Within ten years and the loss of the family fortune, Fanny would be on her own.

In her novels she describes the problems women faced if they attempted to move beyond their narrowly defined roles. Fanny's fictional characters deal with the same issues she faced in real life. Fanny was writing *Family Secret* at the same time she wrote the 1870–72 diary. She refers several times in the diary to *Family Secret* characters—Audley, Julia, George, Uncle Bruen. In the novel there are oblique references to people and events mentioned in Fanny's diary, and a comparison of her diary entries with the novel reveals that she developed characters and situations from her own experiences. The emotional impact of the death of her mother clearly makes its way into *A Family Secret*. Fanny's description of Ruth Harfleur's visit to the grave of Ruth's mother, Nettie, could have been a description of a visit to her own mother's grave—even to the physical description of the "weather-stained cross." Her description of the emotions generated by the fictional Ruth's visit reflects real first-person experience:

[Ruth Harfleur] advanced a step, and looked around; there was no sound save the endless sighing of the wind, no movement save the trailing moss as it swayed to and fro in the breeze. She smiled at her childish terrors, and, opening the gate quickly, went and flung herself at the foot of the weather-stained cross that marked Nettie Harfleur's grave.

You who know what it is to kneel upon a mother's grave in anguish and desolation of spirit: you who have longed to rest your weary heads upon the cold turf above her breast, and to embrace the very clods that hide your treasure from your sight,—you can tell with what hopeless yearning Ruth embraced that senseless stone and poured forth her overflowing heart in prayer to the soul whose flight had made such a great void in her life. There is nothing like a mother's love, in heaven above or earth beneath, save the love that the great Father of us all bears to his children. It is so unobtrusive, so all-pervading, that, like the pure air of heaven, we hardly know what it is till it is gone. Unlike other human affections, it is self-subsisting and indestructible; we could not make our mothers cease to love us if we would. We may repay their affection with baseness and ingratitude, we may wring and break their hearts if we will, but can never harden them against us. The more we wound their bosoms, the closer do they press us to them; the more we are despised, forsaken, and cast off by the world, the wider do they open their arms to receive us. And how few of us ever think of all this, till the time comes when the memory of it mingles our grief with the gall and wormwood of remorse.[34]

Fanny's first novel reveals not only her emotional distress, it also repeats almost verbatim descriptions found in her 1872 diary of Annulet Andrews's death—images also shared in Fanny's letters to her brother Garnett. In the novel, Fanny describes Nettie Harfleur's moment of death: "She [Nettie's daughter, Ruth] heard the old negro say, pointing towards the dawn, 'Her spirit's flew out to meet the light, and the heaven-bells is ringin' for to let her in.'"[35]

In a letter to her brother Garnett on January 25, 1872, two days after the death of their mother, Fanny wrote: "It will be some comfort to you to know that mother died very peacefully: there was not a sigh nor a struggle, but the breath gradually came fainter and fainter, until just at daybreak, she fell asleep, and her spirit flew away to meet the light."[36]

A month after the letter to Garnett, in her diary entry for February 25, 1872, Fanny recorded: "On the 22nd of January, just as the first faint streaks of dawn were breaking in the East, her spirit flew out to meet the light. Never shall I forget the cold cheerless light of that desolate winter morning, as I stood looking out at it from our chamber of mourning, with poor old father weeping at my side, and how I stretched out my hand toward the light, and prayed her to come back."

Several wartime incidents reported in Fanny's diaries appear also in *A Family Secret*. Writing on January 27, 1865, in her earlier diary, the *Wartime Journal*, Fanny describes a story told to her about the horror of the Andersonville prisoner-of-war camp. Andersonville was a major stockade maintained by the Confederate army to hold Union prisoners. The facility became infamous because of the inadequate resources available to the Confederates to care for their prisoners. "Many of the prisoners were stark naked, having not so much as a shirt to their backs. He told a pitiful story of a Pole who had no garment but a shirt, and to make it cover him the better, he put his legs into the sleeves and tied the tail round his neck. The others guyed him so on his appearance, and the poor wretch was so disheartened by suffering, that one day he deliberately stepped over the deadline and stood there till the guard was forced to shoot him."[37]

The same story, retold with a happier ending, appears in *A Family Secret*, as Fanny's hero, Audley Malvern, searches among Andersonville prisoners for a man accused of being a Yankee spy. During their visit to Andersonville, Audley and his friend George Dalton, both Confederate officers, empty their pockets to the prisoners, giving away food, tobacco, and clothing:

> George even parted with his last cigar, after he had given away everything else and though the major vehemently declared that, if he had control of the battery up yonder, he'd have soon have the whole stockade and every d——d Yankee in it blowed to blazes, by Jove: Malvern observed that his hand went often to his pocket, when he thought nobody was looking, and before the close of their expedition he had contrived to get rid of his hat and his overcoat, too. The cause of this self-spoliation on the major's part was a miserable wretch whose wardrobe had become reduced to a single garment, and that a ragged shirt. The destitute creature, shivering with ague, and reduced by want and disease to a mere skeleton, had the better to protect his shrunken limbs, run his legs through the sleeves of the shirt, and tied the tail about his neck. His rude companions, rendered callous and brutal, as men always are, by herding together, saw only a subject for ridicule in the forlorn and abject figure of their comrade. Worn out with sickness, and wearied with their coarse taunts, the unhappy man—a sensitive Pole, who understood just enough English to comprehend their brutality—grew weary of his life, and resolved to end it. Covering his face with his hands, he was about to step over the fatal "dead line," fall under the muskets of the guard, when he was arrested by the major, and covered with the garments of that ferocious rebel. The major seemed very much ashamed at being caught in the act of giving "aid and comfort" to the enemy, and began to excuse himself as earnestly as if he had been detected in some abominable treachery.[38]

The story may also echo Fanny's continuing horror from her experience during the last months of the war when a train on which she was riding passed by the Andersonville prison.[39] She was still processing the Andersonville tragedy in 1908 when she reviewed again the circumstances that created the horror.[40]

*A Family Secret* is written from the perspective of the southern aristocracy, or, as Fanny called the South's elite families, "the 4,000." The novel details the turmoil experienced by the planter class, especially its women, as their world collapsed. Fanny's writing interpreted and reflected the disintegration of her aristocratic world.[41] She addressed in *Family Secret* the problems faced by unmarried upper-class women with no financial resources. *Family Secret* heroine Julia Malvern, a member of a southern planter family made destitute by the war, says of her needs:

> You see people marry for money every day, as well as for love, and they all job along together in pretty much the same humdrum fashion by the time they have been ten years married. The heroine of a love romance must come down at last to minding babies and sewing on buttons, woman's inevitable destiny, as prosaically as any of us; indeed, I am not sure but, in the long run Mrs. Major-General Bagpipe with her velvet and Venice point, her villa on the Hudson, her palace in Madison Square, her brilliant *salons* in Paris, will get quite as much of the romance of married life as any poor little dupe of a love-match, who wakes up after the honeymoon and finds herself tied to one who is but a mortal man after all, and not a hero or a demi-god at all. If no man is a hero to his valet, who can be one to his wife?[42]

Fanny wrote in an 1871 diary entry: "I wish I was like other girls— willing to marry anybody and be done with it. They all job along pretty much the same afterwards and it don't seem to matter much whom they take, so he is not a downright scoundrel."[43]

Fanny's creation, Julia, expresses to her brother George what may well have been Fanny's view that marriage could be a millstone to a woman without money. Julia hated the social pressures under which women of her class and financial situation lived: "'Contented poverty!' she repeated, in a scornful, almost angry tone. 'I hate the canting, ignoble words! Contentment is the virtue of base, contracted minds, and as for poverty, you may be crushed and broken under it, but there is no such thing as contentment with it. I have tried it now for four years, and the more I know of it the less contented I grow.'"[44]

Fanny, like Julia, struggled with the pressures to marry for financial security. She wrote in her diary, in a state of emotion similar to that expressed by her literary creation:

> I believe I will ask father if we are so bad off as to make such a sacrifice [marriage to rich old Sam Wynn] necessary—though I don't believe starvation itself could drive me to it. Yet, he is a very honest, worthy old fellow, spends his money free, and is by no means bad looking for a man of fifty, or thereabouts—but I don't know

what it is—I can't, and I won't. I am afraid my pen has spoilt me: it has opened such a world to me, and I shudder at any kind of a marriage, as a divorce from it.[45]

Probably it was Fanny's frustration with the place of women, their limited options, their restrictions in the culture of the 1870s, that were really being voiced by Julia in *A Family Secret*, when Julia says to her brother, the Confederate officer:

"... but with you men it is so different," interrupted Julia. "There are so many careers open to you, so many doors of escape, that you are not obliged to marry for money. Your career has not been cut short by our reverse of fortune. You have earned glory and fame in spite of our poverty, and that is better than riches. But the social arena is the only one open to woman's ambition; and who can enter there without money? There are no honorable professions open to us; the most we can do for ourselves is to maintain a plodding respectability, and I hate respectability. I would not care if I were a *poissarde*, or a washerwoman, for there is something admirable in the sturdy Bohemianism that snaps its fingers in the face of gentility and lives in blessed ignorance of respectability. Or if I had a literary genius like Mme. de Staël,[46] or a voice like Ruth Harfleur, I could endure being a woman and poor, for genius knows no sex, and I could then shake off the trammels of mine. Even if I were a piece of plodding mediocrity, suited to the mental tread-mill of the school-room, I might be contented and eminently respectable; but being neither a genius nor an imbecile, there is no place for me in the economy of woman's existence. There is no middle ground for us women except marriage—no door of escape from the miseries of poverty and dependence. I have tried every kind of 'honest labor' that a woman in my situation could put her hand to, but am utterly unsuited to them all."[47]

Fanny Andrews was not Julia, but Julia seems to voice Fanny's sensitivity to the realities of being a nineteenth-century woman. Fanny expresses in her diary thankfulness that she was not like her brother's sister-in-law, Mattie Morgan, and other women of their social class, "educated only for show."

After publication of the first novel, Fanny continued to express through fiction her observations and frustrations with her situation and the role of women. In her second novel, *A Mere Adventurer*, she portrays the heroine as an intelligent, scholarly woman saddled with two incompetent brothers.

The older brother has little ambition; the younger is consistently foolish. The salvation of the family falls to the heroine. Once again Fanny's dialogue contains observations dealing with the limited number of professions open to women and the poor pay provided to women doing the same jobs as men. In *Mere Adventurer,* as in *Family Secret,* Andrews, in the end, provides her heroine with an understanding husband who accepts and supports his wife's strengths and intelligence. As Anne Firor Scott observes in her comments about the later novel, Fanny was not subtle. She made a firm statement about the virtue of work for women.[48]

## Family Finances and Mississippi Teaching

In the years after of the South's defeat, the Andrews family's financial situation grew increasingly bleak. Brother Garnett moved to Yazoo City, Mississippi, in an attempt to salvage the family's cotton farm and to establish a legal practice. In spite of his legal and political talents, however, the former colonel could not forestall the inevitable; and the combination of Reconstruction taxes and the recession of the early 1870s forced the sale of the Mississippi farmlands. On the other hand, Colonel Andrews's legal successes were noteworthy, and his law practice flourished. He was eventually elected to the Mississippi legislature, and he authored a law book on the state's legal code that became a standard among aspiring Mississippi lawyers. Garnett's Mississippi sojourn was a mixed experience. He achieved dramatic political and legal successes, but he lost the farm, and his family suffered the loss of their first child, Rose. The family blamed their child's fatal illness on the unhealthy Yazoo environment.[49] Nevertheless, they remained in the delta town for about ten years, always fearing for the health of their other children. In 1881 Garnett closed his Mississippi law practice and moved his family to Chattanooga. There he established one of the city's more successful law firms, and he was elected mayor in 1891.

At the same time Garnett was struggling to save the Mississippi plantation, back home in Georgia, political infighting among the state's Reconstruction politicians was holding up Judge Andrews's salary for months at a time. The Judge's already desperate financial situation worsened, and Fanny felt compelled to provide more support for the family than was then possible from her writing only. As happened with many women of Fanny's social class, she reluctantly agreed to become a teacher, and was hired as the languages and literature instructor for the Washington Seminary. She held the position during her mother's illness and death in the winter of 1871–72. Judge Andrews died less than two years later on August 14, 1873. After the Judge's death, family finances reached the point of crisis, and the children were forced to sell Haywood and their other property.

Fanny left Washington for a Yazoo City teaching position arranged by her brother. Shortly after her arrival in Yazoo City, she was named principal of the city's girls' school, but her time in Yazoo may not have been happy. The superintendent of the Yazoo City schools was, according to family memoirs, an emancipated slave who could neither read nor write. The challenges for a person of Fanny's background in working for a former slave would have been profound.

## Washington and the Seminary

Within two years Fanny returned to Washington to become principal of the Washington Female Seminary, ironically, the same school from which, as a student more than a dozen years before, she had withdrawn under a cloud. Fanny apparently lived, at least for a time, with her sister Metta and Metta's husband, Theodrick Green. In addition to her responsibilities as principal of the girls' school, Fanny resumed her work as a regular contributor to the *Washington Gazette,* and she continued her study of plants. About this time Fanny presented to the Georgia Teachers Association her views on the teaching of botany in a paper entitled, "How to Teach Botany."[50]

The demands of teaching, school administration, and newspaper work were too much. Sometime in 1881 she suffered a debilitating illness that forced her to resign and leave town. She moved for a time to a private hospital in Atlanta, and from Atlanta she took an extended trip to Florida to regain her health. The exact nature of her illness is not clear in the historical record: whether the problem was an emotional or physical breakdown, or both, is not now discernable. However, the breakdown was serious enough to cause a near complete break with the school and community. She did continue writing, and a number of pieces from her six-month trip through Florida in 1884 were published in the *Augusta (Georgia) Chronicle*. She described transportation facilities, the economy and agriculture, the land, people, and the communities she visited, all couched in her personal experiences. As with her other writings, she did not disguise or soften her opinion.[51]

It was during this period of convalescence that she began to pay a great deal of attention to botany, an interest she had maintained from childhood. Andrews began a systematic observation and collection of plants, which she reported in an article appearing in *Popular Science Monthly* in 1886 as "Botany as a Recreation for Invalids."[52]

## Return to the Classroom

Fanny's recuperation in Florida provided her with the time to focus on her flowers, plants, and trees. Botany became a consuming hobby. In the years following the 1886 publication of her first scientific article, she researched, wrote, and saw the publication of more than a dozen journal articles and two textbooks.[53] She advocated studying botany in the field, not from text-books or indoor laboratories.

Wesleyan Female College in Macon awarded Andrews an honorary master's degree in 1882, and in 1885 Fanny returned from Florida to Georgia to join the faculty of Wesleyan as a professor of literature and French. She taught at Wesleyan until her retirement in 1896. The dozen or so years in Macon, Fanny later said, were some of the most pleasant in her life. She taught language and literature and served as school librarian. The summers she devoted to writing, travel, and collecting botanical specimens.

## Retirement

After retiring from Wesleyan, Fanny returned to Washington, accepted a teaching position in the public school, and began work on her first text-book. It was published in 1903 as *Botany All the Year Round*.[54] The Andrews text represented a revolution in the approach to teaching botany. Instead of relying on laboratory equipment and experiments, Fanny's book advo-cated using "the great laboratory of nature." The exercises contained in the text were practical and were based on easily accessible natural materials.

During the late 1890s and early 1900s, Fanny lectured on the Chau-tauqua circuit. She published frequently in the *Chautauquan* and in other periodicals such as *Forum* and *Century*; and she organized and led tours of Europe. In 1898, for example, Fanny led an eighty-five-day tour to historic sites of literary importance. Included in the lengthy itinerary of the $700 ("total cost") tour were stops in Liverpool, Stratford-on-Avon, Genoa, Frankfort, and Venice. The tour brochure suggested that participants read a fairly lengthy list of books before departing New York on the trans-Atlantic steamer, in order to be prepared for the experience.[55]

Fanny left Washington once again in 1903. She moved to Dallas, Texas, where she taught during the 1903–4 school year at the Patton Sem-inary for Girls. In 1911, eight years after the appearance of *Botany All the Year Round*, Fanny published her second textbook, *A Practical Course in Botany*.[56] The second text was translated into French and adopted for use in the French public schools. In addition to her research and writing, Fanny continued to travel extensively. She collected plants from all over the United States and from portions of Mexico and Europe. She moved to Montgomery, Alabama, to be near her younger brother, Daniel Marshall, and his family. It was in 1916, during her Montgomery residency, that Fanny donated her three-thousand-item collection of botanical specimens to the Alabama Department of Agriculture.[57]

Daniel Marshall died in 1918; and, as was done for each of Garnett and Annulet Andrews's children except Cora, his body was returned to Washington for interment in the family's Resthaven Cemetery plot. After Marsh's death, Fanny moved from Alabama to be near cousins in Rome, Georgia. She purchased a small house near downtown Rome; and following her long custom, continued her scientific research and writing while becoming active in the life of the community. Her last article, describing what she coined a "Methuselah of the forest," appeared in 1926 when she was eighty-six.[58]

Shortly after her arrival in Rome she was elected president of the local chapter of the United Daughters of the Confederacy, and she took an active role in several women's civic clubs. From her association with the Garden Club she pushed the city to establish a public forest for the use and enjoyment of Rome's citizens. In her will Fanny designated that the royalties from her botany textbooks go to the city to support the project. The will stipulated that if the forest were not developed within five years after her death, then the royalties were to return to the estate for distribution to her heirs. For reasons now unknown, the Rome city leaders did not take advantage of Fanny's legacy, and the money reverted to the estate.

At some point in the last half of her life, Fanny became a socialist. She began to see African slavery, northern industrialism, and the Civil War in terms of Marxist theory. She wrote in her 1908 introduction to the 1864–65 diary that the transition from chattel to wage slavery was a logical step in human evolution, "just as the transition from wage slavery to free and independent labor will be the next." As a sixty-five-year-old, she saw economic advantage in the transformation. She observed, ". . . capitalists and their retainers are fighting against it with the desperation of the old southern slaveholder against the abolitionist."[59] In 1918 she was serious enough about socialism to be listed in *Who's Who* as a practicing Socialist.

In 1926, when she was eighty-six, Andrews became the only American woman, and at that time only the third American to be nominated for membership in the International Academy of Literature and Science.[60] She declined the membership because of her age and ill health. She claimed her physical condition would not permit travel to Italy to deliver an acceptance speech; and that because of her increasing infirmities she would be unable to take an active part in the academy's activities.

Her travels were slowing considerably when she declined to make the long trip to Italy in 1926. Her visits to the Chattanooga nephews, only an hour or so from Rome by railroad, were also coming to an end. Those visits had been an important part of the family memory. A year or so after her death, Fanny's nephew Garnett remembered fondly Aunt Fanny's trips to Chattanooga with her bicycle, her plant collecting, and her stories of slave times, the war, and Reconstruction.[61] Fanny frequently visited her brother and his children during the last decade of the nineteenth century. Colonel Andrews was taking an active role in the city's political and business life. During his time as Chattanooga mayor, Garnett brought to town their brother Marsh, the civil engineer, to lay out what is now north Chattanooga, across the Tennessee River from Chattanooga's downtown. When Colonel Andrews died in 1903, his sons were becoming business leaders in the community. His son Garnett, Fanny's nephew, played a part in the creation and, until his death in the 1930s, management of the Richmond Hosiery Company, a firm that was part of the foundation of the huge hosiery and related carpet industry that now operates in north Georgia just south of Chattanooga. It was the young Garnett's eleven-year-old daughter Margaret, "Little Miss Mag," for whom a still existent nursery was set up and endowed as a memorial, after "Miss Mag" died from burns received in a kitchen accident at St. Paul's Episcopal Church in Chattanooga.

The son of Fanny's brother Marsh, also named Garnett, moved to Chattanooga and took over the ownership and management of one of the city's leading hotels, the Patten House; and he later became involved in Chattanooga's banking and investment industry.

## Class, Gender and Race

When she was in her sixties, Fanny said that the slave culture in which she was raised was rightly gone and should never be brought back, but she devoted a large measure of her energy to memorializing that bygone way of life. She took an active part in the efforts of the United Daughters of the Confederacy to preserve the history of the Southern Confederacy, a way of life Fanny believed had been made obsolete by what she described as economic evolution.[62]

Jean Berlin's foreword to the 1997 reprint of the *Wartime Journal* criticized the young Fanny Andrews for what Berlin termed Andrews's class-consciousness, her apparent insensitivity to the plight of the southern lower classes, and Andrews's "unabashed racist beliefs." Berlin took special note of Fanny's description and reaction to a "cracker" family written on February 13, 1865, when Andrews described her visit with another woman to recruit children for a Sunday School:

> I was surprised to find the wife of our nearest cracker neighbor, who lives just beyond the lime sink, in a cabin that Brother Troup[63] wouldn't put one of his negroes into, a remarkably handsome woman, in spite of the dirt and ignorance in which she lives. Her features are as regular and delicate as those of a Grecian statue, and her hair of a rich old mahogany color that I suppose an artist would call Titian red. It was so abundant that she could hardly keep it tucked up on her head. She was dirty and unkempt, and her clothing hardly met the requirements of decency, but all that could not conceal her uncommon beauty. I would give half I am worth for her flashing black eyes. We found that her oldest child is thirteen years old, and has never been inside a church, though Mt. Enon is only three miles away. I can't understand what makes these people live so. The father owns 600 acres of good pine land, and if there was anything in him, ought to make a good living for his family.[64]

Berlin wrote in her introduction that such statements revealed Andrews's "complete insensitivity" towards white people less fortunate than herself.[65] A contrasting interpretation is that Fanny, and others of her social standing, were very sensitive to class differences. In her 1908 introduction to the 1864 wartime journal, Fanny wrote: "To use a modern phrase, we were intensely 'class conscious' and this brought about a solidarity of feeling and sentiment almost comparable to that created by family ties. . . ."[66]

Fanny's intense class-consciousness reveals itself frequently in her 1870–72 diary. On July 29, 1871, for example, she described her appearance at a public concert in which the performers were not of her social level in terms that seem to late twentieth-century sensitivities at best quaint and at worst arrogant: "A public appearance on the stage, is, I think of very questionable propriety, unless made in the most immaculate company. I would not be willing to show myself, unless every individual in the company was my social equal. I am even more particular about my associates in any public theatrical or musical enterprise, than in the ordinary intercourse of life, because [in] a public audience containing very mixed, and often disorderly elements, it is very necessary to inspire respect."

However, the young Fanny's class-consciousness may not have signified a hard heart and a "complete" insensitivity, as Berlin claims. Several times during the trip to New Jersey chronicled in the 1870–72 diary, Fanny expressed compassion for beggars and what people of the early twenty-first century call "street people." Her concerns for Newark and New York City beggars, written for no eyes other than her own, seem sincere and from the heart. On the other hand, Andrews knew her place; and her concept of place, class, and character were the reality of her life and her culture.

Fanny's diaries reflect, on the one hand, a person who did not question nineteenth-century racial and gender stereotypes. On the other hand, Fanny refused to accept social pressures to marry and to assume the stereotypical role of a respectable woman of the southern upper-class. She recognized that, for her class and time, teaching was the only profession open to women. But she saw value in such restrictions. Fanny believed society benefited from the limitations placed on women. Commenting to an interviewer in 1911, she said:

> I lived in a period of history when women had to be worth while. Vicissitudes develop character. At the period when I began to work there was no profession open to women of breeding but teaching. Of course women of good social position could do anything honorable and not lose their standing after the war. But so few of us were prepared to work. The contact in the schoolroom with these women of refinement who had been reared in cultured homes was a great advantage to the children. And today the southern schoolrooms are filled with the daughters of women of that class, except that they have been trained to teach and do it better than their mothers did.[67]

It was Fanny Andrews's generation of upper-class women, women of the southern aristocracy of the nineteenth century, who began to break free of the dependence on men and marriage. Women of talent and drive like Fanny Andrews began to break down the traditionally structured, patriarchal culture that, until the mid-nineteenth century, characterized American and European societies. Many of Fanny's attitudes and beliefs changed over time. An older Frances Andrews believed that women of her class laid the foundation for education in the Reconstruction and post-Reconstruction South, if for no other reason than teaching was the only profession open to the best and brightest women of the nineteenth and early twentieth centuries.

Fanny died on January 21, 1931. She was ninety years old. Even in death she wanted things her way. She left instructions that after her final breath, to insure that she was in fact dead, a doctor was to open her chest and sever one of the major arteries to the heart. Her body was then taken home to Washington, Georgia. She was buried in the family plot with her parents; her brothers Garnett, Henry, Frederick, Marsh; Cousin Liza; and other relatives of their generation. Almost in keeping with the wishes she had expressed fifty years before during the visit to Cousin Lilla's, there is no epitaph on the simple marker over Fanny's grave. She had written in her diary entry for April 12, 1870: "I want only a plain granite or marble cross over me when I die, and if any fool does go and put an epitaph there, other than the name and date, I'll haunt him."

## Visiting Yankee Kin

In the summer of 1870 a thirty-year-old Fanny and her younger sister Metta, then twenty-five, traveled from their Washington, Georgia, home to visit Elizabeth Littell Ward, the New Jersey cousin of their mother. Elizabeth, "cousin Lilla" of the diary, was the daughter of Matilda Ball and Hobart Littell. "Aunt Matilda," actually Fanny's great-aunt, was the sister of Fanny's architect grandfather, Frederick. Aunt Matilda had died in 1851, twenty years before the visit. Matilda's daughter, "cousin Lilla," was married to Richmond Ward, one of the leading manufacturers of nineteenth-century Newark. Ward was a successful and wealthy businessman at the time of the visit of his wife's southern relatives. He is credited with developing the patent leather industry in the United States, and his wealth was based on manufacturing and industry—a difficult reality for the aristocratic southern women who came to visit. The Wards lived in a brownstone mansion on Broad Street overlooking a four-acre park in the most fashionable Newark neighborhood of the time. Richmond and Lilla's next-door neighbor, George Clark, and his brother William were the owners of one of Newark's largest manufacturing operations, the Clark Spool Thread Company. It was into this monied world of northern industry that the two southern women, Fanny and Metta Andrews, came in the summer of 1870. Fanny was gaining national exposure as a writer, and she was working on her first novel. She was struggling with the upheaval of her world, and she was beginning to question some of the "truths" on which her old world rested. The sheltered and privileged world in which Fanny had been raised no longer existed—dramatic and significant changes were taking place.

The events leading to the trip to Newark are lost, but the remaining record picks up with a description of the travelers' arrival in Charleston, South Carolina, where they boarded a ship for New York. Young women of Fanny's social class did not travel alone, and during the 1870 trip, the two sisters were under the protection of an older man, a family friend that Fanny names simply as "old Hobbs."

*Journal of a Georgia Woman*

# 1870

(115) . . . number of pleasant acquaintances, and made as many more.* Our special escorts, besides old brother Knowles, were Dr. Ford of Augusta, Mr. Phelps of Warrenton, a perfectly charming fellow, an educated Irishman named Walter Scott, and Captain Francis,[1] the dearest man that ever lived. We arrived in Charleston by six A.M. had an elegant room and breakfast at the Charleston hotel, and then rode about the noble old city till noon. On stepping into a street car, we had our first experience of practical social equality, in the presence of a negro passenger. It was apparent from the conductor's voice and manner, that he was a thoroughbred gentleman, and we soon discovered, in the course of the conversation that he was a nephew of our friend Mr. Tupper.[2] At one o'clock we sailed, and contrary to all expectations, did not feel in the least frightened when I found myself on the broad ocean, with Charleston and Sumter and Moultrie fading into dim specks on the horizon.

We had scarcely crossed Charleston bar, when Metta found herself so seasick that she had to go below, and scarcely raised her head again during the voyage. The motion of the boat was pleasant to me, and I suffered no inconvenience, except from the bad smells that pervaded it, and a headache that lasted me from Sunday night till Monday evening. We were only 50 hours out, and had the smoothest passage ever made: the sea was smooth as a lake, even around stormy Hatteras. The moonlight nights were glorious, and I spent half of them on deck, talking with the gentlemen, and sometimes we all sang. We had services Sunday morning

* The diary begins with page 115. The preceding pages are missing. From the physical evidence, the missing pages were removed with a sharp instrument from the binding of the ledger in which the diary is written. The missing pages, perhaps, contained the original of Andrews's *Wartime Journal of a Georgia Girl*.

and afternoon; nearly all the passengers were Episcopalians, so brother Knowles[3] read the service, and Dr. Vedder of the Huguenot church in Charleston preached.[4] There were a great many charming Carolina people on board, and we had all found each other out, and were good friends before sunset Saturday evening.

There were many Yankees among the passengers, too, and it was amusing to see the tacit understanding by which they and we rebels avoided each other. I offered one of the women who sat near me, the use of my prayer book during service, but had nothing more to do with her. We reached New York harbor just in time to see the famous yacht race. We came upon them just as they were rounding the light ship, accompanied by an immense fleet that looked like a city on the sea. Our Captain counted 43 steamers alone, filled with spectators, besides innumerable smaller craft. When we reached quarantine, we found that all the doctors had gone off to see the race, so we had to wait a couple of hours for papers, and our Captain put about, and joined the frolic. We were scarcely 100 yds from the Magic when she rounded the stake, and her victory was proclaimed by salutes from the battery and all the steam whistles in the harbor. I took very little interest in it, compared to what I might have done, had I known more yachts, still I could not help feeling a little excited, even over a Yankee victory.

We landed at the Charleston wharf in New York harbor, about 5 o'clock on Monday evening and were met by our cousin Mortimer Ward who had heard of the Manhattan's arrival a few minutes after it had been telegraphed from Sandy Hook.[5] He had a pleasant face, with beautiful teeth, but my heart sunk within me when I heard his awful Yankee Lingo. However, he took splendid care of us, and seems to be a real nice fellow, only so intensely Yankee.

We went directly from the steamer to Jersey City, and took the 6-10 train for Newark. I could have cried when I told all our traveling companions good bye, especially Mr. Phelps and Captain Francis, but they promised to see us in a few days—an engagement which Mr. Phelps fulfilled today. I was a little embarrassed when anybody takes trouble to come from a distance to see us, we expect them to stay all day or night, as the case may be, but Yankee ideas of hospitality are very different, and our rich cousin seemed a little embarrassed at having unexpected company to dinner. I like our old slipshod Southern way, that don't mind if things do go a little wrong, much better than this Yankee primness.

Mrs. Ward, cousin Lilla, as we call her, lives in an elegant brown stone mansion facing a beautiful park, on Broad Street.[6] There are great elm trees before and behind, where the birds sing just as they do at home, only we have English sparrows here instead of Mocking birds and Jorees.[7] The house is four stories high, besides the cellar, and though the whole front is not broader than our parlor, there is more available room packed under this narrow roof, than in all our great straggling old house at Haywood. The first floor consists of a hall and an elegant suite of three rooms, all furnished alike, and all very magnificent, with mirrors, paintings, velvet carpets, statuettes, busts, damask hangings, glittering chandeliers, china and glass ornaments—but no piano, and but one case of books. On the second story, are Cousin Lilla's room and ours, with stairway, water closet and bathroom between. Our bedroom is magnificently furnished, with carved mahogany mirrors that reach from floor to ceiling, and all manner of delicate ornaments, that are a terror to me, lest I should break some of them. The handsomest things in the house, to my mind, are the cornices over the windows of our bedroom: they are exquisitely carved in black walnut, and as it is impossible for me to break or damage them, the contemplation of them is an unmixed pleasure to me.

The bath room is another special delight to me, though I am dreadfully afraid of the water cocks, lest I should do some mischief to them, and I am really afraid my digestion will be injured by my fear of putting something out of order in the water closet, and there are two huge plates of imported glass in our dressing closet that are the terror of my life. The pillow cases are trimmed with fluted cambric ruffles, edged with valenciennes lace, and must be taken off every night before we go to bed, and turn where I will, there is some piece of finery that makes me feel like a bull in a china shop. Our cousin wears point lace and diamonds, and drives an elegant pony phaeton. We rode six miles along the Passaic on Tuesday afternoon, and have pleasant expeditions mapped out for each day. The country around here is like a cultivated garden, and so thickly settled, that it is like a village all the way.

Everything is so different from home that I could almost fancy myself across the water. But I like the old home ways best—this is all very grand and rich, but they don't understand genuine comfort here at all. Everybody cleans their teeth over the wash basin, and then turn on the water cock. I can't stand that and long for the slop tubs at home. Then, we never wipe on the same towel twice at home. Here no fresh ones have been put in the room since we came. There we can scatter our clothes about the bedroom & fling a newspaper on the floor when we are done with it, here we have to keep even combs and brushes in the bureau drawers, and the newspapers must all be laid on a particular spot on a certain table, as soon as one has read them, and so I am in constant terror again, lest my disorderly habits may break out sometime, unawares, and shock all my Yankee kin.

---

Cousin Lilla is as sweet and lovely as she can be, and there is a nice old lady, Miss Gardner, living with her, but I am dreadfully afraid of Mr. Ward.[8] He hardly ever comes where we are, and always behaves so queerly, that I cannot help suspecting his mind must be affected. He is very liberal however, and is always sending home some nice thing that he imagines we will like. He is a fine looking man, except for a wen on the right cheek, which, however, is partially concealed by his whiskers.[9] He is a rich manufacturer—cannot be worth less than a million. Our next door neighbor is a rich bachelor—Clarke's[10] spool cotton—a Scotchman, and an awful radical. Think of one of Walter Scott's countrymen being a radical! The Wards are strong Southern sympathizers and abuse the Rads like fury. I say very little, because I know that people very often abuse their own countrymen, when they don't like to hear others do it.

Mortimer Ward's wife Julia called to see us Tuesday.[11] She is a very beautiful woman, very, and fast. I do not think cousin Lilla approves of her very much. She has two shockingly bad children, who are great pets with cousin Lilla. Their mother is a pleasant society [lady], with plenty of small talk and loads of diamonds. Most of the fashionables are out of town at this season, and the bad weather has prevented our seeing much company.

Several persons however, have called already and everybody is so fine, that our clothes look exceedingly plain, though not so old fashioned I thought they would. I don't care atall, for somehow, in spite of all their finery and my poverty, I can't help a feeling of superiority, which places me entirely above all temptation to envy on the one hand, or mortification on the other. I belong to a family of eminence and distinction, and am a much grander personage where I live, than gold or diamonds could make me here, but let that be.

I am sick with a wretched cold, but a letter from home this morning, and Mr. Phelps's visit, have quite set me up. I almost feel like he was kinfolks, and the letter from home—it was charming to think how they missed us. Too dark to write any more, though I still have lots to say.

(121) August 13, Saturday—We intended going over to New York this morning, on a shopping expedition, but were prevented by rain. The weather has been very bad ever since our arrival, and I am sick from being pent up in the house. There are no piazzas[12] in this part of the world, and I never see people sitting on their front stoops, or under the elm trees, though the weather seems to me as hot as at home.

These Yankees, rich as they are have no time to enjoy life. Everybody seems in a hurry. The people on the streets go in a sort of trot that I shall never catch, and children are put through the park in as much haste as if recreation itself were a business.

We took a drive through the city yesterday afternoon, and saw some elegant residences in the suburbs, but they all belong to merchants or manufacturers.

Opposite one of the parks, cousin Lilla pointed out a row of elegant residences, every one of which was owned by some sort of *rich tradesman*. Metta and I could hardly restrain our laughter at the *naiveté* with which she gave information concerning them. "See that brown stone front to your left—two of our most fashionable belles live there—their father is in the leather business." "Mr. Jones built that large double house over the way—he made his money in the shoe business—and there, just beyond it, live the Browns—they are the leaders of our society—manufacturers of spool cotton—worth two million at least. The lady living in that four stories front, behind those elm trees, has the handsomest diamonds in Newark—her husband owns a trunk *factory*—he came here twenty years ago, without a dollar in his pocket." We are expected to admire these men very much, for making their own fortunes, and I pretend to think it all very nice, but can't help thinking to myself all the time, how much more I admire our Southerners for the way they lost theirs, and I can't help contrasting cousin Lilla's ciceroneship, with the way we show places in our part of the world—"That old house in the park, belongs to Judge King—the one who married Judge Pettigrew's daughter—no relation to your Roswell Kings, in Georgia, but a fine old family—Dungenesse, yes, that is the residence of the Nightingales—descendants of Gen. Greene —the Randolphs live over there, in that old brick house they are a branch of the Virginia family."—This is the way we point out places in Carolina and Georgia—without a word or a thought about the negroes formerly owned or the bales of cotton made there.

(123) Cousin Lilla has been showing me her diamonds and laces today, and they are magnificent. She has long pendant earrings, and a broach studded with gems, any one of which would make a handsome solitaire. Even her fan and parasol are covered with real point lace—Brussels point, and she has shawls of lace and cashmere, that almost make me stare with wonder. They sit well on her, because she is a genuine lady in spite of the lingo and the "leather business." She has the blood of the Seaburys in her veins, and what is better still, instincts of nobility in her heart.[13] She is a fine looking woman, and has cultivated manners. But I cannot get over my horror of that abominable lingo that all these Yankees have—It sounds so course, so unrefined,

that I can hardly realize it is the language of ladies and gentlemen—for there are some real ladies and gentlemen, even among the Yankee.

We are beginning to receive visits now from the few people in town, whenever the weather will permit, and I don't believe we have met any but millionaires, as yet. The more we see of Yankee society, the less we like it. This is not mere sectional prejudice, for I leave politics entirely out of the question, in forming my opinions—indeed, most of the people I have met, have spoken very kindly of the South, so I have no reason to fear them a grudge on that score. But there is a stiffness, a want of cordiality, a want of something I can't describe, that makes their manners utterly unlike those of our Southerners who are to the 'manner born.' For instance, when I first met my cousin Mortimer—whom I don't know yet how to address —I thought it would be too stiff and formal, after all our friendly correspondence with his mother to call him Mr. Ward, so after introducing him by that title to some of my friends, I turned to him with a smile, and said "But you must give me a less formal name to call you by, for you know you can't be *Mr. Ward* to your cousin."

"That's so," he replied, through his nose, turned red in the face, commenced playing with his fingers, and said nothing more, so that I don't know to this day what I am to call him. How differently one of my Southern cousins would have done. We'd have had pet names for each other in ten minutes, and he would have been joking me about not giving him a more friendly greeting than a mere shake of the hand. But Yankees never joke. One of the trials of my life here, is, that they will take everything I say in dead earnest, while at the South, every other word we speak is a jest. When cousin Lilla showed me all the modern conveniences about her house, I laughed at myself for not having been accustomed to them before, and humorously exaggerated my own ignorance. But she took it all *au sérieux,* and actually believed me so green, that she came in at night to show me how to turn the gas off! Mett and I buried our heads under the bed clothes and laughed till our sides ached, when she left the room.[14]

There is undoubtedly much to be said in favor of the great conveniences of Yankee housekeeping. I have hardly seen a servant since I came here, while at home, half a dozen darkies are rushing in and out of one's room continually.[15] Everything is served as if by invisible hands in an Aladdin's palace: turn a cock or pull a knob, and all your wants are gratified. But after all, I like our good old slipshod Southern ways the best. Water, sweet and fresh from the well, even if you do have to wait half an hour for a darkey to draw it, is much better than when brought for miles through lead pipes, and I sometimes feel as if I would be glad of a pretext to step out doors, if it were but to call a servant. There is a primness about a Yankee house, that keeps me in constant terror lest I should put something out of order. Everything is so tidy, that I can find no place to throw waste paper, and when I was vainly seeking for some place to brush my teeth over, Cousin Lilla pointed me to the wash basin, and told me just to turn the cock and rinse it out when I was done! Towels are folded up neatly and hung on the rack, everytime they are used, so that the same one is made to serve for ever so long, while we at home, never wipe our faces twice on the same towel. Napkins too, we have fresh at every meal, while here they are all put into silver napkin rings and numbered, so that the same ones will serve for a week. The Yankee way is much more economical and orderly than ours—but, I can't help liking ours best. Their tables are served in such a skimpy way that it looks like starvation, compared with our bountiful Southern boards. There is always enough—but nothing over—it is as if everybody's appetite had been accurately measured and allowance made for it. There is a little skimpy dab of butter in the dish, when we sit down, that I would be mortified to leave behind, on the table at home— and absolutely nothing left when we have finished. Yet I always get enough, and nobody seems ashamed to take the last slice of bread, or the last morsel of butter from a plate—while at the South, we would think it looked miserably stingy if our tables showed any perceptible diminution after feeding a score of people. The Yankees carry out everything on this little sniveling scale. In making change at home, we never think of so small a matter as a dime or a picayune, while here they are scrupulous down to the last copper, it is not uncommon for the children to buy a cent's worth of candy, just as they would a dime's worth with us. I spend all my pennies as they call them, on the beggars and street musicians, since I find they are glad to get them. Most people drive away these vagabonds, but I can't send them off empty handed—especially the poor little children. I dare say I am very green, and these sharp Yankees laugh at me in their sleeves, but I am not used to such scenes and they touch my heart.

The first vagabonds that came in my way were two Italian boys who made very sweet music, and I threw them a quarter—just as we would have done at the South, feeling half ashamed too, at giving so little, but they seemed perfectly amazed at getting so large a sum. That was in the morning: late in the afternoon, as I was standing in the window they passed by again, and looked up at me with a bow and a smile. Next day, came a poor little boy with a fiddle, and began to play. Mr. Ward turned him out into the street: he could speak no English, but began to plead in plaintive notes on the poor old fiddle, that touched my heart more deeply than words, and so came more pennies out of my pocket. The next beggar was a horrid old Irish woman, whom I knew to be an impostor, but gave for the sake of a poor little child she was dragging around with her. Since them, they come so thick and fast that I have to put each one off with a penny. Pennies are not without value here where people think of such little things. I really do believe this little skimpy way of caring for trifles, makes people sniveling and contemptible: I have not seen a manly looking man since I bid good b'ye to our Southern traveling companions on the boat. Mett and I have noticed what miserable little sniveling specimens of humanity pass along the streets: even Mortimer Ward, who is really good looking for a Yankee, is small and stunted, as if he had thought too much about pennies.

We took a long drive this afternoon, through Orange, and the splendid grounds around it. Some of the suburban residences are magnificent, and one, at a place called Montrose, belonging to a New York merchant named Volkes, is arranged in the most perfect taste: it is on a site commanding a beautiful view, and the grounds are perfect.[16] Most of the parks and grounds about here—especially the public ones, have straight angular walks that detract greatly from their beauty, but the walks in Volkes park are serpentine, and the trees are planted in clumps, so as to give a variety of wood and lawn. The turf here is of a vivid green, that we have nothing like at the South, and they have some lovely evergreens, such as Norway spruce, Scotch fir, and yew, that will not live in our climate.

The country around Orange and Montrose is a perfect garden of Eden—but the "trail of the serpent is over it all." The country is a Paradise—but the people!—the more I see of them, the more odious they are to me. Yankee society, the little I have seen of it, is horribly vulgar, and what I have seen, seems to be only a fair specimen of what I have not seen. Almost everyone of the elegant residences that have been pointed out to me are owned by people who have grown suddenly rich by the manufacture of shoe pegs, trunk straps, or some contemptible little thing of that sort—A Yankee manufacturing town like Newark is certainly not the place that one would choose for its society. Give me a thousand times over, our elegant Southerners, with their poor old dilapidated homes. I would rather today, marry a poverty stricken Southerner without a home, than be mistress of one of these splendid establishments with a miserable plebeian who knows nothing beyond the shoe peg and tape business, for its master. It is people, and not their surroundings, that makes society.

(128) AUGUST 14, SUNDAY. Raining all the morning. Mett and I put on waterproofs and went to little Trinity Church in the Park.[17] After dinner we went to see Julia Ward, whom I like more and more everytime I

see her. Several gentlemen were introduced to us there. Julia's brother, Leonard Bruen, is the only handsome man I have seen in Newark. We met a lot of Yankee beaus at Mrs. Thayer's this evening, and they were a 'sorry' looking set, as the Georgia Crackers say. I heard some of them ask cousin Lilla if they might call on Mett and me. I didn't hear her reply, but don't think we shall see many flirtations here. Miss Gardner, the housekeeper, is a nice old lady, but don't approve of men, and cousin Lilla has not much fancy for any of them, except spool cotton Clark who lives next door and is worth half a million.[18] Among the gallants at Mrs. Thayer's I met a Mr. Keene, who once lived in Augusta, and was a nobody there, but seems to be something of a swell here. Of course I keep my thoughts to myself, and am perfectly affable to everybody that is introduced to me—The slim legged gentlemen in spectacles and beaver hats, as well as the big fisted women in diamonds, but Mett and I let out our feelings when we retire to our room at night. It is mean, too, for the people are all just as kind and polite to us as they can be, and cousin Lilla is the very soul of hospitality and kindness, so far as we are concerned. Really, I must overcome my intense antipathy to travel and trades people—especially since one of my own brothers has gone into the business.[19] Well, it isn't their trades that I mind, but all these people do smell so of the shop—and the more diamonds and point lace they pile on, the more vulgar they seem. I am not ungrateful enough to mean any of this for my own relations who are so kind to me, for cousin Lilla is a genuine lady in manner and feeling and Julia is charming, though they do both talk in the harsh Yankee lingo.

Mortimer is quiet and a gentleman, though not an elegant one, like Garnett. But the shoppies they live among are—awful, to use a Yankeeism.

We attended Grace Church tonight, which is called Ritualistic, but I saw nothing to disapprove of except that the prayers were intoned.[20] I think it well enough to sing praises, but not supplications. Cousin Lilla's sister, our cousin Sarah Littell, accompanied us to church. She is a tiresome old lady, but I felt tender towards her because she is so old and feeble.

(130) AUGUST 15. MONDAY. Spent the day in New York, shopping, had no time for sight seeing, except among the shops. Was specially pleased at Macys on Sixth Avenue, and spent nearly all my money there. It is astonishing how soon one's money does give out among New York shops. We went to see our little hair dresser too, on the upper part of Sixth Avenue. She arranged our hair beautifully, and I left my braids with her to be made over. She was a nice accommodating little lady, and I felt quite interested

in meeting her after having sent her so many orders from Georgia. We took dinner at Ganch's, and shopped all over Broadway & Sixth Avenue. It is not worth while to describe here things that were familiar to me before I ever saw them. Stewarts', Arnolds', Fifth Avenue even, did not dazzle me very much, but between Broadway and Fifth Avenue, in front of a row of elegant Brown stone mansions on Fourteenth Street there was something I have never even described, which made a deeper impression on me than all the magnificence of Stewarts' or the prettiness of Macys. It was a poor old blind beggar who sat in a niche of the iron balustrade, with one poor with-ered hand stretched out in mute appeal to the busy throng hurrying by. There was a little placard in his breast, stating that he had been 19 years blind. He uttered no word and made no appeal, save with the poor sightless eyes, and the hand that lay always open on his knee. May God forgive all who know how to resist that mute appeal. I am sorry I gave him so little. It may be confessing myself a great simpleton, but I believe the most vivid impression I have brought from the metropolis of the New World, is the recollection of the poor blind beggar sitting in the street before the splen-did mansions of Fifth Avenue. It was Lazarus at the gate of Dives.[21]

(131) AUGUST 18, THURSDAY. A dispatch from old Hobbs, who is in New York, asking permission to call this evening.[22] Everyday brings crowds of letters—among them a dear sweet, bright little note from Mr. Phelps. My negotiations are still progressing with the New York Weekly. I saw a copy of it today, and it is awfully sensational—worse than the Ledger, if possible. However, I don't care, if it pays well: there is not much difference, in point of dignity between writing mean stories for the New York Weekly, and sloppy politics for the Washington Gazette. The papers say that my old friend the XIX Century has gone over to the Radicals. I feel as if I had been betrayed by a friend, or deceived by a lover. I felt something above mass mercenary interest in the welfare of that periodical: my heart was with it, and my literary career seemed identified with its own. To think, too, what dear sweet letters the rascally editor used to write me. I have not seen the last number, and of course cannot judge whether all that the papers say about its change of politics is true. I shall simply enclose a slip from one of the Georgia papers in an envelope to Mr. Hicks—with the words "Can it be?" and leave him to justify himself. Of course, my connection with the XIX Century must end, if its pages have been prostituted to the dissemina-tion of Radical doctrines, but the parting will be very painful to me.[23]

I shall not drive out with Cousin Lilla this afternoon, on account of letters to write. Yesterday we went 22 miles through Bloomfield and Montclair—

beautiful scenery and elegant residences. Two quaint old ladies called in the evening, and I was delighted with them. They wore beautiful grey veils, and had sweet old fashioned manners. They belong to one of the old Knicker-bocker families, and are not atall shoppy. I thought Miss Gardner was a right nice old lady when I first came, but she turns out to be the grimmest old spin-ster in the world: I am mortally afraid of her. Yesterday Mr. Ward took his first meal with us, and behaved like a bear. I was frightened out of my wits, but Julia Ward, who is one of the few people that can get along with him, told us that we must pretend not to mind him atall, and never let him suspect that we are afraid of him, and he would be affable enough. I followed her advice, and talked away at him all during supper. At first he snubbed me, then he sat passive, and finally was polite as on the first day, when he talked with us for half an hour. I put on a bold face, and pretended to feel perfectly at ease, though my heart misgave me all the time, and once or twice came near betray-ing me by a quiver in my voice. However, I suppose my tactics succeeded, for this morning cousin Lilla brought in two beautiful vials of Lubin's extracts, that he had sent as a present to Mett and me.[24]

He is very liberal, gives cousin Lilla just as much money as she can spend, and is always sending in something nice, but Julia says she is, very unhappy with him—and I don't wonder, if she is as much afraid of him as I am. He is the oddest man I ever saw: I believe his mind is out of order. Even Miss Gardner, who bullies all the rest of us, stands in awe of him. Julia seems to be the only member of the family who is not afraid of him.[25]

(133) AUGUST 21ST SUNDAY. So much to say that I have no time to say it. Spent yesterday in New York, showed around by old Hobbs. Shopped a little on Broadway and Sixth Avenue, then went to Central Park, where we spent the afternoon. I shan't attempt to describe it, for sightseeing, as a business, is a bore to me: I enjoy looking at all the beautiful things, but it tires me to be pushed around and told to see this or hear that. The music in the Park was superb, and there was a motley crowd assembled to hear it. We drove all over the grounds in an open carriage, and were rowed around the largest lake in an American Gondola. Our boatman was a very hand-some, intelligent boy, with a pleasant voice, and I quite enjoyed talking to him. It is perfectly wonderful to think of that large lake made and filled by human industry. There is no water worth speaking of, in the Park, except what is brought there from the Groton Reservoir. The Reservoir itself, an immense sheet covering over 200 acres, is a great ornament to the park. As a work of art Central Park is a wonderful exhibition of human skill and industry, but I like the works of nature better. Such imitations of nature

will do very well for people who can't have the genuine thing, but with all
its art, Central Park is not half so beautiful as the grounds around Haywood. It is admirable in its way, but there is an artificial air about it that
would weary me if confined to it always, as a substitute for Nature. After
the Park, we dined at Taylor's celebrated Restaurant on Broadway, and lin-
gered so long over our roast duck, champagne and ice cream, that we were
too late at the ferry, and did not reach Newark till nearly 10. P.M. Tomorrow, we go to New York again, to shop, and see our little hair dresser, who
is rearranging my braids into an elegant chignon. Today has been quiet.
We went to the Presbyterian church in the morning, out of deference to
the she dragon, Mrs. Gardner, who was beginning to take offense at our
Episcopalian predilections.[26] Tonight, we go to the "House of Prayer"—an
honest downright high church place which will be a relief after our dry
Presbyterian sermon of the morning.[27]

Everyday we have rides and drives and somebody to see. The people
here are perfectly horrid, and all that I see confirms my former impressions
of Yankee society. Money flash, and vulgarity. Thank heaven, I am a Southerner, and have Southerners for my associates. The he-Yankees are as contemptible as their females are vulgar: little sniveling scrubby wretches—it
would take three of them to make a good tall Southerner. The only good
looking men I have seen since landing in N. Y. are the policemen, who are
big and strong at any rate, and I believe the little dressmaker who fashioned my silk cloak, and two poor little milliners across the street, are the
most thorough ladies I have met. Everybody is so loud and flashy. My
cousin is a handsome, lady like person; but she shuts us up in the dark to
keep the sun from fading her carpet, and does other little skimpy Yankee
tricks at home, while she wears point lace and diamonds. There is the difference: we poor rebs make ourselves comfortable if we can't be grand; we
don't wear diamonds, but we don't mind if the carpet gets spoiled: we'll
get a new one, instead of diamonds. In this fine house each person has a
clean towel every Sunday morning—at home, nobody uses the same
towel twice. Everything is as methodical here as clock work: there is one
day in the week for sweeping, another for washing windows, another for
clean table linen &c. At home we sweep the floors and wash the windows
whenever they get dirty, and change table linen everyday. There is my
cousin Mortimer down stairs. I must go.

(135) AUGUST 23, TUESDAY. So much to say that I have no time to say it
in. On Monday, Mett and I undertook our first expedition to N. Y. alone,
and had no difficulty in finding our way. In the evening we had crowds of

company. The fashionables are slowly returning to the city, and the Yankee swells are beginning to call on us. We had three last night, one of them, Mr. Peck, was a really nice gentleman, but there was one little prig named Scott, who entertained us with the exploits of his brother—a staff officer of one of *Beast Butler's*[28] generals—during the war, and informed us, among other things, that his brother was so well pleased "down South," that the family were really very much afraid, at one time, that he was going to marry a Southerner! Smart boy that: I wonder who is his ma?[29]

This evening at the Miller's, we met the nicest Yankee I have seen yet. His name is Leslie, and he really is a polished gentleman, and not a bit shoppy. He is not a millionaire, I believe, and has not been in the shoe peg or paper box manufacturing business. His society, and a letter from Mr. Phelps, enabled me to endure the other people I had to meet. There is no doubt about it, the general tone of society here is perfectly horrid— though of course there are exceptions, like the Bruens,[30] the Garthwaites, Mr. Leslie, and those charming Miller girls. We were out this afternoon returning some of our calls, and among other places, we went to see two old lady cousins, Mrs. Burnet and Mrs. Robinson, or as we call them, cousin Nancy and cousin Hetty. They are two stately old widow ladies, who live together in a great fine house, and wear black satin dresses, with white ruffs. They looked so quaint and grand, that I should have been somewhat over-awed, but the kind cordial welcome they gave me. We have another old lady cousin living in a pretty cottage over on the outskirts of Newark, whom I am particularly charmed with. She is the veritable *Experience Ball*,[31] whose puritan name in the family pedigree once excited so much ridicule among her cavalier cousins in the South, and is a sister of the Hannah Ball, whose name we laughed at too. She has a portrait of Hannah, which is one of the most beautiful things I ever looked at: the face is like a madonna. Cousin Hannah has been dead for a number of years. She was a Mrs. Meade, the wife of a rich man who lived on Fifth Avenue, a Yankee heaven. She was a leader of fashion in her day, went to Europe every summer, and owned one of the most elegant country residences in New Jersey. So much for Hannah, "What's in a Name?" &c.[32]

Experience Ball—cousin Peri[33] as we call her, is a little bright-eyed active old lady of 72—who lives alone with her husband, Mr. Camp,[34] in a little cottage as quaint and prim as her name. The furniture is very handsome, but old fashioned—which is a relief after the brash new gew-gaws of the shoepeg aristocracy, and her garden is filled with bright old fashioned flowers such as marigolds, zinnias, prince's feather, &c. She to [sic] was dressed in black satin, though we surprised her on preserving day, and she keeps no servant. Who but a Yankee could do that? Upon the whole, I like my Yankee kin very much, and to tell the truth, the kindness and consideration with which Mett & I are treated by everybody, makes me feel quite ashamed of way we snub Yankees "down South." I have heard nothing but expressions of kindness and sympathy for the South—except from that fool who didn't know any better: even those who think we were wrong, seem to feel a genuine pity for our misfortunes, and treat us with extra consideration, because we are Southerners, so that I feel quite compunctious to think of the extra contempt I feel for them because they are Yankees. Sometimes, when people who call on me, remark that they have a brother or a sister at the South, I feel half ashamed to think of the contempt with which all Yankees are treated there, and a kind of sneaky feeling comes over me, as if I know something dishonest, in accepting the courtesies that are extended to me, when I have always treated their countrymen with studied indifference and reserve. I am not going to do so any more. Though I hate Yankees in the aggregate, worse than ever, yet I am under obligations to individuals, and I will not be ungrateful. In future, whenever I meet a decent Yankee at the South, I shall make it a point to be polite to him—though of course, I don't mean to have anything to do with carpetbaggers, and school marm's and radicals. But I shan't encourage indiscriminate and wholesale proscription of them any more.[35]

AUGUST 26. FRIDAY. We had a delightful ride this afternoon, to see a glorious view from a place called Eagle Rock,[36] some five or six miles from Newark. How these Yankees do fix up everything! The road up the mountain, as they call it, though it is only a big hill, was beautifully turnpiked, and planted with hedges, and the edge of the precipice all railed in. It was very nice but such evidences of the hand of man seem a little obtrusive in such wild solitudes of Nature. We returned home through a place called Llewellyn Park, that far surpasses the famous Central, of New York. It is on the slope of the hills below Eagle Rock, and is composed of the private grounds and country residences of rich merchants and manufacturers of New York and Newark. Instead of fencing in each lot separately, some dozen or more, are walled in together, making a huge park and a very picturesque one: it is not so artificial as Central Park, but far more beautiful, for that very reason. The natural advantages are fine, and art has done just enough to improve upon, but not supersede nature.[37]

In the evening, we had crowds of company. Julia Ward took tea with us, and among the visitors, were a Mr. and Mrs. Van Antwerp, two of the most charming people I have met in a long time: he lived at the South a great number of years. Our next door neighbor, Spool Cotton Clarke, called too, and I never was more surprised in a man, in all my life. Instead of a vulgar old codger, with no thought beyond making money, I found him one of the most intelligent and cultivated men I ever met. He staid [*sic*] till nearly twelve o'clock, and I was perfectly delighted with him, though he is stout and bald headed, and a radical. But he has never been naturalized, and can't vote, so that don't hurt: he has just the faintest little touch of Scotch brogue in his voice, which is very pretty. I am not going to call him Spool Cotton Clarke any more, but, George A. or George W., or whatever his name may be. It shows he has good taste never being naturalized: I don't see why any man should ever want to give up his English birthright to become one of this horrid Yankee nation.

AUGUST 27. SATURDAY. Spent the day in New York, and visited Green-wood Cemetery: old Hobbs for escort, of course.[38] He carried us to Mrs. Parmelu's in Brooklyn, and got Mrs. Hanson to go with us. We stopped at the gate of the cemetery, and took lunch in a restaurant which advertises itself in a card after this fashion:

Fifth Avenue Ice Cream
Saloon Opposite Funeral
Entrance to Greenwood Cemetery.

I thought that was an incongruous jumbling of festivity and mortality; however, the ice cream was very good, and we did not feel atall funeral while eating it. Greenwood, like everything else about New York, has been described to me in such exaggerated terms, that the reality hardly came up to my expectations. Of course we saw the famous Canda monument, all discolored now, from neglect. We asked the guide if he knew what had become of the parents of the young girl who lay beneath.[39]

They are dead and buried in France, I believe: that is why the monument is so dirty, they always kept it clean, and took a power of care of it when they were living.

There was something very touching to me, in the thought. There are none, it seems, so beautiful and bright in life, so tenderly loved and mourned in death, but must come at last to share the common doom—neglect and oblivion. The handsomest monument in the cemetery at present, is over two of James Gordon Bennett's children.[40] It cost $50,000 the guide told us, and is really a splendid piece of work. It is the figure of a woman with clasped hands, kneeling before a pedestal upon which stands an angel, bearing off a child. The female figure is life size, and its drapery so perfect, that even the meshes of a lace shawl thrown over her head and shoulders, are perfectly distinct.

There are a number [of] other splendid monuments and mausoleums, in white marble, granite, and brown stone. The most costly of the vaults is a Byzantine structure in white marble, that cost $30,000, and the prettiest, to my taste, a gothic edifice on a hill, belonging to Stephen Somebody—one of the richest men in New York. So much for splendid tombs. I have forgotten his name already. The garish splendors of Greenwood affect me unpleasantly: they impress one so with the utter impotence of all human efforts to escape the leveling hand of death. After all, a great name is the only monument worth having: it makes any other unnecessary, and a great monument to a small name, is so belittling to both. I cannot describe the feeling that came over me when the guide would point out a splendid mausoleum, and inform us, "That's the family vault by John G. Smith—he's in the hat and glove business—one of our richest men;" or, "That monument Mr. Samuel Jones raised over his wife he made his fortune in the pin and needle business." I am not sure that I altogether approve of splendid funeral monuments, anyway: it seems so presumptuous to flaunt our pitiful show of finery in the very face of death. To my mind, the dust and mold on Miss Canda's monument are more impressive than the shining marbles of the Bennett tomb, and the rude little blocks of stone in the church yard of Stoke Poges will be memorable longer than either.[41] Humility is most becoming in the presence of death. I want only a plain granite or marble cross over me when I die, and if any fool does go and put an epitaph there, other than the name and date, I'll haunt him. We saw some absurd attempts at simplicity in Greenwood. On one tombstone was engraved simply the word "Pa." Another had "Harry's Grave," while there were "Our Fathers" and "Our Mothers" enough to have populated the earth, it seemed to me. I really think there ought to be a censor to inspect the inscriptions in public burying grounds, and keep silly friends from making ridiculous, poor people who are dead and can't help themselves.[42]

We dined again at Taylors, and then went to see the Pneumatic Railway, but it was closed to visitors for the day.[43] We walked down Wall Street, rode through Bowery past the Tombs, and many other places of note, but hardly saw anything unfamiliar: I have seen so much of New York in books and pictures, that I believe I really know more about it than some of the people who live there. I told Mr. Clarke the other night about several objects of interest in England that he had never heard of—particularly the little church in the Isle of Wight. I had a nice little chat with him on the back stoop this evening. He was sitting on his, reading the paper; I didn't know he was there, and started down Cousin Lilla's back steps to walk in a little slip of ground behind the house they call a yard. He put down his paper, and accosted me, and we both leaned over the railing and were having a nice little chat, but I caught a glimpse of the "lynx"[44] gliding through the reception room, and was so afraid of having all the properties down on me at once, that I left him abruptly, and closed the blinds, and tried to look as though I hadn't seen anybody, and when she reached the drawing room, I was deeply engrossed with a photograph album. She found the sash up however, but as I professed much surprise, and said I had been wondering what made it so cool in there, she never discovered my guilt. She is the most dreadful old lady I ever knew. She wears velvet slippers without any heels, and glides about the house as noiselessly as a cat, so that we have no warning of her approach, and is sure to come upon me just as I have drawn aside the curtain—which is never permitted here lest the lace should get crumpled —or spilt water on the carpet, or taken a book out of its place, or committed some other heinous offense against propriety. When we have company, she sits like a statue in the next room, and never budges till the last visitor is gone. She looks sour if they stay late, and savage if they are men. She says she don't like men and never did, and the feeling seems to have been mutual. She is a grim Presbyterian, and seems to consider it a personal injury that Mett and I are Episcopalians: in fact, she has been so severe upon that score, that we have hardly dared to enter our own church since we came here, and dare not mention the Catholic cathedral, which we are very desirous of attending, but we should vex her righteous soul beyond endurance. We have been running about to all sorts of places, when we would so gladly have entered the open doors of little Trinity, and last Sunday, we even went to her church, and heard a grim Presbyterian sermon, for the salvation of our souls. Still, I believe she thinks us past redemption, because we can't hide that we love to talk to the men. I don't wonder that Thackeray had such a horror of old women: his "motherinlaw" must have been a Gardner.

(144) AUGUST 28. SUNDAY. I would have given the world to go to the Cathedral this morning and hear Bishop Bayley,[45] who has just returned from the Ecumenical Council, preach his sermon on the Promulgation of Infallibility, but there is such a horror of Romanism pervading this house, that I am afraid old Miss Gardner would have wanted to fumigate us, if we had gone, so I didn't dare to make my wishes known, but went poking after cousin Lilla to the Market Street Methodist Church,[46] which she was particularly anxious to show me, because it is so big and fine. Some people

have precious little idea of what is really worth seeing and hearing, but when one is the guest of such people, one has no right to grumble, especially when they are so kind and I am indebted to them for so much.

After dinner, cousin Lilla went to sleep, and we had a rest from sight seeing, so Metta and I slipped off to little Trinity, and enjoyed a good orthodox service, without giving offense to anybody, for we never let the *lynx* know we were going, and as she spends Sunday afternoons up in the third story, meditating on the infinite mercy of God in damning little babes, I don't think she detected us. I thought until I came here that cousin Lilla was an Episcopalian, but she is not a communicant of any church, and attends the Dutch Reformed. At night we were carried to the "House of Prayer", a tawdry little edifice with all sorts of cheap flashy coloring on the walls, where all sorts of Ritualistic flummery is carried on. I do not object to many parts of the Ritualistic service that other people find fault with, but to depart from the beautiful simplicity of the prayer book, and substitute for the 'fair white linen cloth' of the rubric, a lot of cheap embroidery and gilt and pasteboard ornaments, is degrading the offices of our church.

I like the choral service, and see no signs of damnation in a boy choir, even when they wear surplices and bow their heads at the *Gloria*. On the contrary, I think their sweet childish faces and innocent voices ought to put good thoughts into any heart: but a choir ought always to be composed of little boys, with innocent faces. In the "House of Prayer" choir, I saw one big boy with a vicious face and a red head who was a rock of offense to me throughout the service.

Cousin Lilla talks of taking us to Long Branch, and paying all our expenses. That is very kind and generous, but we don't encourage the plan, because our poor shabby wardrobes would never pass muster there.[47] Not that we care, on our own account, for nobody at the Branch knows us, nor do we care a snap what those shoppies might think of us, but cousin Lilla herself is gotten up in such magnificent style and thinks so much of fine clothes, that I am afraid our shabbiness might be a mortification to her. We can barely stand fire, here, at the most unfashionable season—and among the flash assemblage at Long Branch—it makes me laugh to think what we would look like. So far as I am concerned, I would like to go, and see the sights, even with my meager outfit, but I would not like to make my good generous friends ashamed.

(146) Ah, there is one point on which I can truly boast of Southern superiority—nobody is ashamed of shabby clothes there: some of our greatest and most influential ladies in Georgia would pass for nobodies here, on

account of their clothes—But enough—this sounds ungrateful—these Yankees are overwhelming us with hospitality and attention, though they do talk a vast deal about money and clothes. Still, their actions often belie their words.

AUGUST 29. MONDAY. I never in my life had so much to say, or less satisfaction in saying it, because I have no time. What with writing home, and seeing sights and receiving visitors, I have no time for anything else. This afternoon we visited Tuscan Hall the old square stone house built by my great-great-grandfather, a hundred years ago.[48] It was a grand residence in those old revolutionary times, and its hospitality was extended to many a patriot soldier, but today, is sadly fallen from its proud estate. It is situated on the outskirts of a little place called Middleville, about 7 miles from Newark, and is at present the property of a wealthy German brewer of the latter place. It is inhabited by a family of German laborers who work on the farm attached, and is dirty and neglected, but the stout old stone walls resist the worst efforts of time and man. Two children belonging to the work people, understood a little English, and interpreted for us. Their elders flocked around, and received us with a heartiness that would not shame the memory of my hospitable ancestors. When they understood the object of our visit, it seemed as though they could not do enough for us. The Frau took off her shoes, and led us all over the quaint old house, up the break neck staircase, through quaint little old bedrooms, and into old lobbies and closets, where the mold and dust of years lay thick upon the wall—enough to rouse several generations of my notable old grandmothers out of their graves. We went into the kitchen, and saw the oven where such famous dinners were cooked 100 years ago, and where many an old revolutionary soldier had found warmth and rest and food in the olden time. What would the shades of those good old ancestors think if they had known that two of their descendants were standing there, who had given food and shelter and rest, and prayers and blessings too, to soldiers who fought against the flag those old heroes had loved? We have all been rebels together—only their rebellion was successful—ours was not. The old Dutch woman showed us a loaf of her making baked in my great-grandmother's oven. I would fain have tasted some, but could not, for the stomach's sake, for it was black as the chimney, and heavy as a stone: I wonder the shades of my worthy ancestresses could rest. We went into the quaint old parlor, ornamented with carved wood in the ceiling, like Haywood and saw the spot where cousin Lilla's mother, aunt Matilda, stood to be married. Then we went to the garden— a perfect wilderness, now, of weeds and wild flowers, except where the

Dutch laborers have planted a few cabbages and onions. The children hastened to gather us bouquets, while the older people brought grapes, and pears from trees perhaps, that my ancestors had planted. On one side the garden was a clump of huge boxwood as tall as an ordinary doorway, that I am sure must have been planted there by my great-great grand-mother, ["100" erased in the original] years ago. There was a hollow space walled in between them, that the old frau called a *soomer fix*. I broke some cuttings of the box to carry home and plant alongside the rosemary from my great-great-grandmother Appleton's garden. The poor laborers rushed about here and there, hunting for flowers and fruits to give us and chatter-ing away in Dutch of which we understood not a word, and we answered in English, of which they understood not a word, and so the conversation was highly edifying to both sides; at any rate, it was very friendly and jolly too, for they laughed at us, and we at them. They wanted to bring us some sweet milk, but we contented ourselves with a draught from the well where our ancestors had slaked their thirst, and I thought of David and the water from the well at Bethlehem. It was the coolest, purest water I ever tasted, and I loved to think that perhaps Washington's soldiers had watered their horses there. I wish Lee's soldiers had too.

High up in the Eastern wall was a stone larger than the others with an inscription, but the date, 1773, and detached letters E. F. B. and M. and the number 17 were all we could make out of it. We gave the little Dutch children some money and trinkets when we left them. Unfortu-nately, we did not know what sort of people we were going to meet, and were unprovided except with a fan and a ribbon & a little change that we happened to carry about us. However, they were very grateful and pressed our hands as fervently as if they had bestowed saintly blessings. They could not speak, but as the carriage drove off they waved their hands at us, and then pressed them to their hearts. Such hearty good will, such honest simplicity and good nature, I never saw before, and will long remember it. However their homely peasants' fare may contrast with the sumptuous hospitality of my ancestors, I am sure their simple kindly hearts are worthy successors to the noblest that ever beat. I do not con-sider that the "hall of my forefathers" is degraded by having become a peasants' hut. Altogether, it is the pleasantest expedition I ever made, and one that I will never forget: that alone, would pay me for coming from Georgia, if I had had no other pleasure.

The evening we spent at Julia's. Her brother George was there, with his wife and is a splendid musician, and a real nice fellow: I like all the Bruens we have met thus far.

**AUGUST 30.** Spent the day in New York, with Julia and cousin Lilla, and had a nice time: went everywhere, and saw everything: rode in the Pneumatic Railway as far as it is finished, and heard the omnibuses of Broadway rolling over our heads. They have a fine station there underground, with a fountain, mirrors &c: but I can't begin to describe all I see. We visited the Groton Reservoir, and it seemed to me like the walls of Babylon: rode up and walked down Fifth Avenue, saw Stewarts' fine house, dined at Delmonicos, visited all the grand shops—cousin Lilla bought an India shawl, and I tried on one worth $5,000: saw lots of pretty things, but bought nothing because my money has all run out, but barely enough for traveling expenses. We spend Thursday night in New York to see Rip Van Winkle, and then start up the Hudson, with old Hobbs, on our way to Niagara. No time for descriptions. Oh, dear, how I do wish I had some more money!

**SEPT 1ST. THURSDAY.** New York Hotel. We left Newark at 3 P.M., walked about Broadway & 14th St. till six, and met one of our Manhattan friends, Miss Browne, of Carolina with Miss Brougham of Florida. Dined at six o'clock, then went to Booth's Theatre, and saw Jefferson in Rip Van Winkle. Mrs. Ellen Hanson and Charley Parmelie came over from Brooklyn and accompanied us. It was splendid.

(151) **ALBANY. N. Y. SEPT 2ND.** Left New York at 9 A.M. on the Hudson River steamboat, Daniel Drew. It was a floating palace [and] revived my recollection of the splendors of Alabama and Mississippi steamers. There was a band of music onboard, and everything else that could contribute to the pleasure of a tourist—except good company.

There was an immense crowd of passengers—and some nice people among them, as I found by experience—but the sharp harsh Yankee brogue, with the inevitable "I guess" was to be heard in every direction. The "nice" people did not single each other out instinctively as it were, and affiliate without ceremony, as we do at the South, but each party kept to itself, and stared at the rest. Accident brought me in contact with a nice old gentleman from New Jersey, named Douglas. He was very polite to me, and we soon became good friends. He introduced his wife, who was a real nice lady, and we adopted them into our party at once. They only came as far as Albany, but added materially to our pleasure during that part of the journey. Mr. Douglas, I soon discovered, was a radical, so I took the first opportunity to let him know that we were Southerners. He understood the hint, and both parties by tacit consent, avoided every approach to dangerous topics. Mr. Douglas has been up and down the Hudson repeatedly, and could point out all places of interest much better than the guide book. It is a glorious river, and the scenery on its banks is beyond all description: well is it called the Rhine of America. And yet, I like the flowery swamps, the wild tangled scenery of our Southern rivers better. The dear old South, in its wild uncultivated state, has more of Nature: the hand of man does not obtrude itself there in every corner as it does here. The miserable, money loving wretches that these Yankees are: they even have the impudence to paint their advertisements of paper collars and patent medicines upon the Palisades and the rocks that jut from the Highlands of the Hudson.

There was a party of negroes on board the steamer, but they were perfectly respectful, and I do not object to social equality at the North, because here, it is not a symbol of my country's degradation, and besides, there are not enough negroes to make the question one of any practical importance. A mulatto girl sat next to me at dinner, and I only felt amused. The fact is, I like negroes so much better than Yankees, that the sight of a black face in a crowd, gives me positive pleasure: it looks like home.

We reached Albany about 7 P.M., and walked to the Delavan House— one of the best and prettiest hotels I ever stopped at. The waiters are all negroes, the rooms delightful, and the parlours and dining saloons arranged with more taste and elegance than in any hotel I have seen in all my travels, North or South. The parlor is filled with nice people, travelers like ourselves. We leave at 10½ P.M. on the New York Central, for Niagara.

NIAGARA. SEPT. 3RD. I won't try to describe the falls: language here would be as impertinent as it is impotent. My first view of them revealed only a great column of white mist rising in the air. It has been a bad rainy day, and my first glimpse of the falls was under a cloud—but Niagara is Niagara, in cloud or sunshine. We reached here at noon, and put up at the Cataract House, a hotel that is only equaled by the one at Albany. The waiters are all black, but the maids are white—some of them exceedingly handsome, and none of them very respectful or attentive. The night journey from Albany was horrible. In spite of our protestations, old Hobbs would persist in packing us into a sleeping car, hoops, chignons, and all. The berth was hardly wide enough for one, nor high enough to rise on your elbow in, yet Mett and I both had to crawl into it. I would as soon have been put to sleep in a coffin with the lid shut down. We nearly suffocated, did not sleep a wink, but spent the night abusing old Hobbs, and the man that invented sleeping cars for the torture of poor innocent mortals who never did him any harm. If I were a despot, I would hang him. In the morning we passed through Syracuse, Rochester, and some other towns that are put down in the school geographies in answer to the question, "What cities [are located] in the Western part of New York?" I felt as though I had a passing acquaintance with Syracuse and Rochester on the strength of the geographical introduction. I would have liked to improve it, some, what, at the latter place, where we stopped for breakfast, but these rapid Yankee schedules allow no time for anything of that sort. A fifteen minutes breakfast or dinner is a barbarity that would be unheard of out of Yankeedom.

Well, at all events, the Yankees have Niagara, and that is a possession a world might be proud of—though they have done their best to spoil that. Above the falls on the American side, the river is disfigured with paper mills, and all sorts of ugly manufacturing houses—it rained so all the afternoon that we could not go very far; however, we put on overshoes and waterproofs, descended the chasm on the American side, then went over to Goat Island, and saw all the points of interest and beauty there. It was all glorious and grand, but everywhere the hand of man was too obtrusive. I would like to see Niagara a wild solitude, as Châteaubriand saw it. It is one of Nature's sublimest spots, and the pitiful efforts of man to improve and beautify it, are simply contemptible. There ought not to be a house within ten miles of Niagara, and as for suspension bridges over chasms and steam elevators upon the sides of precipices of a thousand feet, they are very convenient to tourists, but not consonant with my ideas of congruity. I believe I would rather risk my neck clambering down the sides of precipices as we did at Tallulah in Georgia, than see the grand gorge at Niagara disfigured with an unsightly wooden structure for my convenience. But those suspension bridges are grand: when one sees them spanning the awful chasm at Niagara with the ease of a deck plank over a wet weather run, one is almost tempted to exclaim with the old women who saw the first cotton gin "Truly, the works of God is great, but the works of man is greater."

(155) After supper we trotted round the village of Niagara, where a great many curiosities and knick knacks of Indian workmanship—so called— are exposed for sale. We bought some beautiful feather fans, and a number of other ornaments for the people at home. Our hotel is splendid: we have elegant rooms, and better fare, and some charming people sit opposite us at table. There are several Southerners here, and an English nobleman— Lord Wodenhouse, I believe, but I suppose he looks just like other people, as he traveled with us from Albany, and I have not singled him out from the rest of the crowd yet, nor tried to do so.

**BUFFALO N.Y. SEPT 4. SUNDAY.** I had not seen Niagara last night. I knew nothing of its glories, for I had not seen it from the Canada side and there is no real view of the falls from the American. The weather has been glorious today, cool clear and bracing, like October at home. The trees in these Northern woods are already beginning to assume autumn hues. We spent the entire morning driving round to see the different views of Niagara, and found many other parties doing the same thing. I was sorry, but with our limited time, and still more limited means, we could not afford to observe the Sabbath at the rate of $5.00 a day. One does not see Niagara every Sunday, and after all, it preaches a loftier sermon that ever a man spoke. We had our first full view of it from the middle of the Upper Suspension Bridge, and I rose to my feet, in an ecstasy: I could have fallen upon my knees there, and thanked God for letting me behold such a sight. I could not sit down, but stood up in the carriage till it stopped before the Museum in Canada, where we were to change clothes and be conducted under the falls. I was a most absurd looking figure, I daresay, in blue stockings with holes in them, India rubbers so large for me that they flapped the ground at every step, and a yellow oil skin coat and cap, but in the presence of Niagara, one forgets self, and even a woman can forget looks. That expedition under the falls was something of a humbug, still I am glad I saw Niagara in every aspect—the grand, glorious beautiful awful tremendous thing! How pitiful it seems to pull out your purse and pay a dollar or two for every new view of that incalculable wonder! I would rather pay twice as much and say it was for something else—but to pay for looking at Niagara—what a desecration! What a pitiful thing human nature must be, that it can be mean and sniveling under the very thunders of Niagara. I wish I knew some words to describe Niagara in—but I won't try: language here would be as impertinent as it is impotent. I have seen Niagara—that would be a comfortable thought if the world were blotted from existence tomorrow.

We visited the Museum in Canada, and saw many very interesting things —among others, a quantity of poor old Confederate money displayed among their coins of all nations. There were the skeletons of whales, and casts of basreliefs from Egypt and Nineveh, that interested me very much, and there were stuffed animals and eggs from all countries. Two Englishmen there were very kind in pointing out to me the coins of their country that I read about so much in books. I like English people and everything English, and drew my breath so gaily in the free air of an English Colony.

We drove about all the morning, seeing sights and returned to the hotel just in time to dine at 4 P.M. At 5. we left on the Lake Shore R. R. for Buffalo, which we reached between six and seven. The ride was delightful along the banks of the Niagara River, and the shores of Lake Erie. The air was cool and fresh as pure water, clear skies, and open hilly country could make it: we were in a splendid palace car, which gave us full benefit of the scenery. We were recommended to the Continental Hotel in Buffalo, as being near the Erie R. R. depot. It is a nasty hole—frowsy company and bad fare, but our room is good. We would not have come here if we had known better, but it is not worth while to make a change now—especially as we don't know where to go and old Hobbs is too pokey to find out. I hope it may never be my ill luck to travel with such an old codger again. After supper, we went to St. John's Episcopal Church, we heard good music and a poor sermon.

(157) **SEPT 5. MONDAY.** Left Buffalo at 7 A.M. and traveled till 10 P.M. over the Erie R. R. a distance of more than 300 miles. The scenery is perfectly magnificent. The road winds in and out among the gorges of the Catskill mountains, following the valleys of rivers, and sometimes making such sudden turns that we were nearly thrown from our seats in rounding them. I believe they average an accident every day on that road, but fortunately our train escaped. It was the through express, from Buffalo to N. Y. and we took places in the palace car, which was even handsomer than the one from Buffalo to Niagara. There were some very pleasant people among the passengers, and we struck up acquaintance with several of our fellow passengers; one of them, a gentleman who sat near us, reminded me of Captain Francis.

At Gnoguchamna, where we dined, a rascally Yankee trick was played upon us. In barbarous Yankee fashion, we had only fifteen minutes for dinner. It was an elegant eating house, and we were ravenously hungry after a 5 o'clock breakfast and a mean one at that. After bolting a few mouthfuls, we were startled by the cry "All aboard," and there was a general rush for the cars. There stood all the train officials and the hotel proprietor, enjoying the joke, but not one of them volunteered to inform us that we had still 8 minutes—and we did not find it out till we had paid our fare, and were on board again. There were some angry travelers then. I mean. If I had time, I would write an account of it to the World, and expose their rascality. It is all a humbug about the cheapness of travel at the North. It is true, a R. R. or steam boat ticket can be bought for less than half of what it costs to travel the same distance in my country, but there are so many extras that by the time one has traveled a hundred miles, he is swindled out of more than would carry him a thousand at the South. When you buy your ticket at the South, you pay for everything, but here they won't look at a piece of baggage without charging extra for it, nor let you look at anything else. They are a nasty, miserable, sniveling, driveling cheating, swindling, humbugging, vulgar minded set of snobs and skinflints, these Yankees, and if there is another rasping expletive in the language, I wish somebody would tell it to me, for I have exhausted my vocabulary.

The Erie depot is in Hoboken. We crossed over the Chambers St. ferry to New York, then down to Courtland street for Jersey City, and reached Newark. Cousin Mortimer, like a dear good fellow that he is, was at the Centre St. depot to meet us, and a crowd of letters waiting on our bureau at home—one from the World with last month's pay, and another from father with a check for $50.

(159) SEPT 7TH WEDNESDAY. A nice quiet day and a charming evening. Julia and Morty took tea, Mr. and Mrs. George Bruen, Mr. Clark, and the Howells called afterward. Mr. Bruen is perfectly charming, and old Mr. Howell is as fat and jolly as he can be, and I like him though he is an awful Radical. He behaved like a gentleman, and carefully avoided all allusion to disagreeable subjects, but one of his daughters, Lizzie, took a seat near me, and commenced conversations about the war. I made one or two efforts to change the subject, but she kept returning to it, and alluded to the South in a sneering manner that nearly made me boil over. However, I managed to contain myself and to answer her as much as possible in mono-syllables, and I told her some rare lies too. She kept asking if I was not dreadfully afraid when the United States soldiers came where I was—and I told her no, I wasn't a bit afraid of them—which was about as flat a false-hood as ever passed my lips. I had a great mind to add that I was too much concerned about higher matters, to tremble at the prospect of having spoons stolen. Finally with the assistance of Mr. Clark who sat in on the other side of me, the conversation was turned to Niagara Falls, which she too, has just visited for the first time. She spent three months in Europe last spring, and was constantly bragging in allusions to things abroad that she thought I could not understand: everything that was mentioned, she would hop to compare with something abroad, and was so anxious to bring in her foreign travels, that she did it once at the expense of comparing the elevator at Niagara with the steps in the Tower of London. She tried to talk over me to Mr. Clark, but he studiously addressed himself to me—only making a polite rejoinder to her remarks, and then appealing to me so as not to leave me out of the conversation. It was worthy of a Southerner: I felt so grateful to him, and fortunately, my reading has made me so famil-iar with all the real points of interest in Europe that I was really more capable of keeping pace with Mr. Clark than was Miss Howell, and had the pleasure of turning her down two or three times. She is an awful snob, and

like all these Yanks, measures everything by money: I saw her give a long contemptuous stare at my poor old Japanese poplin, and when I looked at her elegant Paris made dress, banded with exquisite lace and then thought of my own shabby toilet, I began to think she had the upper hand of me then, and the battle was lost on that ground. But luckily, she soon uncovered her weak point, and then I brought up my reserves, and gained at least a partial victory. I don't know whether it was accidental or intentional, but she contrived some way, to expose her feet. They were no bigger than all the other women have in this region, but perfect clodhoppers compared to an average Southern foot. I saw my chance at once, her shoes were beautiful bronzeo, trimmed elaborately with bows and buckles: mine, only simple black kids with a little embroidery about the tips, but very pretty, and I know that my feet would look like pigmies in them compared with hers as I contrived while talking very earnestly to Mr. Clark, to put my feet out from under my dress—very carelessly, as if I were perfectly unconscious of the act, and let them rest straight alongside of hers—still talking earnestly all the time, as if perfectly unconscious of what my lower extremities were about. Presently she looked down, and I could hardly keep from laughing out, to see how quickly she drew her clodhoppers in. Oh, what wretches we women are—and yet, it is fine fun. I never engage in these ridiculous contests voluntarily, but when challenged to it by a Yankee shoppy, I'll fight to the death. I wouldn't mind her snickering at my poor dress, but when she presses to turn up her pitiful Yankee nose at my country and to speak sneeringly of my beloved South, I'll put her down, if I die for it.

Miss Howell returned to her politics after awhile and very gratuitously boasted that she was a Republican, pitched into the Democrats, and finally sneered at some man she had met on the steamer as nothing but a Southern Judge. I am no more of a Democrat than I am of a Republican, but as the Democrats are allies of the South, and I the daughter of a Southern Judge, her remarks were more personal perhaps than she intended. I said nothing to provoke a quarrel, but, secretly resolved to pass a few hot shots into her the first good chance that offered. It was not long before my turn came: I found occasion in telling some little anecdote or reminiscence, to make some off hand allusion to "respectable merchant sort of people—prosperous tradesmen and manufacturers you know, very worthy people of course, whom I am always careful to treat politely, but not, you know—" &c &c. taking care to address her as if taking for granted that she was one of the *elite*, who was entitled to look down on vulgar prosperity, though I know, as well as she did, that her father made his fortune in the leather business—that is, as a tanner on a large scale. I wouldn't have made such a snobby speech to anybody but a snobby fool, and took care that nobody else should hear—but it served my purpose: I think she will hold her tongue about Southern Judges in future, if she finds out that I am the daughter of one. After talking off a few distinguished names at her, such as Semmes, Hampton, Randolph, &c. with a due intermingling of aristocratic jargon, I wound up, as Mr. Clark opened conversations with me again, and I did not care to make a fool of myself before him—though even then, I could not resist sending out one more shaft.

As soon as Mr. Clark rejoined us, Miss Howell returned to her European tour, and commenced gushing over the dear old ruined castles of the Rhine, and lamenting that we had nothing like them in this country. "If you will go to Charleston or Atlanta," I said, "you may contemplate ruins to your hearts content." I must have been a little excited when I said it, for everybody turned and looked at me. I was afraid I had committed a *faux pas*, so turned it off as quickly as possible, by gliding into a description of the old Circular Church in Charleston, and the beautiful ruin it makes. Pretty soon, I became absorbed in conversation with Mr. Clark and Mrs. Bruen, and Miss Howell turned upon Mett. I know she would come off second best there, for Mett is equal to anybody. Then too, she had Mr. Bruen and cousin Morty for allies, and it is easy enough to triumph over another woman, when all the men are on your side.

Mr. Clark is just the nicest old fellow in the world. He says that I must go down some day and visit his factory, and he will show me some very wonderful and very interesting machinery. He is a thorough gentleman, and just as witty and intelligent as can be: he has traveled everywhere and read everything, and never obtrudes his radical sentiments upon me. Miss Howell is the only person who has done that as yet, and I don't think she gained much by it.

SEPT. 12TH. MONDAY. Spent the morning in New York. Called at Fulton Street and had a blow up with the Weekly for not returning certain mss. not intended for them to keep. The corresponding editor away, and things in a mess generally: think our negotiations will come to naught. At Stern Bros. I invested in some elegant point lace, and have ordered a bonnet from Mrs. Anderson. It is foolish and extravagant I know, but I made the money, and I never can resist lace.

On returning to Newark, I found many letters—one from home full of bad news. Cora Rose, aunt Cornelia,[49] and our good natured darkey[50] all sick, and the newspapers abusing father. He has been making some report to Bullock[51] about the disorders of the country. If I had been there, I might either have stopped the mischief, or modified it, but now all the papers are down on my poor dear old father, and he is down on my poor dear country, and so I am perfectly miserable. I sat down and took a good hard cry over one bitter piece that I read. I could not blame the editor, I could not blame father. I ought to have staid [*sic*] at home: I have only shirked its duties and not avoided its troubles for here they are trooping after me, a thousand miles from home.

After my crying spell, the carriage came, and we all went, as pre-arranged, to visit Mr. Clark's spool thread mill. He was there to receive us, showed us all over the place, explained the machinery, and when we left, gave us each a pretty little box of thread. I kept my face shaded, so that nobody, I think, could detect a trace of tears. It was a very interesting visit —and heavens! how it opened my eyes! I will never turn up my nose again at a manufacturing of spool thread. Cotton planting is nothing to it. It is a really manly business to command such an establishment so that, and still more so, to understand all about it as Mr. Clark does—and still find time, with all that on his hands, to be one of the most cultivated and sensible gentlemen I ever met! What a fool I have been! I know now that cotton planting and soldiering are not the only occupations for gentlemen, and I have found out that rich manufacturers are not necessarily shoppies and upstarts. A spool of sewing thread seems a very insignificant thing but the process of making it is anything but insignificant. I'll never make a fool of myself again by feeling contempt for manufacturers.

Verily, travel is a great liberalizer: no son of a planter that I ever knew, can surpass in general culture, elegance of manners, and geniality of mind, the manufacturer of "George A. Clark & Co." spool cotton. Manufacturers are not here what they are at the South. If Mr. Clark only was not a Radical, what a splendid old fellow he would be! And yet, one of the things I most admire about him, is the delicacy with which he avoids all allusion to his political tenets in my presence: he does not sneak around and pretend to be half rebel just out of deference to me, but steers clear of the subject altogether—I would not know that he had any politics if others had not told me, and I don't think he can be enough of a radical to hurt. At any rate, he had the good sense and good taste to prefer the dignity of English citizenship and evidently don't care enough for American politics to dirty his fingers with them, for he has never been naturalized. I think the reason why so many nice people at the North are Radicals, is because the Irish laborers are all Democrats, and capital and labor seem naturally to assay themselves against each other. The Irish bedevil the native Americans and others of the upper ranks of society, just as the negroes do us at the South, and hence the fight between them. I would be a Rad myself, if I had to deal long with the Baddies and the Paddies, and could forget the niggers and scalawags down South.

(166) SEPT 14TH. WEDNESDAY. All the morning in New York—shopping, visiting, and looking around. Mett bought the guitar I gave her, at Ponds, and then we visited Ball and Blacks great jewelry store: they were very polite in showing us around, though I told them at the outset we could buy nothing. I am glad enough Mett has that nice guitar, for I wanted to give her something that she will keep always. In the afternoon, we made calls, with our beautiful new bonnets on: they are lovely—guipure[52] of black and white neapolitan, Mett's with pink roses, blue feather and black thread lace, mine white roses, feather and point lace—cost altogether $18 each, and extremely becoming. With that and my handsome silk sack, I feel competent to pass muster even among the Yankees. After tea, we went to the Broad St. Presbyterian Church, and Mr. George Bruen played for us on the organ till bed time. A select company of his friends were invited to meet us, and we had a nice time. The youngest of the Bruen brothers, Leonard Bruen, or Leone, so they call him is the handsomest and nicest fellow that ever lived. He sat by me nearly all the time, and walked with me on our way home: his manners are just like a Southerner's, and his voice as sweet and soft as if he . . . *

(171) . . . [T]he party that opposed the negroes; Irish aggression was a much nearer evil to Northern conservatives than negro emancipation, so they arrayed themselves against it, and thus found themselves accidentally the allies of Bucher and Greeley. The bulk of Northern Radicals care nothing about Southern politics, and never consider the principles of their party as they affect us. Mr. Howell's daughter was not aware that negroes could vote at the South until I told her, and was very much shocked at it! I enlightened her then as to some of the other things they do. I am very certain that the same considerations that make Mr. Clark and Mr. Howell Radicals here, would make the best rebels of them in my country.

SEPT. 20. Mett and I went to New York this morning, and saw cousin Jim and Sallie: the hotels are all filled with friends of ours from the South: I wish we were just coming on now, instead of just going away. We leave tomorrow night on the 9-30—express, with Mr. Phelps. This has been a day of business—we have received 3 telegrams, and half a dozen letters. After dinner, we had a long drive with Ella Miller. The Millers are very nice people in their way, but my feelings towards them have cooled very much, since I have learned that their father was in Sherman's army: of course his daughters are so pretty and pleasant as ever and it wasn't their fault if their father burnt people's houses and stole their property, but it is

---

*Pages 167 through 170 are missing—apparently torn from the book. The text picks up with diary page 171.

against my principles to cultivate such acquaintances, though, of course, for cousin Lilla's sake, I would not be rude.[53]

In the morning we had lots of company. I wore my white muslin with the point lace, looped up over my Japanese poplin, and it looked real nice. Mr. Clark staid [sic] later than anybody else, and was a great deal pleasanter: he brought over some beautiful pictures to show us, and a some sort of *scope* to look at them through.[54] Of course they were beautiful—everything he has, and everything he does, is in perfect taste.

(172) SEPT 26, MONDAY. HOME. I am back in the old track already, and so busy, that I can only give a bare outline of our delightful journey home. We were very busy packing, all day Wednesday, and had crowds of visitors too: everybody coming to say good b'ye. Belle Gift, from Albany arrived in Newark a few days before we left and called to spend the morning, and in the evening, a dozen people ran in before the train left, to say good b'ye. Those Yankees were right good to us, and some of them seemed really to think a great deal of us. Mr. Phelps and his sister came over from N.Y. and spent the evening so as to start with us from Newark. Cousin Morty kissed us, and cousin Lilla cried, when she bid us good b'ye, which was very sweet —especially, as the very last thing I did before leaving her house, was to break a vase. It was too bad to think I had spent six weeks among all that finery without doing any mischief, and then to go and lose my character at the eleventh hour. It was worse than turning over the ink stand on Mr. Jenning's linen sheet: I would rather burn down the house of a Southerner than break a pin belonging to a Yankee: they have no tact, and do make one feel so dreadfully. Cousin Lilla never once said, "oh it don't matter," or "I don't care half as much as you do," as any poor starving rebel would have done, if I had broken his last plate with his last dinner on it, but said "what a pity"—and "you didn't mean to do it, of course." and "I hoped it was nothing more than the lamp shade, when I heard the crash", and finally wound up my pleasant feelings by saying "I wouldn't mind it so much if I had not painted the vase myself—it was my own work."

I said nothing, but inwardly resolved to replace that vase if it took the last dollar out of father's pocket—I didn't have any in my own. Fortunately, at our journey's end, Mr. Phelps returned me 12 dollars that were left from my traveling fund. The vase I broke could not have been worth more than $2.00 at the outside, for I saw its counterpart at the Dollar Store but I will replace it with a $12.00 pair, and I will give them as a present not as a reparation— that will be doing things like a Southerner, and I thank the Lord I am not a Yankee, whatever other faults I may have. They have not a particle of tact: the very best of them say the most dreadful things without any intention of

---

being rude, because they [are a horrid vulgar minded race and][55] don't know what true politeness is. Mr. Phelps and Alice were delayed in New York on Wednesday, so that although we waited tea for them some time, they did not arrive till we were half through. Instead of inviting them right down, with a joke at our own expense, in not having waited for them, Cousin Lilla and the old Lynx fell into an awful flurry, sent us up stairs to ask if they had been to tea, kept them waiting half an hour, while she had the table entirely rearranged, and then came up to inform the guests that she had entirely given them out, just as I had told them that we had been expecting them for the last two hours, but that our appetites had finally got the better of our manners, so we had gone into the supper ahead of them. Her remark made them feel uncomfortable, and Mr. Phelps began to apologize for being so late. I undertook to smooth matters over by saying, "Oh, it don't matter, you are just in time for the oysters—we have not eaten them all up yet." and was quenched by cousin Lilla's inviting them down to supper with the remark that it would have been a great deal better if it had not been kept waiting so long. She did not mean to be rude, for she is really one of the kindest hearted women in the world—but she is a Yankee, and had not tact enough to abstain from apologizing for her [smudged] at the expense of her guests feelings. [The truth is, Yankees have not a spark of genuine hospitality about them.][56] A Southerner will share the poorest dinner he ever sits down to, with a friend, and bid him welcome, but a Yankee only entertains for his own credit—to display his fine things and make a show: he is selfish, even in his hospitality. At the South, we entertain for the pleasure of it, and think more of making our guests comfortable than of making a creditable display for ourselves. I never heard mother apologize for a dinner in my life, though company has often taken us unawares, and during the war, our fare was often of the poorest, and there were many good reasons why it was no better—but the reasons were never given—our guests fared as we did, and were supposed to be content. [But Yankees are a vulgar minded set of whangsniffling—My goodness, it is base ingratitude for me to talk so, when I have been treated so kindly by them, and owe so much to their hospitality and generosity. I won't do it anymore. Cousin Lilla is just as sweet as she can be, and Julia, I love dearly, and if Mortimer only would let whiskey alone, he would be the finest fellow North of the Potomac, and as for their being Yankees and talking whang-nosed, they were born there and couldn't help it.][57]

Old Ward, never appeared to take leave of us—he had been on the verge of a big spree for three days. The mystery about him was solved long ago. He is horrible dissipated, gets drunk, keeps women, and does all sorts of bad things, and treats his wife like a brute. Sometimes he won't speak to her for six weeks, and he never lets cousin Sarah, her only sister, enter the house, if he knows it. Cousin L. told me a great deal about her troubles before I left her, and she could never speak of her husband without crying. Julia says he is the worst devil that ever lived, but she is not afraid of him, and is the only person in the world who has any influence over him. Sometimes, she told us when he gets drunk, one would think he would tear the house down. Fortunately, he seemed to take a fancy to us, and was always sending presents or doing something on the sly to promote our pleasure, though he scarcely ever showed himself to us, and was as likely to snub us as not, if he did. Altogether, he is a curious compound: he lavishes upon cousin Lilla all that money can bestow, and yet treats her like a brute. He has pride, too, about his own appearance—was always dressed beautifully, whenever I saw him—his shoes and gloves, in particular, attracted my attention, his nails were always faultless, and he used the most delicious perfumes, and yet, at heart he was a beast—but enough about the Yankees —I wish I was with them still, for I had a fine time there, upon the whole, and I always have anxieties at home.

The journey here was perfectly delightful. We slept all the way from Newark to Washington D. C., but when we got on board the Potomac steamer, we found a host of acquaintances from Georgia and Alabama; they introduced us to others and by the time we reached Acquia Creek, there were enough of us to fill a car. It was delightful—almost like being in a private drawing room with a party of friends. Through all the changes between Washington & Augusta, we contrived to keep in the same car, and a delightful trip it was. We came from Richmond by the Charlotte and Columbia route breakfasting in one place and dining at the other. The eating. . . .[*]

(191) . . . had arranged for a rehearsal in our drawing room and besides, the weather is so bad it would all be knocked up anyway. I should not be surprised if we had to give up our theatricals, on account of the public disorders. The elections begin on the 20th and the riots have already begun. There was one at the depot yesterday just as the cars came in which two negroes were killed. The Ku Klux were there to give a cowbell, and probably a cowhide reception to some radical speakers who were expected on the train: fortunately they did not come, but the Ku Klux and the negroes had a row which resulted fatally to two poor wretches. There will be a Yankee garrison here next week, of course and that will keep things quiet.[58]

[*] Pages 175 though 190 are missing—apparently torn from the diary. The text picks up with diary page 191.

The negroes are very much exasperated, but the poor creatures are too stupid and defenseless to do any harm: they do not know how to organize for their own defense. If we should act our play next Friday, as anticipated, I am a little afraid they might take advantage of the occasion to attempt some terrible revenge, such as burning the house down, or a general massacre, but I dare say the white people will provide against that. I am sorry to say that my clever young friend, Willie Toombs[59] and others of the same class, were leaders in the riot. Charles Irvin[60] is captain of the Ku Klux in this county, and Dudley DuBose our candidate for congress, is said to be the 'Grand [Cyclops—marked out and replaced with Titan]' head director and general for all this region.[61] They ought to be ashamed of themselves—at least Charley ought, but I don't believe Dudley DuBose has sense enough to know there is anything disgraceful in heading a gang of rowdies and assassins. I am very uneasy about father for his official position will compel him to attempt some measures against these people, and I am afraid they will Ku Klux him. However, the popularity of the ladies in the family, and the politics of the boys may protect him. I don't think anybody about here would willingly hurt Mett or me, and they would have to kill both of us before they should touch a hair of the dear old father's head. I think he is strong in the protection of our weakness for I never heard of a Southerner so bad as to hurt or to insult a woman except a Yankee or a nigger—and the worst of them ought to be ashamed to do that.

Oh, dear, here is my nice quiet day all broken up: yonder comes Henry Slaton and a lot of men to talk about the riot, and more of them are coming tonight, to see about the theatricals. Henry Slaton is one of our Democratic candidates who was very popular with the darkies, and he will be dreadfully worried at the damage the riot has done his cause.[62]

(192) **DEC. 17. SATURDAY.** A very exciting week this has been. The negroes have been in a state that causes great alarm. On Sunday evening, at William Harris's[63] funeral, they wrought themselves up to a fearful pitch of excitement against the whites, and by nightfall, 500 men had collected in Cannan, one of the negro suburbs, and were threatening to march upon our village, and burn and massacre everything in their way.[64] A secret deputation waited on father at dusk, and informed him of the danger. Henry and Fred[65] set off at once to rouse the white men of the village and in less than an hour, 100 of them were under arms and organized. Henry and Captain Erwin[66] taking command. They stationed pickets in every direction agreed upon a set. . . .*

* Pages 193 through 235 are missing—removed from the binding.

# 1871

(236)* . . . the play of Hamlet with the part of Hamlet left out: scarcely a word about Magna Carta, and a great deal of buncombe and bad grammar.[1] Yet, he expressed himself with great force, sometimes with eloquence, and I can well see could have great influence over the common people. Upon the whole, I think him a more forcible speaker than Mr. Stephens,[2] but not as polished.

There was a party at the Waddey's[3] in the evening, and I had to go though half sick, because father says Mett and I have declined too many invitations recently, and must go out more frequently. Who should I have for an escort, but old Sam Wynn! a very decided step in his part.[4] I thought it was his son, young Sam, when the note came and could hardly keep from laughing out, when I came down in evening dress and found the old gentleman waiting for me, Mr. Simmons, of Atlanta called at the same time, and I invited him to accompany us, but he withdrew, and left the field to old Sam. The party was stupid—a lot of strange women there, and entirely too hot to dance, so I came away at 12 M. Old Sam told me he intended to take a trip to Canada, and a lot of other places, this summer, but that he didn't want to go alone, &c. &c. I saw through the mill stone, but didn't give him a chance to say what he wanted. I don't pretend to say that I haven't got my price, but old Sam Wynn, with all his money, isn't rich enough to pay it. It would take a round hundred thousand to make his "onst" and his "trial" and his "ten mile" go down with me, to say nothing of his silly daughter. I wish I was like other girls—willing to marry anybody and be done with it. They all job along pretty much the same afterwards, and it don't seem to matter much whom they take, so he is not a downright scoundrel. There is poor Lilla Legriel[5] now, would give her head for a good pull at old Sam's purse,

* The text picks up with diary page 236.

and the Presbyterians are after him like a pack of hounds for little Bessie Walthour, while I, who am just as poor and needy as any of them, can't make up my mind to take the plunge they are all dying to make, and ugh! the more I think of it, the further I am from making up my mind to it. Even school teaching, bad as it is, can't bring me to terms. Mett and I were talking about it the other day; she has been trying for six months to make up her mind to take old Hobbs,[6] but then he is a far worse case than old Sam, though he has got more money, and I won't try to encourage her to take any such desperate step as that. I don't know what is to become of us: all the men that are worth having for their own sakes, are too poor to be thought of, and I can't make up my mind to the others. I believe I will ask father if we are so bad off as to make such a sacrifice necessary—though I don't believe starvation itself could drive me to it. Yet, he is a very honest, worthy old fellow, spends his money freely, and is by no means bad looking for a man of fifty, or thereabouts—but I don't know what it is—I can't, and I won't. I am afraid my pen has spoilt me: it has opened such a world to me, and I shudder at any kind of a Marriage, as a divorce from it.

(237) JULY 15TH SATURDAY. Belle Nash[7] and the Barnetts spent the evening. Yesterday we had Mrs. Hunter, and found her hopelessly stupid. Mr. Hunter likes Washington so well, that he has sent his wife and children to spend the summer: they are boarding with the Robertsons.[8] His children are not as bad as preacher's children usually are—but how did he contrive to get such a stupid wife? It is like pulling teeth to get any talk out of her.

General DuBose came here the other day, with Captain Edwards of Elbert, and spent two hours trying to pump me as to what I mean to do with old Mr. Wynn, but I wouldn't give him any satisfaction. He says that old Sam told him he meant to know before the end of this year, whether he could get me. The Terrys, who live with him, are so certain of a change in the *ménage*, that they are looking out for a house of their own. Now that is jolly: I like to astonish people. I don't go as cheap as most poor schoolteachers. Talent, social position and good looks—or at least an elegant appearance when I am dressed up, people say are something in my side of the balance, and I must have their full value in money, when I sell. However, I must write to Garnett. It may be that the family affairs are in such a fix as to require—but I know Garnett is a highminded fellow, and won't be apt to advise anything very dreadful—That is why I always like to take him into council: he nearly always thinks just as I do.

Lettie left today for the Virginia Springs she and aunt Cornelia,[9] and the Navy Hunters[10] spent last evening with us.

(238) July 23rd Sunday. I have been busy all the week nursing Mrs. Hunter's sick children. They are both on the mend; but little Julian Edings is like to die, and I think I shall be called upon to sit up with him tonight.[11] I think I had as well get married; my main reason for staying single, was to get rid of being bothered with children, but I believe the only difference is that now I have the care of other people's instead of my own. Somehow, I feel for little children a great deal more now, since darling little Rose[12] died: their sufferings seem to come nearer home to me. I want all that I do for them, hence forth, to be in her name and for her sake, as a sort of memento of the little darling, to keep the thought of her fresh in my heart, and to make her memory live in acts of kindness to other little children.

I had an overwhelmingly complimentary letter last week from the editor of the Southern Magazine about my article on "The Novel as a Work of Art." & word of encouragement comes in very opportunely just now, for I was afraid my mind had begun to degenerate since I commenced school teaching. I see by the papers, that any prophesy about the time when our sewing would be done for us by steam, is about to be fulfilled: the machines in Stewarts establishment are already worked by steam.

Lilla Legriel writes me that she and her mother can't make me their promised visit. I would like to see dear Mrs. Muller, but I am truly glad we shall escape a visitation from that wretched boy.

I mean to try and fix up a match between Lilla and old Sam Wynn; he couldn't put his money to a better use than taking care of some poor little helpless woman like her or Mattie Morgan.[13] If he just would take a fancy to one of them, it would be the very thing. I have had my eye on him for Mattie a long time, but men are so stupid, they never will fall in love with the right person.

Last week we had a house full of lawyers come over to a special court. Strange to say, Mr. Gidell, a Pennsylvania Yankee by birth and a Hart countian by adoption, proved one of our pleasantest guests, and I took a great fancy to him. He fought in our army all through the war, and was reared an Episcopalian, which accounts for it all. There is no doubt about it, the church does exercise a refining influence over the manners, as well as over morals.

(240) July 29 Saturday. It has been a week of dissipation. Tuesday the brass band gave a concert and invited all the musical ladies of the village to assist, but as the band is composed of men who are not of our station, we did not participate except as spectators, or rather, auditors, though several of our acquaintance did. A public appearance on the stage, is, I think of very questionable propriety, unless made in the most immaculate company.

I would not be willing to show myself, unless every individual in the company was my social equal. I am even more particular about my associates in any public theatrical or musical enterprise, than in the ordinary intercourse of life, because a public audience containing very mixed, and often disorderly elements, it is very necessary to inspire respect.

Wednesday, I spent the night at Cornelia Slaton's,[14] and went to a big country barbecue on Thursday. Henry Slaton[15] came for me in his fine new buggy, with his splendid thoroughbred: it is the finest turnout in the county what a pity he is such a poke himself. I believe I will give up trying to marry him off, because I don't believe he is going to do it, anyway, and then I find him so convenient, always ready to be made use of. When Gen'l DuBose offered to drive me home from the barbecue, he made no difficulty about it, and though the General's horse and buggy are not near so fine as my good country cousin's, he is a much pleasanter companion for a twelve mile ride. Yet, he hasn't half as much sense as cousin Henry, if the poor fellow only knew how to show it. Why is it that brains count for so little in the social market—that they really do seem to be of so little practical use in the art of making oneself agreeable? It was a Herculean task, on Wednesday afternoon, to spin out twelve miles of talk to poor cousin Henry, with a horse that flew over ground like lightening, while on Thursday, though Gen'l DuBose walked his horse every step of the way on purpose to take a long time, we were both as full of talk when we rolled up the avenue at Haywood, as when we left Frank Slaton's door. And yet, while the General was making his glib speech at the barbecue, I was laughing in my sleeve all the time, and wondering how on earth he could continue to say nothing in such fine words, and I admired so much more cousin Henry's good sense when he was called on by the crowd for a speech, and got up and said, "Ladies and gentlemen, you will have to excuse me—I am not a public speaker." Now, that was the difference between pinchbeck and rough diamond—but in society as in dress, pinchbeck makes the most show. What would one do with an unpolished gem in a ring? For my part, I am afraid I am like the vulgar herd, and prefer the pinchbeck—if the gilding don't rub off. A gem might as well be no gem for me, if its beauties have got to stay in a crating of rough clay.

We got home on Thursday, just in time to dress for a large party at Mrs. Arnolds. My dress suited me better than any I have worn in a long time, though I did have to dash it on in a hurry. It was lilac with white llama lace overskirt, waist and sleeves trimmed with print lace, skirt and basque of the dress covered all over with plaited flounces, that made me look like a big purple dahlia, Cora said. My gloves and ribbons were all of lilac,

trimmed with white lace, and I wore an elegant cluster of white mar-
guerites in my hair. Everybody said it was the richest dress in the room. I
enjoyed the party only so so—the company was not well selected.

I had Col. Alston talking to me most of the evening. I found that he
could talk about his family, so I wound him up and set him going, and
believe he would have gone on forever like the Dutchman's cork leg, if
somebody hadn't sent Wilkes Saunders to the rescue. Yesterday Mett and
I paid up a number of duty visits. This evening we are expecting Col.
Alston, and I am going to sit up all night with the Edings baby, and am half
sick to begin with. Tomorrow will be a day of much needed rest.

AUGUST 6. SUNDAY. If my diary were a newspaper, it might well be
named "The Sunday Times," or something of that sort, for I never find time
to write in it, except on Sunday. I have been trying all the week to make
progress in my story, but what with one thing, and what with another, I can
give only the afternoons to it, and not all of them. On Thursday, Cousin
Henry came in his fine turnout to carry me to a country school exhibition,
near Smyrna, about six miles from town. It was a delightful little trip: we
started at six, and returned home about midnight, by a glorious moon.
Everybody was there: I think there was a caravan of. . . .*

(243) . . . was curtained off for the stage, and everything was conducted
with classic simplicity. Thespis himself could not have been more independent of scenic accessories. The drop curtain consisted of two old chintz
bedspreads—one of them with a patch on it—sewed together and fastened
to a pole, which was raised or lowered at need, by two tall countrymen who
stood at either end, and lifted the pole, when in technical language we
would say the curtain was down, and dropped the pole when the curtain
was "up" which in this case meant down. For lights, the teacher stood on
one corner of the stage with a lamp in his hand, and two old codgers at the
other with tallow candles, while the parquet, as I suppose I may term the
brush arbor where the audience sat, had only the moon.

The entertainment consisted of poems, speeches and dialogues recited
by the country children with occasional interludes from the brass band. I
was sometimes ready to burst with laughter at the quaint mechanical ges-
tures and sing-song tones of the little youngsters, but I did my laughing in
my sleeve, and pleased the honest country folks around by praising everything I saw.

* The bottom of the diary page is torn away here. The text picks up at the top of
  diary page 243.

Next day, Friday, came a huge watermelon from old Sam Wynn, meant as an antidote, I suppose, to the moonlight ride with cousin Henry. It is jolly to have both our county members "waiting on" me, as the country folks have it. . . .*

(248) . . . elegant, but the company too young to be agreeable to a venerable spinster like myself.

SEPT. 3RD. SUNDAY. I find school teaching less odious to me than it was last term: I have begun by being very strict, and find it saves me much trouble. I have taken Maude[16] in, and think she is going to be bright about her books. I shall do my best to give her a good education, for it is all I shall ever be able to give her, I expect, and it will make her independent.

What would become of me now, if I were like Mattie Morgan, and most other girls of my class in society, who were educated only for show?

Mett and I have spent nearly every afternoon this week, making calls. Mrs. Hunter has gone back to Augusta without returning any of her visits, and we have to go round and do it for her, besides making a good many on our own account. Annie Maxwell is at the Dunwoody's looking so seedy and poverty stricken that it saddens my heart when I remember how elegantly she used to dress: before the deluge, she was very rich.[17] Tuesday evening, we spent at the bank, with quite a large company, and had a charming time: Wednesday and Thursday evenings we had company at home. Friday and Saturday I always keep free from engagements if possible. The Edingses have moved away, but Mr. Edings says his business will bring him back here very often, so we shall not have to give him up entirely.

OCT. 1ST. SUNDAY. I do not know what would become of me if it were not for this blessed seventh day: and yet, I am afraid I regard it less as a day of religious privilege, than as a time of perfect rest for body and mind. I get so worn out during the week that I don't believe I could live out half my days, if it were not for Sunday. Today I have done nothing but stay at home and coddle myself. I have been suffering all the week with a wretched cold, and believe I would have lost myself entirely if these two blessed days of rest had not intervened. I have been so hoarse since Tuesday that I can scarcely speak: I am better today, but talking to the children, lecturing and explaining will bring it all back next week, I am afraid. Added to school, an unusual streak of gaiety seems to have lighted on our little town. I was

---

* The bottom of this page is torn away. The text picks up at the top of diary page 248.

invited out every evening during the week, except two, when I had company at home. On Wednesday we had quite a large party, and I felt so sick, I had to go to bed before the company left. Week before last, we had invitations at the rate of two an evening, and there were a lot of people to be called on. I really do think when a poor mortal has to teach school, she ought to be excused from society, but somehow I can't get rid of it.

Father has come home from Elbert and Hart, broken down with fatiguing courts, and I am too hoarse to read for him, so he lies on the sitting room sofa, doing the best he can for himself. Generally, the happiest part of my life, is the Sunday afternoons when he comes into the library for me to read what I have written during the week. It is very wrong, I am afraid, but we poor working people have no other time. Father is as eager after my story as ever the public were for Dickens's; the first thing he asks when he comes home from court, is "Have you anything to read to me?" Poor father, it isn't often I have anything, for it takes me three or four weeks to write a single chapter. Saturday afternoons are the only times I have for writing, and not always the whole of them. We no longer have one session on Fridays now, so that cuts off half my play time. My poor eyes are so weak that I can never use them at night, and have to let whole hours of precious time slip by unemployed. I think it very hard sometimes, that I, who have so much for eyesight, should have had such a meager portion allotted to me. I said something to that effect last night, when father was complaining that I got on so slowly with my story. He told me then, that Judge Thomas when on his death bed exclaimed, "What the h'll does God Almighty want to come and kill me for? Why can't he take some d'nd rascal like Joe Miller that ain't no use to himself nor anybody else, and leave me alone?"

I thought it the most shocking thing I had ever heard—and yet, I am doing something of the same sort whenever I complain of my poor eyes. To see atall is better than I deserve, and I ought to be only too thankful that my eyes are not defective in a way to blind or disfigure me. Perhaps after all, it is best, for even now, when I know that I can't put down a word until Saturday I find my head constantly filling itself with all sorts of fancies when it ought to be digging away at realities, and if I know that I could take up my pen every night, I am afraid I would never get out out [sic] of dreamland. As it is, I sometimes wake from a brilliant *jeu d'esprit* between Audley Malvern and his sister, or a delicious love scene between Julia and George, only to find myself face to face with a black-board and twenty stupid children![18] Heavens, what a drudgery teaching is then!

I have written my book a dozen times over in my head. I can't help living in my romance at all odd moments, as when I am walking, or sewing, or sitting idle at night, but the trouble is, that I never think it twice alike. Sometimes I make out an exciting scene, or a sprightly conversation, and when I come to write it down, it is all different from what I thought: I get the very words fixed in my head, and then, don't even use the ideas. So characters and events change under my hand in the same way. People that I meant to be very important, sink into insignificance, and others that I hardly intended to mention by name, grow into the most prominent characters in the story. In short, I don't manage the tale atall, but it manages me, and the very people I make in my own head, take the reins out of my hand and turn out something very different from what I intended them to be. I don't know what will come of it: if I had time to sit down and put my story in proper trim and mold it according to a fixed model in my head, it might turn out something worth writing, but cobbled up in this irregular piecemeal fashion, I do not know that it will ever serve any other purpose than to amuse me and father. I do wish it would turn out a famous story, just to see how delighted father would be—but that is a wild thought—it takes genius to make famous stories—and it is not likely that a little country school mistress should have genius—or rather that one should have genius and be nothing better than a country school teacher. Mercy! how I do hate that schoolroom and what slavery it is to be poor! And there are those miserable wretches in Atlanta withholding father's salary for some miserable squabble of their own. Angier, the state treasurer, and Bullock, have been at dagger's points a long time. The latter has been traveling all summer, and his long absence and neglect of business, causes a great deal of grumbling. Angier takes advantage of the opportunity to increase the public discontent by refusing to pay out any money without the Governor's signature, which of course can't be had during his absence. None of the state officials can draw their salaries, and father's drafts have all come back from Atlanta protested—the first time such a thing ever happened to him. Mr. Irvin has taken my salary to help pay for his house, and heaven only knows when I shall get anything from that quarter. Mett and I can't buy a rag of winter clothing: we are all in a desperate strait—father can't even pay the servants' wages, nor can we buy so much as a paper of pins or a spool of thread, because forsooth, the state treasurer chooses to spite the governor. When thieves fall out, honest men don't always get their own.

OCT. 22. SUNDAY. I have not had the heart to open my journal for a long time. Mother has been sick all this week, and shows no signs of getting better. I don't believe she has ever been confined to bed before, since I can remember, and it makes me wretchedly unhappy. I could stand anything else, but to see mother and father gradually fading away under my eyes, withers my very heart. Mett and I lie awake every night, thinking about our troubles: we don't talk much, but when I hear her turn over in the middle of the night, and sigh wearily, I know that the same thoughts are in her mind that fill my own with visions worse than nightmare. Mett went to Mrs. Mattox's on Friday to see about a situation as governess that I think she can get, but if mother continues sick she will have to stay at home and look after the housekeeping, for I could not possibly do it and teach too. I am worked so hard now that I have lost half my interest in life: seven hours in the school room then buckle down to needle and thread the moment I get home, the dairy before breakfast, and after it gets too dark to sew, leave me little time for anything else—and with it all, my back gives ominous symptoms of breaking down. I am writing now, half lying down, to rest it, for Sunday is the only time I have to rest. I am up by daylight every morning, and must work although my back breaks. Fred has lost his place and though father is still able to perform his duties, I dread lest every turn of the court may be his last: he comes home from his sittings, so tired and worn out that it sickens my heart to see him. He scarcely eats anything, but is very fond of milk, and I always fill his glass half full of cream, so that it is very nutritious. We have succeeded in getting the P.O. for Mr. Morgan, and it is a great relief to my mind to get him provided for. Thom Pope is here at present—he is not as good a boy as Fred, but aunty wants him to stay here, and a demand upon one's hospitality can never be refused.[19] We shall have a real hospital of invalids, when cousin comes home in November: she writes that her health is worse than ever.[20] Dear me, I hope my back will be stronger in winter. I shall have such need of robust health. Company, we have not had much of since Belle Nash left.[21] Mett and I have absolutely sworn off from society—it is impossible to meet its demands, and all the others crowding upon us too—and to tell the truth, I have no heart for it. When Lettie and Lucy[22] come over, full of their summer's tour, and their projects for the winter, I wonder how on earth anybody can interest themselves in all that, and yet, there was a time when nobody cared more for all that than I. Society was not made for poor devils who have to gain their living by the sweat of their brows and it is a wise provision of Providence that working people lose their taste for company. It is a positive bore to me now; I will get off from a party on any pretense, and when the young men request permission to call in the evenings, we actually make up lies, and pretend previous engagements to get rid of them. I can hardly believe that I am myself, when I think how fond of gaiety I use to be—and the golden visions of my youth—where have they all ended? In poverty and obscurity. An overworked brain has no room for visions, and an overworked body no fancy for recreation—except the recreation of doing nothing. I look upon a state of utter inanity as the sweetest recreation in which I can indulge. My poor story hardly gets a thought: every Sunday father asks eagerly—"What have you got to read to me?" and Sunday after Sunday comes the same response, "nothing." My mind seems to have grown sluggish. Sometimes a bright thought will come to me, but I have to wait so long before I find time to put it on paper, that it fades away, or gets buried and obliterated under the rubbish heaps of my over burdened mind—the cares and anxieties, the pinchings and screwings to make both ends meet, the nasty little calculations for saving a dime here, a dime there, to say nothing of the wearisome lessons, that form the bulk of my mental food. And yet, after all my worry, the old home gets dingier and barer every day, and father and mother keep fading away before my eyes, carried off on the relentless tide of destiny, till they are borne over the great Niagara—all under my very eyes, and I cannot stay one single wave of the stream that is bearing us on. The helplessness of poor humanity is a terrible thing.

OCT. 29TH. Oh the blessed day of rest! I never realized the merciful provision of God for poor overworked humanity, till I came myself to be one of the working class. Sunday used to be a tedious day with me, and I half dreaded it as an interruption to my plans and pleasures, but now I hail it as the best of all days, and thank my merciful father for its institution. To think that today, it is actually my duty to rest—actually incumbent on me to do nothing, me, whose duty all the week is toil, toil, toil, till the soul is weary and the hands are faint, who can hardly sit down to eat my bread in comfort, for thought of the work that is waiting for me. True, I don't keep the Sabbath as rigidly as I used to, for many things are works of "necessity" with me now, that were not so formerly, and many a little labor of love that might perhaps lie heavy on my conscience if I had time for them during the six days of labor—labor so dull and heavy to me. I never open my journal on any other day and all my letters of luxury—for so I call those to friends, in distinction to business letters, bear the same date, and I sometimes steal a choice bit of secular reading that I could never enjoy but for Sunday. It is my only day for standing by the open windows and drinking in the beautiful weather, lounging lazily on the door step after dinner, for idle strolls among the autumn roses, and for a thousand other things that I never esteemed as actual pleasures, till the enjoyment of them became so rare. Perhaps after all, my Sundays are as well spent as when I used to read religiously, the long lessons appointed in the prayer book, and why may not a little recreation be a fitting celebration of the close of creation? I

believe now, since I have tasted so fully the sweets of a day of rest, that
there was a compassionate forethought in the Creator's mind for the generations of poor plodding overburdened humanity, that were to come upon
the earth.

Mother is no better, and I am afraid will not be for many weeks to
come. Henry thinks she has disease of the heart, but I can't think it possible that anything so dangerous should be the matter with mother. She
has never been sick before, that I know of, and she is not old enough to
fail from age: she is only sixty, and people often live to be seventy-five or
eighty. I hope nothing dangerous is the matter with her, but I can't help
being very miserable. I never had such feelings in my life, as I did last Monday morning when the seminary bell rang and I had to leave mother in the
midst of a dreadful paroxysm, and saw my poor old, feeble father, at the
same time, starting off for Lincoln court in the rain. The Seminary is at
least a mile from our house, so that I can never come home in recess, and
though I have a pretty path through the woods that shortens the distance
nearly one half, I never dare to walk it alone, for fear of stray niggers. One
hears so many dreadful things of them now, that I would sooner meet a
lion in a lonely place, than a "nigger fellow." That Monday morning was a
wretched time to me, but the weather faired off by noon and set my heart
at rest about father, and I found mother easy when I came home to dinner. Since then by the constant use of opiates, we have succeeded in keeping her quiet, until this morning, when she undertook to have her bed
changed, and the exertion brought on the worst attack she has had. Anything that quickens her pulse atall, brings on these dreadful paroxysms,
and we have to keep the house as quiet as a church to guard against the
least excitement, with mental or physical. She sees no one but the family,
and then but one or two at a time. Mett and I take it by turns to sit in the
room and nurse her, and we sleep there on alternate nights. She is such a
patient uncomplaining sufferer, that her nurses find little to do, and hardly
know, even when she is in pain—but oh, it makes the house so desolate—
I would rather all the rest of us should be sick at once. She used to meet
me at the little stile under the cedars everyday when I came from school,
and now I come into the sitting room and find her chair empty. God grant
it may not be so long.

Mett attends mostly to the housekeeping. I help about it here and
there, when I can, and do all the family darning on Saturdays. It takes me
all the morning, for the boys do wear awful holes in their stockings. I tried
yesterday to work a little on my story, over the darning: I had the skeleton
of a sprightly conversation between Audley Malvern and Claude Harfleur

in my head, and I undertook to fill it out, and put it in language over my sewing—but with the ragged stocking heels before my eyes, and a sick mother on my heart, made sad work of it—everything got into a hopeless jumble in my brain, and I almost despair of its ever coming right again. Poverty and sickness are poor incentives to romance—alas, there is too much stern reality about them. I am afraid I must bid a long adieu to Ruth and Audley, George Dalton, and Uncle Bruen, and shake hands once more with the commonplace people of everyday life. I do not know if it will not be a lasting farewell—that is, I fear they will take leave of me—my romance will rot on my brain, as it were, and spoil for long keeping.[23] Bright visions and vivid conceptions ought to be seized and committed to paper—the author's canvas—his lyre, while they are fresh in the heart, where my poor conceptions fade and grow dim, and sometimes die entirely out, and have to be renewed, before I find a spare moment to write them down. But a mother is more than a romance, more than the dearest children of one's brain, and God has called me to other work. I have often feared that it was a sin for me to write, because it makes the common duties of life so hard, and tempts so to neglect them, but I cannot resolve to lay aside my pen forever. When I think of it, the thing seems as impossible as to divorce myself from myself. This little steel tipped staff of pine is my fairy wand, that charms all cares away: as soon might an opium eater relinquish his drug—as soon might the flowers bid adieu to sunshine, as I give up the one friend that has never failed me.

This reminds me of a touching little incident I read the other day. A poor forlorn little old school mistress, had a female friend—the only living being that cared for her, to whom she used to write a letter every week. This correspondence was kept up many years, and was the only solace the poor little worn out school miss had amid all her cares. In course of time, the friend died, but the habit of the weekly letter was so fixed, the yearning for confidence and sympathy so strong, that the poor school mistress continued, every Saturday to write the accustomed letter, and at her own death, her little cabinet was found filled with letters, sealed and stamped, and addressed to her dead friend. What a commentary on the human heart those neglected letters must have been? I could almost weep, when I think of the poor solitary soul, turning for companionship to the dead. That is the way it will be with me when my poor old father is gone. These Sunday entries are my weekly letters—but it is time for me to go to mother. Mett has been in the room ever since dinner.

**NOVEMBER 5TH. SUNDAY.** Mother still the same. No material change in her, either for better or worse. We have holiday in our school next week, on account of the fair, which will bring crowds and is to be a time [of] general jubilation. The Agricultural Society has applied to me to act as reporter on the occasion, but I doubt whether I shall be able even to visit the grounds. We are to have a lot of company staying at our house, and cousin is coming home besides, and she is, equal to half a dozen ordinary invalids.[24] As it is, I see nothing of the outside world, except in passing to and from the Seminary. As soon as I come home from school every day, I take my sewing into mother's room, and sit there till time to start to school again. Saturdays, I do the darning for the family, and it occupies me nearly the whole morning: Marsh and Fred wear such big holes in their stocking heels, that I could almost be buried alive in them. I am so pushed for time, that I hem cup towels and dish cloths by feeling while I am sitting alone with mother at night, in the dark, with a wet cloth over my eyes, to relieve the burning. I have become so expert, that I can sew up straight seams and turn narrow hems almost as well in the dark as in the light, and occupation of any sort relieves the tedium of my long watches, very much. I generally sit with mother at night, to give Mett an opportunity of keeping up her music, as that is the only time she has to practice. Sometimes, when Fred is reading aloud to father a particularly interesting article from the Living Age or some of the English reviews, she keeps watch and lets me listen. This morning, went over to the cottage, and played along time on the organ myself. It is the first time in four weeks that I have indulged in such a pleasure, and then I was interrupted in the midst of it by poor Miss Wary, who came over from the Baptist Church to sit and talk with me. Since my time has become so precious to me, I think I have been particularly beset with unusual demands upon it. All sorts of out of the way people have taken it into their heads to branch out and call on me, or write letters. My correspondents never were so active as now, when my weekly bulletins to absent members of the family, about mother's health occupy the best part of every Sunday, and who should come poking to see me the other day, but Sue Norman, and the two Mrs. Colleys, quiet obsolete sort of people that I haven't visited for years, and living at the remotest extremities of the village, in opposite directions.

(261) But the last three days have been charming. Friday, the children and I were all in high spirits at the prospect of a week's holiday. A troop of them came home with me, along my beautiful path through the woods, and I stopped and played with them a long time under a great locust tree on the hillside, and helped them gather locusts, and even ate some of the trash with them.[25] The children and I get along splendidly together out of

school, where I don't have to manage them. I didn't know before, that there was such a strong love of children latent in my breast: I am perfectly devoted to my little scholars, and am growing more and more attached to them every day. I bring some of them home with me nearly every day, and the happiest part of the 24 hours is that walk over the hills with the joyous little souls. We all feel so good at being free, and high spirits and freedom and out of doors and children all go well together. I never like children so well as on a walk through the meadows, and I never enjoy Nature so well as when visiting her in company with children. The weather, too, is and has been enchanting: I never knew our after summer as beautiful; the flowers are blooming even more luxuriantly than in spring, and the air is so delicious that I want to open my mouth and drink it in. It is true, I can't enjoy it out of doors atall, except on my walks to and from school, but it is a blessing and a privilege just to look out of the windows [at] such weather as this. The views from mother's room are lovely in every direction, and as I sit alone by the window at the head of her bed, and look abroad over the joyous, free earth, I thank my God that I am permitted even to look upon so much beauty.

(262) NOV. 9 THURSDAY. A glorious November rain and nobody here. I went to the fair grounds yesterday and was both surprised and pleased to see what a smart show our county makes. The display of stock and vegetables is particularly fine. The finest thing among the flowers is the pyramid Lucy Pope and I made, and every body says it will certainly take a premium, especially as I made a little Confederate flag to put at the top. It is three feet high, a foot and a half in diameter at the base, and made over wet earth so that the flowers will keep fresh a week. We had 31 different kinds of plants, without counting the different varieties of roses and asters, all blooming in the open air. I had a nice time at the fair grounds, watching the races and meeting so many people. I had not expected to go at all, but the committee sent me a complimentary ticket and insisted so upon my going out that I could not well refuse. They appointed me and Mrs. Hogue to make the wreath for the queen of love and beauty who is to be crowned at the tournament today, but I have a dress to make for poor old Miss Fanny Andrews, who is much more needy than the queen, so I declined, on plea of having to stay with mother. Love and beauty always find plenty of people to think for them and wear their crowns, but the poor little school mistresses and their calico gowns have to take care of themselves.

I have an event to chronicle. Who should pounce in upon us last night, but Robert Ball—the veritable Robert, of awful memory, and what is more surprising still, the reckless youth has grown up into a fine looking man, and holds a most responsible and honorable position as general agent for the Macon & Brunswick and Atlantic & Gulf RRs.[26] He arrived here at 3 o'clock this afternoon, on RR. business, which he dispatched in a most business-like manner, and hurried off again at 9. P.M. He found time to call to see us after supper, and staid [sic] till the train left. He met me so affectionately, and seemed so glad to see me that my heart quite warmed towards him, and I began to repent of all the hard things I have thought and said of him. The poor fellow has had a great deal of trouble since I saw him. Some poor girl was foolish enough to marry him, and now she is in the lunatic asylum, and he has two poor little helpless children knocking about the world, with the taint of hereditary insanity, and satanity too I am afraid, in their blood. He has led the roving vagabond life for which alone he is fitted ever since he left us. [He] was on the surveying corps of the great Pacific R. R., and the last time I heard of him, before he popped in upon us, he was vibrating between Salt Lake City and San Francisco. His account of himself is not altogether reliable, as his characteristic inveracity still clings to him, and it is not easy to sift truth from falsehood in his narrative, as internal evidence is all we have to test it by. When he told us how often the sheriff had sold him out, I could believe unreservedly, but I was rather more dubious about the elegant houses and furniture that were disposed of. His present responsible and important position is a puzzle to all of us. I would dismiss it as a myth if I had only his word for it, but there are the printed circulars of the RR. association and its flaming posters, with the name R. Jamison Ball, in great awe inspiring capitals. Is there really reason to hope that the powerful energies of his nature which have so long run to waste, have at last been turned into some useful channel?

Upon the whole, I think the man is an improvement upon the boy: want of education is his worst fault; he would talk very well, barring the lies, if he did not try to use so many words that he don't know the meaning of, and to talk about so many books that he has not read.

Later. I have had such a delicious day that I can't help chronicling it. Everybody went off to the tournament, where by the way, Mett was crowned queen, leaving father and me in sole possession.[27] Mother was well enough for me to sit in the next room and write, which I did all the morning, and then we had such a delightful little dinner, with rich strong chocolate, the only beverage to which I could ever become slavishly addicted.

In the afternoon, Cousin arrived, and everybody came back from the tournament in a state of glorification over Mett's honors, and she did look magnificent with her crown of white flowers. They have all gone off tonight to Mattie's grand concert, leaving me in charge of the two invalids. Mett likes to go out and I don't care much about it, so I stay at home in her place when I don't have to go to school.

DEC. 3RD. A cold drizzly gray day, but full of intellectual sunshine for me. I sat by the fire in mother's room all the morning, reading that delicious book, so admirable in its honest, straight forward homely simplicity, *My Schools and Masters* by Hugh Miller.[28] Annie Barnett has lent me *Les Miserables* in French, which I read whenever I can steal a moment during the week. As it does not greatly interest me, I don't care much for interruptions. After next week our winter vacation begins, and then I think I shall take up my own story again. I have pretty well given up all idea of going to Florida as mother's health does not improve in the least, and father shows symptoms of breaking down again. We have put two beds in the room and nurse them both there together. My winter things have arrived from N. Y., but I have neither occasion nor inclination to wear them. In the way of luxuries, I got myself a pretty set of furs (Siberian squirrel), an elegant point appliqué collar, a set of tortoise shell ornaments, and have sent to get a package of visiting cards engraved. The rest of my half year's salary, I shall invest in a sewing machine for the benefit of the family. Next Thursday and Friday, Bishop Beckwith is to be here with Mr. Weed rector of the Church of the Good Shepherd at the Sand Hills.[29] Mr. Hunter has gone to take charge of the church in Columbus, so we shall lose him: I don't think I shall ever be satisfied with anybody else. Marsh had a lot of boys to dinner.

(265) DECEMBER 10. SUNDAY. It is with a heavy heart that I open my journal today. Mother is so ill that Henry has telegraphed for Garnett and written for sister [30] to come home. She seems utterly prostrated and is out of her head all the time. Fred Pope[31] is here sick with chills, Maude and Cora have both been in bed all the week, and I laid up with a strained ankle. The old grey cat got under my feet the other night as I was coming down stairs in the dark and tripped me so that I fell from the turn to the bottom. Fortunately school closed on Friday, in the winter vacation, and I can hobble about the house on a crutch very well. The Bishop's visit, with all this turmoil, was very unsatisfactory. He staid [sic] only one night and preached such a splendid sermon against modern infidelity that I feel fortified against the *Westminster Review* for six months to come. Yesterday the agent brought my sewing machine to me. It is a first class Wheeler and Wilson, which I prefer to every other make. It can do everything but walk and talk.

It costs me 90 dollars with all the new attachments, but it is an investment that will pay. I determined ever since I first began teaching and found how hard pressed I would be for time that I would buy a machine with the first money I got, and since mother's sickness has given us so much more work, I feel double the necessity of having a machine. My pay for the half year will be something over $215, so that I can afford to buy one and I want always to spend part of my salary so as to be of use to the rest of the family. If mother ever does get well, she will like so to sew on it, but she shall never sew any more except for amusement. I believe I am even more troubled about Mattie Morgan just now than about mother. She has been acting for some time in a way that scandalized the whole community and overwhelmed Cora and Henry with mortification. She runs the streets all day long, loafs about on the square with men that she ought not even to know, and acts in a way that seemed altogether unaccountable until yesterday. A friend of the family who thought her relations ought to know of it, commissioned me to tell Henry that she has actually taken to hard drink and is half the time in a state of utter intoxication. She got at it from drinking lager beer for her health. I was so shocked and horrified when I heard it, that I felt right faint, and yet the thing has long been a matter of public notoriety in the village, and I am afraid it must be true, for nothing else will or can account for the things she says and does, short of sheer insanity.[32] I feel that Henry ought to know it, and I have been trying all day to make up my mind, and lay awake over it all night. My God, what will come upon us next? As if poor Fred's case wasn't dreadful enough to have now a drunken woman in the family![33] Merciful heaven, what have we all done that such curses should come upon us! I must try and tell Henry tonight, and yet I am so sorry for the poor fellow, with all his troubles, that I can't find the heart to do it. And yet there is another chance to save the poor girl. The habit is not yet an old one and might possibly be broken. She starts for Alabama on Friday, and her relations there ought to be warned. No pains, no severity even, ought to be spared to save Mattie from such a horrible fate, for a fall of another kind will be apt to follow this. Old Mr. Morgan is shut up in the P.O. all day and, for many reasons, would never find out by himself, anymore than I did. Henry is so incensed at her carryings on, that he has refused to hold any intercourse with her, except what is barely necessary, for two months. Next to old Mr. Morgan, he is her nearest male relative, and if he knew all, would pity and try to save her.[34] Poor girl, the effort must be made; they say she is already a laughing stock and a bye-word to the whole town, and the "uncs gude" [?] are beginning to look askance at her. Mett and cousin say that I am the proper person to tell Henry, as he has already confided his domestic truths to me. I wish mother was well—she would know just what to do, but all these dreadful things must be kept from her.

(268) **DEC. 24TH SUNDAY.** The past two weeks have been so full of wretchedness that I have not had the heart to open my journal. Mother grew steadily worse until Tuesday, when she had such an ill turn that even the doctors gave her up, and we sent for Mr. Tupper to read the prayers for the dying over her. She rallied, however, and her physical condition seems to be slowly improving, but there is no comfort in that since her mind is hopelessly gone. She barely retains consciousness enough to know when a stranger comes about her. She will not even bear aunty or Cora in the room. Fortunately sister came on Monday and can help Mett and me nurse her. She will allow no one else except father and the boys to come near her. We three take it by turns to sit up with her at night, and we all sit together and grieve over her all day. I sat up last night and have been sent off to rest this morning, but I find greater relief in telling my troubles. Whoever sits up with mother attends to father, too. He is very feeble, and since mother's sickness [Father] has been moved into the big room over the parlor, which is very cold, so that in bad weather we keep a fire burning all night, and put warm bricks to him. We try to economize each other's strength as much as possible, for we don't want anybody else to nurse mother.

We may not have the privilege of waiting on her long, and want to do all we can while we can. Besides, I don't want anybody else to see mother in her poor demented state. Her delirium is so sacred to me, and an outsider might repeat her vagaries and gossip about her infirmities. I remember once hearing somebody repeat, in mother's presence the wandering vagaries of some poor bed-ridden old lady, and when the officious gossip was gone, mother turned to me and said, "That is what people come to when they get old and infirm. I hope, my child, when I come to be a crazy old woman, that you will never let my infirmities be gossiped about in that style." When her mind first began to wander, I would sometimes in the night mistake her mutterings for a call to me and ask what she wanted. The sound of my voice would bring her to herself, and she would say, "Oh, I was wandering in my mind. I'm glad I have my children to nurse me, for you will excuse all my nonsense, and not repeat or talk about it." I know that she dreaded above all things the failure of her mind, and I respect her failing faculties now more than I did her most sparkling efforts of wit in her best days. I never knew before how much I loved mother. It almost breaks my heart to see her in this dreadful condition of utter imbecility, varied by attacks of fearful delirium, in which she drives us all from her with shrieks and can only be quieted with stupefying drugs. The death that I dreaded at first is nothing to this. Mother was a person of such remarkable intellectual vigor, so strong and self-reliant, so looked up to and admired by all who know her, that the contrast between what she was and is, is perfectly heart-rending. I first fully realized it about a week ago. I went into her room with a bottle of wine. She was sitting propped up in bed, trying to eat her breakfast, looking as sick and listless that the very sight of her brought tears to my eyes. Several of the family were already in the room. She was not then past recognizing us, and still would try to say something pleasant to each of us that came about her. As I entered, she turned to me with a vacant look that tried to be smiling in spite of the weariness and suffering it wore, and said, "Here you all come, dropping in one by one." It was such a melancholy ghost of the old half playful, half chiding way in which I have so often heard her say those very words when we lazy children [would come] into the dining room, one by one, late for breakfast, that I dropped the bottle and rushed out of the room to keep from bursting into tears before her very eyes. Since then I have wept until the fountain of tears seems exhausted, and I have learned to sit down dry eyed, face to face with this blackest of miseries—mother hopelessly out of her mind. When I thought she was going to die, it was very dreadful, but nothing like this endless misery. I know from the whole tenor of her past life that she must be ready for death, but I wanted some further assurance of it. Monday night, the King of the Terrors seemed drawing near, and Mett and I who were watching beside her, prayed all night that the Lord would give us some sign that she was ready. I know that I was a miserable sinner and had no right to ask for such grace, but, oh, I did want it so! and sure enough, Tuesday morning when we thought she was dying, she came to herself long enough to express her faith in Christ, and to let us know that she was perfectly willing to go. Mr. Tupper talked with her and says she is prepared to die at any moment. That is a great comfort, for if she should live for years, her time for preparation is now past.

(271) A few nights before that dreadful day, Mett was watching beside her. It was warm and she threw off most of the cover, but towards morning, she began to be cold, and the chill gave an awful turn to her wanderings; Mett heard her say, "There are the tall monuments and handsome tombstones gleaming in the sunshine, but there they all lie, there they lie, under the cold moss, oh, it's so cold in the grave—cover me up, cover me up." Mett

hastened to rouse her, and to draw up the cover, but there are those awful words to haunt us till our dying day. How can we ever put mother into the ground after that? We have not told any of the others about it, because it would make them so unhappy, but the echo of those words has added bitterness to my tears many a night since.

Monday was the last time she called me by name and recognized me. She often calls me to her now, but when I answer, receives me with a blank vacant look, and asks who I am, and when I tell her "Fanny" she will tell me to go away or ask with a puzzled air, "What Fanny." Oh, what human heart can stand all this?

Almost the last rational words she ever spoke were to me to take care of Fred. It was Tuesday when she seemed to be dying—she had been begging us all to take care of Marsh, and I said, "Yes, mother, we will all take care of Marsh." "And Fred, too." She said "poor little Freddy—how I have thought of that boy." Fred went to her. She patted him on the head and said, "poor little Freddy." She had got back into her wandering and thought Fred was a little boy. Poor Fred, poor miserable Fred, do what I can, I can never be what mother was to him.

# 1872

(272) **FEB. 25. 1872. SUNDAY.** It has all been over for more than a month, and yet I can hardly find it in my heart to trace over that dreadful time. The world has seemed an utter blank to me ever since, and if it were not for father, life would not seem worth the having. Instead of growing lighter, the trouble becomes harder to bear; as time moves, I seem to have no interest in life and feel as if nothing could ever give me pleasure anymore. I can't enjoy the beautiful weather because mother is shut out from it, and it seems like a sin to make ourselves [ink blotted] in the house in cold wet nights, because she is left out in the rain. I lie awake long hours in the night thinking about her, and sometimes it seems as if I shall die or go mad from grief.

On the 22nd of January, just as the first faint streaks of dawn were breaking in the East, her spirit flew out to meet the light. Never shall I forget the cold cheerless light of that desolate winter morning, as I stood looking out at it from our chamber of mourning, with poor old father weeping at my side, and how I stretched out my hand toward the light, and prayed her to come back. I hope it wasn't a sin, but I can very well understand now why the Romanists pray to their dead for them, and sweet and comforting thought it is. I have so long coupled the names of father and mother together in my prayers, that even now, I very often put in her name before I know it, but she doesn't need my prayers now.

She was dying all day Sunday, and we didn't know it. She had been gradually sinking into a stupor all the week, and it gradually became more and more profound until she never waked from it again. Sunday night was my turn to sit up, and mother was so low that for the first time we called in outside help and sent for old Mrs. Ellington to come and watch with me. About eight o'clock I went to my own room, took my bath as usual, put on my dressing wrapper, and went back to mother's bedside. I had not been out more than an hour, but there was a change in mother's face that shocked me, and a rattling sound, whose meaning I guessed only too well, accompanied the slow measured breathing. I called old Mrs. Ellington and asked her if mother was dying. "Yes, my child," she said, in her simple straight-forward way, "I think she is. I don't want to grieve you, but it's got to come, and there ain't no use deceiving you." What my feelings were then I can never describe, nor the scenes of that awful night. Aunty was sick in bed and could not be with us, and we determined not to call poor old father till the very last; it would all come upon him soon enough. I stole into his room once to see if he needed anything and found him sleeping as peacefully as a little child. I said to myself, "Sleep on now, and take your rest," and stole out of the room. When I went back again, at 2 o'clock, it was charged with a terrible message. He was still sleeping, but waked with a start at my touch. He knew what I had come for before I spoke and the groan that he uttered will sound in my ears till I die. I cannot describe what followed; it can never be written down save on the tables of my heart.

About 4 o'clock, I went back into father's room to warm my feet, for it was very cold, and the watchers surrounded mother's hearth. I had sat there some half an hour when sister came in and touched me on the shoulder. "Come sis," she said, "Mother is going very fast."

I went back to the bedside where I had watched for so many weeks, and watched again for the last time while her breathing grew slower and fainter, till there came one long deep sigh. Then all was still, save the ringing of the old town clock, as it struck six: then we were all led out of the room; and she was left to strangers.

The weather was so cold that we kept her two whole days before we buried her. She was the most beautiful creature after death that I ever laid my eyes on. Every trace of suffering had disappeared, and the light of heaven was on her face. She looked scarcely twenty years old, and father almost fainted when we carried him in to look at her. He said she was so like when he first married her. Father had her photograph taken, but the picture was not like her; that heavenly light, no created sun could fix. We kept her all the time surrounded with flowers, and her own greenhouse plants were put around the white couch on which she lay. A beautiful calla blossomed out just in time to be placed in her coffin, with the violets and hyacinths and white camellias that were put there to wither beside her. Lucy made a beautiful crown of violets, and Lettie a cross of hyacinths for her coffin, and some kind friend even decorated the top of the hearse with white flowers. Everybody was as good to us as they could be; people were coming in all the time to see what they could do for us, and Lettie and Lilla, and cousin Will,[1] and Mr. Tupper, and plain good old Mrs. Ellington were like angels sent from heaven. Mr. Tupper said more to comfort me than I had ever thought could be said for the loss of mother. One pretty thought of his will always be with me. When we carried him into the parlor to look at mother, he smiled pleasantly, and said, "This is one of your treasures laid up in heaven." I shall try to think of her henceforth, not as locked in the tomb, but as my "treasure in heaven." I love to look at her as she lay in her still heavenly beauty. I was always afraid of dead people, but I never felt afraid of mother. I couldn't stay out of the room where she lay. At night before I went to bed I would go in and look at her and talk to her, and put flowers to her lips, and ask if they were not sweet, just as if she were alive, and who shall say she did not hear me? One night I sat and watched her till I fancied I saw her breathe; then I imagined I saw her lips move, and the fancy took such strong possession of me, that, although I had till that moment purposely refrained from touching her, I felt that I must break the wild illusion—and laid my hand on her forehead. I shall regret to my dying day that I did so; it was cold as marble and sent a shudder through my very soul. Those wandering words of hers came back to my mind, "There they all lie, there they lie, under the cold moss. It's so cold, cover me up," and they will ring in my ears till judgment day.

The memory of those days is almost a great black blank to me. At the funeral I remember there were a great many poor people trudging along behind the long procession of carriages, and their presence gratified me more than all the honors paid her by the rich. I thought of the time when Dorcas lay dead, and the poor stood around her weeping and showing the garments she had made, and when I remembered all the good she had done to them, I felt that her words did indeed follow her, and that every tear shed upon her tomb by the poor she had succored would add a precious jewel to her crown.[2] The most desolate of all was the return to our empty home after the funeral, and empty now, it will always seem, no matter how many are here. I hear of people losing their mothers every day, but I never knew what it was before. I thought when I saw mother lying on her bed with her mind entirely gone, and capable only of suffering, that I was willing for her to go. I even persuaded myself that I would rather she should die than live in that state, but now that she is gone, I know how sadly I deceived myself, for I would give up every hope I ever had in life just to have her back even as she was then—just to look at her and wait on her.

For the last month we have been busy getting ready our mourning and receiving visits of condolence, but mother has never been out of my thoughts one moment. We have received letters from all parts of the country and all the papers have noticed our affliction and now, these conventionalities dispensed of, the world is ready to forget her. The crape is taken off the door, and everything goes on about the house as usual and people come here and laugh and talk with us as if nothing had happened, but, oh, how different the house is. I keep her chair and work basket and table just as they use to be. Her sick room is the only thing that has been changed—the associations connected with that are painful enough at best. Everywhere I turn, there is something to remind me of her. Only yesterday, in looking over my things, I came upon some caps that I had cut out and never finished. She was buried in a white dress cap I had made for her when she was first taken sick, never dreaming to what use it would be put. I try to keep myself busy and to occupy my mind with other things, but the great trouble hangs upon like a dead weight all the time, and if at any moment I am surprised into a laugh, I start half shocked at myself, and the old sorrow comes rushing back stronger than ever. The next week after mother was buried, I took out my story, interrupted for so long, and tried to write on it but in the whole week got over only two pages. I started fresh in the middle of a chapter, at the broken word where I had laid down my pen to run and do something for mother, and it was hard to bind together the broken thread of thought, broken by such a rude shock. I was over three weeks finishing that chapter, but when at last I read it to father, he was so highly entertained, and laughed so heartily at my "old Judge's" freaks, that I felt my interest revive, and every day to the work. Those hours are almost the only happy ones I know. Father takes such an intense interest in the story, that somehow I associate the work in my mind with him, and feel as if I were doing it for his sake. I believe now it is the greatest desire of his heart to see that story finished, and he looks so feeble that there is a feeling in my heart that I had better hurry if I want to gratify him. I don't know that I could ever have the heart to finish it, unless I do so before he goes away where mother is.[3]

Yet there is no telling that last chapter I wrote when my heart was so sad is one of the most humorous in the story, and made father laugh almost the only real genuine laugh he has enjoyed since our troubles came upon us. I am not teaching this year, and I have a spleen. . . . *

(281) . . . their time. Cora is going to New Orleans if Henry can raise the money to have her eyes operated on by cousin Bolling.[4] I told him to take the $100 that I had saved from my last year's salary to buy a watch, but Mr. Morgan has promised to pay her expenses as far as Montgomery, and father or Mr. Ben Micon will fix up the rest.[5]

Garnett has just left us. He too, came on a sad errand: to bring poor little Rose's remains. We had a grave dug just at the foot of mother's, and met the train that brought him at the cemetery. The weather had been horrible ever since mother died nothing but sleet and rain and cold for three weeks, and the ground was so saturated with moisture that the little grave filled with water almost as fast as it could be bailed out. A terrible storm came up just as the train arrived and added its own horrors to the gloom of the occasion. We must have presented a gloomy spectacle to the people in the cars, we four women shrouded in black and covered with long black veils, standing there under the pines by the cemetery stile with the little group of gentlemen who had come to assist us. The precious little coffin was brought out under the black sky, and put away in its damp grave while pelting rain drops packed down the wet clods that were shoveled upon it. I hope I shall never never again be called upon to see and to suffer what I did that day. When all was done, and the gentlemen went away, we dressed both graves in camellias and white hyacinths, and then came sadly home. Garnett's visit did father a great deal of good. He looks stronger and better than he has done since the great calamity. He says now that he thinks he shall be able to get through his circuit, which begins next Monday. Mett and I have been doing our best to bolster him ready for his courts. We sleep in a little room next to him, so that we can attend to him at night, and put hot bricks to him when the weather is cold. I run down to the sitting room early in the morning to see it made comfortable, and some of us stay with him all day, for he never likes to be left alone now. I hope his mind will be diverted when the courts open, for he is devoted to his profession, and always seems better in the society of lawyers. Next to Garnett's visit, I think an evening Mr. Lumpkin, his new solicitor, spent with us diverted him more than anything that has happened for a long time. I expect Mrs. Elzey and Touch will be with us in

* Pages 279 through 280 are missing. The text picks up with page 281.

April, and I am expecting great things for us all from their visit. They are spending the winter in Montgomery, for Touch's health. Sister leaves next week, but father will be on the circuit then, and I hope won't miss her. We are to have another loss, too, in our dear friends the Tuppers; they are going to Richmond to live. Mrs. Tupper is down stairs now, waiting to see me, so I must close this long entry. I don't know when I shall ever make another, or even if I shall ever have the heart to keep a journal again.[*]

[*] This is the last entry on the last page of the journal.

Metta Andrews, Fanny's younger sister and traveling companion during the period of the Wartime Journal and the 1870 trip to Newark. Reprinted from the Frances Andrews photograph album, MSS004, Lupton Library Special Collections, University of Tennessee at Chattanooga.

Park Place, fronting Military Park, Newark, New Jersey, c. 1875. Fanny wrote, "Mrs. Ward, cousin Lilla, as we call her, lives in an elegant brown stone mansion facing a beautiful park, on Broad Street. There are great elm trees before and behind, where the birds sing just as they do at home. . . ." Reprinted from the Robert Dennis Collection of Stereoscopic Views, Photography Collection, Miriam and Ira D. Wallach Division of Art, Prints and Photographs, The New York Public Library.

Broadway from the footbridge, New York City, c. 1870–75. "It is astonishing how soon one's money does give out among New York shops." Reprinted from the Robert Dennis Collection of Stereoscopic Views, Photography Collection, Miriam and Ira D. Wallach Division of Art, Prints and Photographs, The New York Public Library.

Bennett Monument, Greenwood Cemetery. "The handsomest monument in the cemetery at present, is over two of James Gordon Bennett's children. It cost $50,000 the guide told us, and is really a splendid piece of work. It is the figure of a woman with clasped hands, kneeling before a pedestal upon which stands an angel, bearing off a child." Reprinted from the Robert Dennis Collection of Stereoscopic Views, Photography Collection, Miriam and Ira D. Wallach Division of Art, Prints and Photographs, The New York Public Library.

Tourists at Niagara, c. 1872. "My first view of them revealed only a great column of white mist rising in the air. It has been a bad rainy day, and my first glimpse of the falls was under a cloud—but Niagara is Niagara. . . ." Reprinted from the Robert Dennis Collection of Stereoscopic Views, Photography Collection, Miriam and Ira D. Wallach Division of Art, Prints and Photographs, The New York Public Library.

Annulet Ball Andrews, Fanny's mother. "Mother was a person of such remarkable intellectual vigor, so strong and self-reliant, so looked up to and admired by all who knew her. . . ." Reprinted from the Frances Andrews photograph album, MSS004, Lupton Library Special Collections, University of Tennessee at Chattanooga.

Judge Garnett Andrews, Fanny's father. An engraved portrait of Judge Andrews, at forty years, that appeared in the *Sunny South* (Atlanta, Georgia), Saturday, August 3, 1878. Reprinted from the Garnett Andrews Collection, folio 1839, box 2, Southern Historical Collection, Wilson Library, The University of North Carolina at Chapel Hill.

Marshall Andrews, Fanny's younger brother, c. 1864. This wartime photograph is labeled in Fanny's album, "Little Marshall and his pet dog, Toby. The boy is dressed in a full suit of Confederate handmade clothing. The left leg is stretched out behind in a childish effort to hide the home made brogan shoes, which were a sore mortification to him thus bringing both the leg and the shoe into awkward prominence." Reprinted from the Frances Andrews photograph album, MSS004, Lupton Library Special Collections, University of Tennessee at Chattanooga.

Wilkes County Courthouse, Georgia, c. 1855. Fanny's grandfather Frederick Ball served as the architect for Washington's first brick courthouse. The courthouse and the nearby "old bank" were torn down around the turn of the twentieth century and replaced with a "modern" structure. Reprinted from the Frances Andrews photograph album, MSS004, Lupton Library Special Collections, University of Tennessee at Chattanooga.

Haywood's front gate, summer 1867. Fanny captioned this photograph in her album, "Haywood in summer. This photo was taken in 1867." Reprinted from the Frances Andrews photograph album, MSS004, Lupton Library Special Collections, University of Tennessee at Chattanooga.

Site of Haywood's front gate, summer 1999. Now called Greens Grove, the modern roadway follows the path to the site of the Haywood mansion.

Col. Garnett Andrews, Fanny's brother. "I know Garnett is a highminded fellow, and won't be apt to advise anything very dreadful—That is why I always like to take him into council: he nearly always thinks just as I do." Reprinted from the Metta Andrews Green photograph album in the private collection of David Harris, Washington, Georgia.

Frederick Andrews, c. 1860, Fanny's brother. "Poor Fred, poor miserable Fred, do what I can, I can never be what mother was to him." Reprinted from the Frances Andrews photograph album, MSS004, Lupton Library Special Collections, University of Tennessee at Chattanooga.

Rosalie Beirne Andrews, c. 1869, Garnett's wife and the mother of "darling little Rose." Reprinted from the Frances Andrews photograph album, MSS004, Lupton Library Special Collections, University of Tennessee at Chattanooga.

Julia Butler Toombs, Fanny's niece, the daughter of Fanny's older sister Cora and Troup Butler. Reprinted from the Metta Andrews Green photograph album in the private collection of David Harris, Washington, Georgia.

Cora Andrews Butler, Fanny's older sister. It was to Cora's and Troup's plantation that Fanny and Metta traveled to escape Sherman's invading army, an incident detailed in Fanny's earlier diary, *Wartime Journal of a Georgia Girl: 1864–1865*. Reprinted from the Frances Andrews photograph album, MSS004, Lupton Library Special Collections, University of Tennessee at Chattanooga.

Capt. Troup Butler, c. 1870, cotton planter,
Confederate army veteran and husband of
Fanny's sister Cora. Reprinted from the
Frances Andrews photograph album,
MSS004, Lupton Library Special
Collections, University of
Tennessee at Chattanooga.

Arnold "Touch" Elzey Jr., the
son of General Arnold Elzey,
c. 1872. Touch, during the last
days of the war, brought news to
the Andrews family that Garnett
had been wounded in Salisbury,
North Carolina. Reprinted from
the Frances Andrews photograph
album, MSS004, Lupton Library
Special Collections, University of
Tennessee at Chattanooga.

General Arnold Elzey, c. 1864. Andrews family friend and the patriarch of the family from whom Fanny took her pen name. Reprinted from the Frances Andrews photograph album, MSS004, Lupton Library Special Collections, University of Tennessee at Chattanooga.

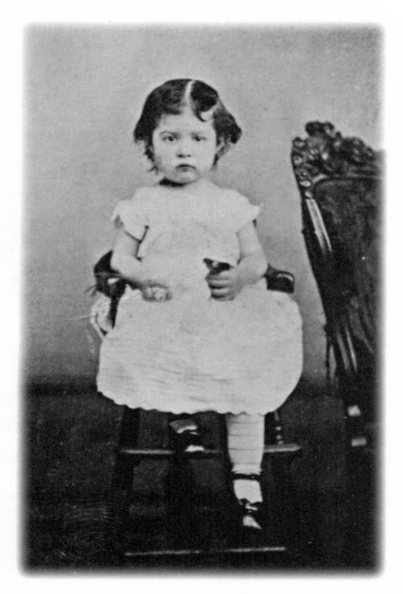

Maude Andrews, the daughter of Fanny's brother Henry and sister-in-law Cora. "I have taken Maude in, and think she is going to be bright about her books. I shall do my best to give her a good education, for it is all I shall ever be able to give her, I expect, and it will make her independent." Maude grew up to be an early twentieth-century journalist. She was a columnist for many years with the *Atlanta Constitution*. Reprinted from the Frances Andrews photograph album, MSS004, Lupton Library Special Collections, University of Tennessee at Chattanooga.

Fanny, c. 1879, about the time
of her third novel, *A Mere
Adventurer*. Reprinted from
the bookplate of *A Mere
Adventurer*, Lupton Library
Special Collections,
University of Tennessee
at Chattanooga.

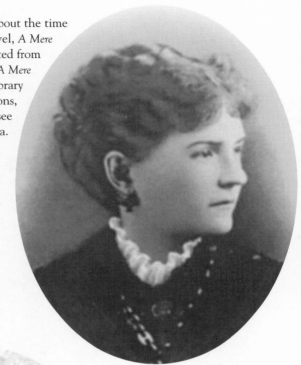

Cousin Lucy Pope. "The finest thing
among the flowers is the pyramid
Lucy Pope and I made, and every
body says it will certainly take a
premium, especially as I made a little
Confederate flag to put at the top."
Reprinted from the Frances Andrews
photograph album, MSS004, Lupton
Library Special Collections, University
of Tennessee at Chattanooga.

Cousin Will Pope, c. 1869. Fanny wrote to her brother Garnett after their mother's death, "Cousin Will, too, was so good that I can't find any word strong enough to express it." Reprinted from the Frances Andrews photograph album, MSS004, Lupton Library Special Collections, University of Tennessee at Chattanooga.

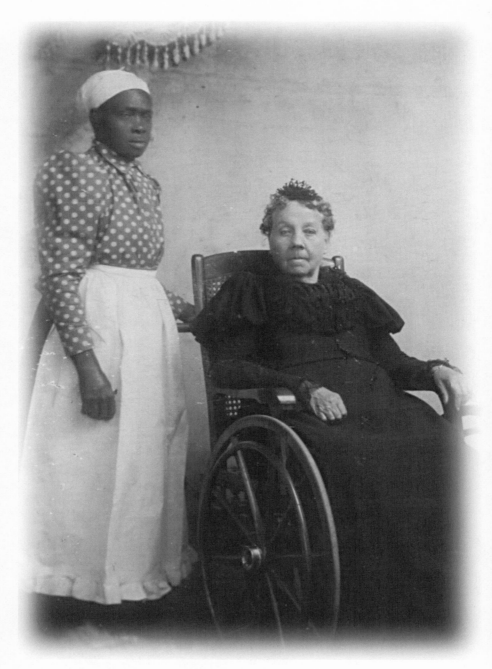

Aunt Cornelia (Cornelia Ball Pope), Annulet's sister with "faithful servant." Aunt Cornelia was the mother of Cousin Lettie and Cousin Lucy and the step-mother of Cousin Will. She was certainly one of the strong-willed women in the world surrounding Fanny Andrews. Reprinted from the Frances Andrews photograph album, MSS004, Lupton Library Special Collections, University of Tennessee at Chattanooga.

Sophia, "Mammy Sophia." Fanny wrote of Sophia in the *Wartime Journal,*
"my dear old mammy—Sophia by name . . . so superior, and as genuine a
'lady' as I ever knew. . . ." Reprinted from the Frances Andrews photograph
album, MSS004, Lupton Library Special Collections, University of
Tennessee at Chattanooga.

Hobbs, c. 1870. This may be a photograph of the "old Hobbs" who served as chaperone to Metta and Fanny during the Newark trip. "Old Hobbs" may also be the Captain Richard Hobbs mentioned by Fanny in her wartime journal. Civil War records indicate that Capt. Hobbs of Albany, Georgia, lost an arm in the war. The left sleeve is empty in this photograph from the album of Metta Andrews. Reprinted from the Metta Andrews Green photograph album in the private collection of David Harris, Washington, Georgia.

General DuBose. "I don't believe Dudley DuBose has sense enough to know there is anything disgraceful in heading a gang of rowdies and assassins." Reprinted from the Metta Andrews Green photograph album in the private collection of David Harris, Washington, Georgia.

Andrews family servants, 1906. A note in Fanny's album indicates that the aging Andrews family servants shown in this 1906 photograph were still living on the Andrews property and were being supported by Metta Andrews Green. Reprinted from the Frances Andrews photograph album, MSS004, Lupton Library Special Collections, University of Tennessee at Chattanooga.

Andrews family plot, Resthaven Cemetery, Washington, Georgia. In the rear of the obelisk that marks the Andrews plot in Washington's Resthaven Cemetery are (left to right): Frederick Andrews, Annulet Ball Andrews, and Judge Garnett Andrews. Fanny's granite headstone is to the left below. Not shown in this photograph, but at the foot of Annulet's grave, is the gravestone for three-year-old Rose.

Fanny's grave. A granite headstone engraved only with the initials E. F. A. marks Fanny's grave. "I want only a plain granite or marble cross over me when I die, and if any fool does go and put an epitaph there, other than the name and date, I'll haunt him." Fanny's name is also on the obelisk with the names of her brother Garnett and Garnett's wife, Rosalie.

# Articles by Eliza Frances Andrews

## Romance of Robbery

NEW YORK WORLD, August 21, 1865

*Details of the Recent Extraordinary Operations at*
*Washington, Ga.—Curious Glimpses of Life in the*
*New South—Justice Done to Brute in Shoulder Straps*

(From our own Correspondent)

Washington, Ga., August 10 (1865).*

The little village of Washington, Ga., has, for several months past, been the scene of many stirring events, few of which have excited deeper interest than the robberies committed in and around the town. Immense treasures have been disposed of there, and gold has passed through scenes that would embellish a romance.[1] Tradition will, no doubt, hand down to posterity fabulous tales of buried treasure surpassing anything we have heard of the famous Captain Kidd; and, as thousands upon thousands of the lost moneys are still unaccounted for, future discoveries may tend to increase the marvels of tradition.

### A Bad Habit

The fashion of plundering was first started by some disorderly cavalry, when the surrendered armies were passing through Washington, *en route* for their distant homes. They "cleaned out" the commissary quartermaster

---

* Garnett Andrews Collection, folio 1839, box 2, Southern Historical Collection, The University of North Carolina, Chapel Hill.

and ordnance stores which had been collected there for the use of the so-called confederate government, in order, they said, to prevent them falling into the hands of the Yankees. Powder, shot, and shell were strewn along the streets to be collected by negroes and school-boys; and for a long time such large quantities were scattered about the railroad depot that it was dangerous to walk there lest some stray spark from a locomotive or a cigar should ignite the whole and cause a terrible explosion. What the soldiers could not make way with themselves, they distributed to whoever would take it. Ladies walking on the streets during the days of the riot had reams of villainous letter-paper and worse pens pitched at them by rough hands, with an injunction to use them in writing to their sweethearts. A taste for plunder once started, it did not rest with the soldiers alone, but negroes, boys, and "mean whites" helped themselves to whatever they could find, and the federal authorities afterwards discovered government wagons, bacon, &c., in the hands of well-to-do country farmers.

**A Horse For Any Price**

Horses were in great demand among the returning soldiers, and so many were stolen by them that all the country people, from Charlotte to Washington, came to regard every man in uniform as a horse-thief. Many were stolen by soldiers who had no need of them, merely for the pleasure of selling or trading them off, and as Washington is the beginning of an unbroken line of railway communication with the West, horses there cease to be of use to many. In spite of the thieving which had almost stripped the country of stock, the market became so gorged, that horses were sold at prices varying from $2.50 to $5 and $25, and I know of one instance in which a good mule sold for twenty-five cents.

**Money "Lying Around Loose"**

The next system of plundering was on a grander scale. The confederate treasury, or a great part of it, scattered between Abbeville and Washington, was pillaged by that bane of the rebel armies, their undisciplined cavalry. Some of it, not actually pillaged, was so strongly threatened by its guard that the officers where obliged to divide it among them. The same old excuse was given: the confederacy had "gone up the spout," to use the favorite rebel slang, and the money would fall into the hands of the Yankees if "our boys" did not take it. Most of the money was carried West by the soldiers into whose possession it had fallen, but some of it remained behind and negroes were seen on the streets of Washington with bars of gold and silver in their hands.

## Romance of the Dollars

Some of it met with a singular fate. A party of cavalry who had possessed themselves of four or five thousand dollars, took panic, and fancied they were hotly pressed by a large body of Yankees. As they went flying through the streets of Washington, expecting every moment to be overtaken by their imaginary pursuers, they threw their money into Robert Toombs's yard—whether merely to keep it from the Yankees, or for the double purposes of cha [unreadable] them and aggrandizing Toombs, must forever remain a matter of doubt. Toombs, among whose failings dishonesty can never be reckoned, collected the gold, and turned it over to Captain Lot Abraham, the first federal provost-marshal of the place, who promised to spend it in buying rations for the paroled rebel soldiers, at the time passing through the village in large numbers.

## Friends or Enemies

Washington was doomed to escape neither Scylia nor Charybdis. After the rebel soldiers, came the federals, and as no public stores were left for them to pillage; they fell upon private property. Little mischief was done by them in the village, where Captain Abraham's garrison maintained pretty good order, and protected the citizens; but the country around suffered severely. I saw many of the soldiers who passed by the house where I was lodging with ladies bracelets on their arms, silver cake baskets and teapots tied to the pommels of their saddles, and ruffled linen pillow cases—the pride and joy of country housewives—fat with plunder tied on behind. Some had women's drawers tied up at both ends, the legs filled with booty and slung astride their horses. They hung men up by the neck to extort confessions of concealed treasure, and stripped some plantations of what horses the rebels had left. A curious accident happened to a country planter, who had hoarded a little gold through all the reign of paper money. On hearing of the approach of the Yankees, he hastened out to conceal his treasure, and was sliding along the side of a hedge, when he spied a party of them coming toward him. With the forlorn hope of saving his money, he pitched the bag containing it over the hedge, when, lo, it hit a Yankee soldier plump on the head.

## A Royal Robbery

But the grand finale of all these robberies came off in May, when the paroled men had pretty nearly all passed through. It is a deed which surpasses, in the audacity of its accomplishment, the magnitude of its consequences and mystery of its surroundings, all the exploits of Robin Hood or Shan O'Neil. It contains robberies within robberies, wheels within wheels, a perfect labyrinth of roguery and knavishness which no Theseus has yet been able to thread. Amid the present upturned state of things, in a country where public and private veracity seem to have fallen in the general overthrow, it is almost impossible to learn the exact truth concerning events which take place under our very noses, but after carefully collecting and sifting facts, I think I can give something very like a true account of this notorious bank robbery, which occurred not twenty miles from the place where I have been sojourning for six months.

### Half a Million in Gold

Nearly half a million in money and jewelry had been sent by one of the Virginia banks, for safekeeping, to the secluded little town of Washington, which no one ever imagined would be drawn into the grand march of events. The treasure remained secret and secure in the village bank, amid all the plundering that went on around, but Taylor and Weissiger, the men who had it in charge, began to grow impatient to get it back to Richmond. They were urgently recommended by the cashier of the bank at Washington, and other men of sense and experience, to wait until the country became more settled, or, at least, to avail themselves of the transportation which the federal authorities offered by way of Augusta and Savannah. But their advice was disregarded, and the treasure, in the face of sense, reason and experience, packed into wagons and started, with an insufficient guard, for Abbeville. A soldier in town saw the wagons packed, and believing them to contain confederate treasure, hurried off and gave notice to two men named Maston and other stray cavalry from East Tennessee. These soldiers, having received no pay for a long time, concluded, to help themselves from what they believed to be government money—that being considered lawful plunder. It is thought they were assisted by others, whose identity, like many things connected with the robbery, is as yet involved in mystery.

### How It Was Done

The bank officers and their party halted at night near the Savannah river, and, stationing a guard over their camp, betook themselves to rest. The story goes that the guard fell asleep also, when the robbers fell upon them, and made off with the treasure. Next day the news reached Washington, and excited great indignation; for it was understood that the property of many widows and orphans of rebel soldiers was invested in the bank.

Taylor and Weissiger offered a reward of five thousand dollars, and ten per cent of all the money that should be recovered. The first clue towards discovery was given by a bright, new silver quarter—something uncommon in these poverty-stricken regions—which a man spent at a settlement called Danburg, in the "dark corner" of Wilkes county. Four men from Danburg pursued the suspicious owner of twenty-five cents, and overtook him on the road to Washington. He gave up four or five thousand dollars, and named other parties concerned in the robbery.

Weissiger, assisted by some nineteen or twenty men from the region about Danburg, then went out and arrested several robbers, recovered from $15,000 to $17,000, and learned the names of other guilty parties. It was understood that these others were well armed, and would fight if any attempt were made to arrest them; so Weissiger's party retired to improve their own equipments. In the meantime, one of the Chenaults, of whom we shall have more hereafter, was sent by the thieves to negotiate for them. Having learned that the money was private property they agreed to give up their portion and influence their associates to bring in the balance, in return for which the bank officers promised not to have them arrested. They then collected from their hiding places in the old fields and branches about $70,000. One hundred and eleven thousand dollars, in all, was recovered and safely locked up in the bank at Washington.

**Capture of the Thieves**

Three or four days after this, the rebel general, E. P. Alexander, with a party of paroled men upon whom he could rely, went out to apprehend the rogues, and succeeded in capturing most of them. He rested for the night near Danburg, not far from where the robbery was committed. Some of the inhabitants of that region, including several of the men who were out with Weissiger offered to assist General Alexander in guarding his prisoners—an offer which he gladly accepted. No sooner had they gained his confidence than they turned traitor, and rescued the prisoners. This act seems to implicate them with the robbery, but they cleared themselves by saying that the arrest of the highwaymen was a breach of Weissiger's contract, and they were honor bound to release them. Some of the men engaged in the rescue were, no doubt, prompted by honorable feelings, but I cannot answer for the motives of all; many people suspect very ugly things. There is certainly great rascality somewhere, and the trouble is that nobody can meddle in the business, even with purest intentions, without getting his fingers or his reputation soiled. Many stories are afloat in Washington about various countrymen having been seen with large sums in specie, and it is said that the Danburgers call their country California, and speak jocosely of mining; but these are merely rumors, and should be treated with little respect in times when everybody suspects everybody, and Truth seems to have turned her back upon mankind.

There is some place in the vicinity of Washington, which may be regarded as a miniature California, for over $200,000 is unaccounted for up to this time.

### Plundering All Round

The first robbers were plundered in their turn, and much of the money found its way into the hands of negroes, who watched them visiting their treasure. But all the privileges recently conferred upon the negro could not secure him from pillage. A fresh band of highwaymen collected together, who went about the country whipping negroes and hanging them up by the thumbs to extort treasure from them, and four thousand dollars were actually taken from one black man. At last, one Mrs. Moree, upon whose servants the freebooters began to exercise their "mining" skill, came to town and demanded protection of the federal authorities. General Wild, who was at that time inaugurating his reign of terror in the village, went out with a party of soldiers and proceeded to arrest various persons whom he considered "guilty of being suspected." Then was perpetrated a series of atrocities unheard of in civilized lands since the days of King James II and his thumb screws.

### Outrageous Proceedings

The most conspicuous personages arrested by General Wild were the Chenault family—two brothers, their wives, the son and two daughters of the elder brother. They were people of wealth and standing in their part of the world. Dionysius Chenault, familiarly known as "Nish," had been for years the glory of camp-meetings and country barbecues. He is a sort of Methodist preacher—what they call a local preacher, I believe, but unlike the Patriarchs of old, loves good company and good cheer. I have been in a tent at camp meetings, and always found the cream of country society under his shed, the biggest puddings and fattest pigs on his table. He lives in a large country house in real old southern planter style, and hospitably entertained Mrs. Davis and her party on their sad journey through Georgia. But "Nish's" glory departed under the iron hand of General Wild. He hung up the three Chenaults by the thumbs, until "Nish," a large fat man, weighing over two hundred pounds, fainted under the operation. The other brother, John, who is already half dead with consumption, was tied up by the thumbs with his hands behind him, an attitude which rendered the torture excruciating. The three men were hung up where they could hear each other's groans and shrieks, a circumstance which almost doubled their torture.

### Disgracing the Uniform

While General Wild was regaling himself with the spectacle, a scene equally atrocious was enacting among the ladies who had been arrested by a subaltern. They were confined in a room to be searched by a negro woman, but the federal lieutenant stood looking on at a window to see that it was well done. The ladies stripped off to their chemise, and then, in the name of decency, protested against going any further, but the lieutenant forced them to drop the last garment below their waists, and exhibit themselves almost in a state of nudity before he could be satisfied that his task was accomplished. The house was searched. One hundred and twenty dollars in money and Miss Chenault's watch taken from them, and they were detained in the woods a whole day before being brought to Washington. They were confined several days with other ladies in the court-house, although a citizen of Washington offered bail to any amount, or even to entertain a Yankee guard, if the ladies could be permitted to lodge at his house. They were all finally reduced to a diet of bread and water—a proceeding which met with so little approbation, even from common soldiers, that the Yankee guard smuggled fruits and melons to their prisoners.

### A Brute Come to Grief

General Wild's career was cut short at this point by the arrival of Colonel Dayton, of General Steedman's staff with orders for his arrest, and he left the village amid the general rejoicing of both rebels and Yankees. If the South is to be conciliated, it is not to such men as Wild that the work should be confided. Certainly, hanging up men by the thumbs and stripping women naked is not very conciliatory policy.

The arrest of Wild [?] provided satisfaction to the [?] ing that there is protection for [?] under the shadow of the old flag. I heard a rebel say that it gave him greater respect for the Yankees than he had ever thought it positive for him to feel. With such men as Steedman and the present provost-marshal the conciliation of the South may soon be effected. It is better to lead than to drive a spirited people, and nothing wins the confidence of the rebels and quells their discontent, like manners and justice on the part of the federal authorities.

---

## Georgia: The Elections, A Peep Behind the Scenes

THE NEW YORK WORLD

Pine Wood, near Albany, Ga., November 6 (1865).[*]

As elections seem to be the centre of interest just now, especially at the South, where a new political system is just beginning to operate, a few particulars concerning the recent elections in this State may not be unwelcome to Northern readers. The telegraph has, of course, acquainted everybody with the main result long ere this, but a little local gossip as to how those results were brought about may not, even now, come too late to be of interest. Residing on a large plantation, in one of the most flourishing cotton regions of the South, I have as fine a post of observation as could be wished for my present purpose.

On all the plantations which I have visited in this section, the most friendly relations seem to prevail between the owners and their employees, and on that one which I now reside, sixty of the planter's former slaves— all attached old family servants—have remained with him, ever since their emancipation. Though they all belong to the "Loyal League"[2] they talk to their old master about their political affairs with more candor than might be expected, and candor on their part is met with liberty on his. Not only was no effort made to induce them to vote against the Radical ticket, or to follow his own example of not voting at all, but every facility was afforded them for reaching the polls, and the same was done, on all the neighboring plantations. The Pinewood estate is some thirteen or fourteen miles from the county seat, too far for walking, so on the second day of the election the planter's mules and wagons were placed at the disposal of the new lords of creation. They were off by daybreak with a mighty trolling of horns and explosion of old blunderbusses. The fondness of negroes for

[*] Garnett Andrews Folio, Southern Historical Collection, The University of North Carolina, Chapel Hill.

noise and powder smoke is wonderful. It is the height of every man's ambition, to possess something that he can shoot off and make a fuss with, and they never turn out for any celebration, civil, political, or religious, without a great show of military weapons. Very little importance is attached to these demonstrations, for the negro with his gun, is like a boy with his first tin sword, when he struts out to look big, and attack imaginary dragons in turkey cocks, or giants in gate posts. Even if the real intentions of the negroes were as redoubtable as they would like to believe, their achievements could not amount to much in the present state of their equipment and discipline, for the greater part of their cherished weapons are rusty old blunderbusses that would not kill a cricket at two paces, and their management of these is so awkward that to hit a pine tree at ten paces is considered quite a feat among negro marksmen. But, harmless as these demonstrations may appear at the present, they can hardly fail to bring about mischievous results in the end by fostering a spirit of violence and insubordination.

It can hardly be expected that the negroes should see the absurdity of all this bluster when those to whom they look for guidance and instruction thought it necessary to guard the polls with United States muskets at every precinct of importance; though the supreme indifference manifested by Southern whites during the election days ought to have convinced even the bitterest radicals that the aid of firearms was not needed to secure their majority. Respectable white people throughout the State refrained from voting and went about their business as quietly as though they were in no wise concerned with the election—as, in fact, they were not, being so greatly overpowered by negroes and radicals that their suffrages could make little difference, one way or another. The negroes seemed somewhat perplexed at the refusal of the white people to vote, but to one who has attentively observed the events of the past few days, it will hardly seem a matter of surprise, that respectable men should look with contempt upon an institution which has been so degraded and abused as the ballot, in the five military districts. When the negroes have played with their new liberty a little longer, and find that it never fills an empty stomach, they may learn to value it as little as do the Southern whites. In this county, the son of a radical candidate was the only white man who voted, and in the neighboring town of Albany, a blundering Irishman, who voted by mistake, and a radical candidate who voted for himself, filled the list of white voters. In several counties as Clay and Sumter, there was not a single white vote polled, while in Bibbe, with its flourishing city of Macon, there were only eight. This apathy on the part of the whites caused serious anxiety to the radicals, for when the three days originally appointed for the election had expired, it was feared that a majority of the registered electors in the State, had not voted as required by the Reconstruction Act, and so their measures might have gone by the board, after all, had not General Pope lent them a helping hand, and extended the election two days longer.

Had this been the only means employed for increasing the Radical vote, the other party, accustomed to such arbitrary proceedings, would have thought little of the matter: yet the frauds and deceptions that were practiced can not be overlooked. In the border counties, negroes were brought over from Alabama and Carolina to swell the colored vote of Georgia, while many, after voting in their own county, repeated the operation in an adjoining one. I know at least three on this plantation who went to Albany and voted after their votes had been thrown out on account of non-registry in their own county. The negroes are too ignorant to be held responsible for these frauds; but the falsehoods that were practiced upon their simplicity and credulity will ever remain a black chapter against their perpetrators in the books of the recording angel. On the plantation from which I write there are several quiet old negroes who did not care to vote, and remained comfortably at home, while the others trotted off to the polls. They were greatly disconcerted when their comrades returned, and brought them word that a heavy fine was the penalty for not voting at all; but their master—or "boss" as the negro language of the day will have it— failing to convince them of the absurdity of this story, finally pacified them by promising to pay their fines himself. As this story failed of its purpose, the negroes were next day informed through some mysterious channel, that if they did not vote they would be taken from their families, and sent off to work on the Pacific Railroad, thousands of miles away. I undertook to reason with one old fellow, who came to seek his master in great consternation after hearing this new report.

"You call yourself a free man, now, don't you, Uncle Jack?" said I.

"Dat's what dey all tell me, dat I free," he answered as if not quite sure of the fact himself.

"Well, I never heard before of anybody's taking up a free man, and sending him off to work on the railroad just because he didn't choose to vote. Your Mass B. has not voted, and you know he is not going off to work on any railroad. How can you call yourself free, if anybody has a right to treat you in that fashion?"

"Dat do look might strange," said the old man, scratching his head in great perplexity; but, as he was still unconvinced, his "Mass B." told him to take a horse and go to town and satisfy himself—which he did. In some places the negroes were told that they would be sold back into slavery if they did not vote the Radical ticket, while in others the story ran that non-voting was a penitentiary offense. It is no matter of wonder that the Southern whites never succeeded and seldom attempted to convince the negroes of the falsity of such reports; for they have been taught to believe that their former owners have no wish but to entrap and deceive them. I myself once heard a Radical editor in addressing a negro mob, tell them they must not believe what was said to them by white people at the South, except radicals. "Some of these people," he said, "will tell you that registration is only a trick to get your names, in order to make you pay taxes. Now, you all know that is a lie, and you see these people won't do to be trusted." Thus artfully, was the deception that had been practiced by one or two unworthy Democrats or the joke perhaps, of some wag—for wags are very fond of poking fun at Cuffee—turned into a weapon against all Southern people who happen not to have followed the example of such creatures and Joe Brown³ and his like.

The negroes are as often the dupes of their own blindness and ignorance as of the machinations of evil men. One can hardly tell whether to laugh or to sigh, at the part they have been playing during the past week. If such grave interests were not at stake, this last act of the reconstruction comedy, would be the most laughable ever presented to the world. The effort of keeping up with their own names, was one of the main difficulties that many colored voters had to contend with. The negroes have not yet got used to the grandeur of possessing surnames, or "entitles," as they call them, and change their appellations so often, that it is impossible to keep the run of them at all. One man Jimboy, for instance, is Mr. Tate in the cotton patch, and Mr. Jones when he gets his Sunday clothes on; while Scipio, is Mr. Fields one month, Mr. Robinson the next, and Mr. More the third. These changes occur so frequently, that many of the negroes not only alter, but forget entirely, the names or "entitles" under which they registered. Legality would require that the votes of such should be thrown out, but in many places, the only consequence was, that they voted under as many of their names as they could remember—casting a vote for each one, and thus materially swelling the Radical majority. Those negroes who were able to give their own names correctly, could not do as much for their candidates. On at least one large plantation to my certain knowledge, there is not a solitary negro that can tell who or what he voted for, or has any distinct idea what voting means. On Sunday after the election, one of the new sovereigns asked me to write a letter for him. After the usual preliminaries about sending "these few lines to let you know that we are all

enjoying good health, and hoping these few lines may find you," etc., the
task of dictation became painfully laborious, and the letter became nothing but a string of messages, such as, "Tell Phillis, Psyche sends how d'ye
to her; and Pollo says tell Dinah how d'ye. Give my compliments to
mother and sister Rose, and tell Pompey how d'ye." After a page or two,
even this resource seemed to fail, and Cuffee scratched his head so nerv-
ously, and looked so helpless, that, touched with compassion, I tried to
assist him a little, and suggested that the brother to whom he was writing,
might be interested in knowing what sort of crop he was making. "Oh yes,
tell 'em dat," he cried, delighted at the idea—and, scratching his head
more piteously than ever, when, with the benevolent intention of render-
ing fresh assistance, I suggested that he should tell about the election, and
what he did when he went down to C——, to vote. But this seemed only
to involve him in deeper perplexity. "Why you see," he said, as if in apology for not adopting my suggestion, "I can't tell notin' 'tall 'bout none o'
dat, cause I aint never yet got at de sense of it to have no 'magination to
see what it's all 'bout. You see when we went dar to vote, de man what was
dar to 'tend to it all, he giv'us tickets and tell us what to do wit em, and we
all done justd alike he tole us, and now we's done voted, we's just got to
wait and see what'll come uf it." I asked the three foremen of this plantation, the most intelligent negroes on it, whom they had voted for, and not
one of them could tell. "De man dar just gi' us tickets wid the right names
wrote on 'em, and tole us what do wid 'em so we knows we done voted
right," was the reply of all three. Could a herd of cattle be driven more pas-
sively than these ignorant, credulous beings? A few days before the election, one of the negroes, fresh from a meeting of the Loyal League, and
trying to explain the political intentions of that powerful brotherhood,
told me that they were going to vote a man in for a year, and then, if he
didn't do right, they would vote him out, again. When I asked what he
meant by *doing right*, he could only fumble with his hat, and say "well, you
see, if he do anything that ain't right, we'll vote him *out* again." One venerable "uncle" on the Pinewood plantation gravely declared his intention
of voting for "missus," "cause," he said, "she be sure to do what's right: she
gib old Cæsar fine new bed-quilt t'other day—she gib him victuals from
white folks dinner ebery day—missus be sure to do what's right."

Here, I think we have some glimmering of what the negroes mean by
"doin' right" When asked what they voted for, their almost invariable reply
is, "to git our rights." I have never heard one of them answer the question,
"what do you mean by getting your rights?" but it is plain, from various indications, that "getting their rights," is, in their minds, equivalent to getting

their hands into other people's pockets. The only tickets they ever heard of before, were circus and railroad tickets, and they have an idea that the "Radical ticket" will admit them to something much better than a show of the horses, or a ride in a railroad car. So general was this conviction, that in many places, negroes appeared at the polls with halters in their hands, to lead home the mules and horses, which they confidently expected to receive, as a reward for casting a vote. Even though the hope of immediate gain has been disappointed, they still cling to the belief that there is some hidden virtue in the mere act of voting which is to dispense with labor and raise them all in some mysterious way, to wealth and prosperity, and in the meantime they neglect the only legitimate means by which wealth and prosperity are to be attained. Cotton lies wasting on the ground for want of hands to gather it, while these new lords of creation are devoting their time and attention to the affairs of the country. The mere act of leaving their business to vote is a small matter, but I certainly do not think it conducive to the prosperity of any country that its laboring population should be forever galloping off to hear political speeches, attend meetings of loyal leagues, or play soldier with rusty blunderbusses and pocket-pistols; and the effect of these demoralizing influences is apparent all over the South. Not many days ago, when riding with a friend through a part of the country I had not visited before, we came upon a dreary waste, covered with broom sedge and blackberry bushes, which I pointed out, as fulfilling my idea of the wild moors we had read about in English books. "Why, that is uncle Cato's cotton patch," explained my companion with a laugh; and on closely inspecting the "wild moor" I could discern a few little stunted balls of cotton, peeping up here and there from under the sedge. The field was part of a farm that had been rented to a negro on his own responsibility, and is a fair sample of every one, without a single exception that I have seen; entrusted entirely to the care of blacks, without the superintendence of a white man; so it is plain what we have to expect, if Thad Stevens's confiscation scheme should ever be carried out.[4] If only those negroes who are entitled to vote, were tempted away from their proper business by the novelty of political excitement and the constantly recurring celebrations and demonstrations, the planters would not have so much reason to complain, but even the children would grow obstreperously loyal on such occasions, and the women turn out to display their parasols and artificial *chignons.* By the way, the radicals made a great mistake in neglecting to bestow the right of suffrage on negro women for they will always be cheap instruments, even after the men become too wise to be managed with cocks and bulls. A red silk parasol, and an artificial waterfall of fair blonde hair would buy the vote of the last one of them, from the most respectable old "mammy" down to the rawest Dinah in the cornfield. Think of it, Messrs. Sumner and Stevens, before you lose your majority in Congress.

I am not a planter, and have no personal interests whatever to serve in writing this communication—neither have I recorded the foregoing facts from any feelings of unfriendliness towards the negro, for I have none; nor do I wish to deny those good qualities which he really possesses. The negro is affectionate, kind-hearted, and confiding, but these virtues alone will not make statesmen, and it is plain that in his present state of civilization the services of the negro are much more useful to his country in the cotton field than in the cabinet. When he is enlightened by education and experience—when he learns that industry, not theft and agrarianism, is the only legitimate source of wealth—then perhaps it may not be unwise to entrust him with a proper share in the government of the nation, but in his present state of ignorance and credulity, which render him but a tool in the hands of others, he is neither a fit nor safe receptacle for the overwhelming power that has been placed in his hands. How the experiment in Congress may end, or what effects it may produce, is not in the power of man to devine. Like Cuffee with his voting, "we ain't never yet got at de sense of all dat, to have no 'magination to see what it's all 'bout," and like him, we can only "wait and see what will come of it."

# Dress Under Difficulties; or, Passages from the Blockade Experience of Rebel Women
*by Elzey Hay, of Georgia*

GODEY'S LADY'S BOOK AND MAGAZINE, 1866

I have somewhere seen an account of the inmates of the Millbank prison, in England, and, among other things, it was noted how women's instinctive love of dress clung to them through all the difficulties of their situation. Some of them displayed wonderful ingenuity in the arrangement of their prison dresses, making them appear as graceful and becoming—or, rather, as little ungraceful and unbecoming—as possible, and gave the keepers much trouble by their continual efforts to alter the prescribed uniform into something like a faint shadow of prevailing fashions. One would electrify the little community by some cunning device for a hoop-skirt; another drove it wild with the discovery of a way to make corsets out of bed-ticking; while a third raised an excitement which might rival that produced by the introduction of the *waterfall,* when she rouged her cheeks with red threads, cunningly drawn from some cloth on which she was sewing. The matrons, and other officials, whose business it was to prevent these little infringements of prison regulations, were baffled and outwitted in spite of their most rigid discipline. Although shut out from the world, with none to note or care how they were dressed, these poor reprobates took the same pleasure in exciting the envy and admiration of each other, that any city belle feels in outshining a rival. They would slyly twist their wiry locks into fanciful coiffures, purloin tallow candles for pomade, and a bit of looking glass was more precious in their sight than gold.

The struggles of these humble worshippers of fashion are a faint representation, on a small scale, of what we Southern women went through with during the blockade. Let those who have never experienced it set their imaginations to work, and conceive, if they possibly can, what must have been the condition of ladies in society—and very gay society, too—cut off for four years from their supplies of new dresses, shoes, gloves, linen, buttons, pins, and needles, ribbons, trimmings, and laces, not to mention the more urgent necessities of new bonnets, hoop-skirts, and fashion-plates! How we patched, and pieced, and ripped, and altered; how we cut, and turned, and twisted; how we made one new dress out of two old ones; how we squeezed new waists out of single breadths taken from skirts which could ill spare a single fold; how we worked and strained to find out new fashion, and then worked and strained still harder to adopt them—all these things form chapters in the lives of most of us, which will not be easily forgotten. Those who wish to learn economy in perfection, as well as those who interest themselves in curious inventions, will do well to study the experience of a blockaded devotee of fashion.

We managed pretty well during the first year of the war, for although we were too "patriotic," as we called it, to buy any "new Yankee goods," most of us had on hand a large supply of clothing. Planters were rich men in those days; and their wives and daughters always had more clothes than they could wear out. As soon as we became tired of any article, we would give it to some of our servants, and often, towards the close of the war, have I seen my "mammy" or my maid in cast-off dresses that I fairly grudged them, wondering how I could ever have been so foolish as to give away anything so little worn. Before the blockade was raised, we all learned to wear every garment to the very last rag that would hang on our backs.

In the first burst of our "patriotic" enthusiasm, we started a fashion which it would have been wise to keep up. We were going to encourage home manufacture—we would develop our own resources, so we bought homespun dresses, had them fashionably made, and wore them instead of "outlandish finery." The soldiers praised our spirit, and vowed that we looked prettier in homespun than other women in silk and velvet. A word from them was enough to seal the triumph of homespun gowns. Every device was resorted to for beautifying a material, in itself course and ugly. Our homemade dyes, of barks and roots, gave poor, dingy colors, that would have made a pitiful show among the dazzling hues of Northern bazaars, but the blockade effectually shut off all the fine things that might have put our *"patriotism"* out of countenance. One old lady made a really brilliant dye by dipping wool in pokeberry juice, and then inclosing it for several days where Peter put his wife—in a pumpkin shell. The color obtained was a brilliant red, but this process was too tedious for anything that had to be dyed in large quantities. Various shades of brown and drab, with some very ugly blue, were the chief colors used by us in our homespun dresses. Before things came to be very bad, we used to buy Turkey red, and have our homespuns striped with it. Some had the patience to ravel out scraps of red flannel, which was respun and used for striping dress goods. It is almost incredible, the number and variety of patterns that could be manufactured by an old woman with a hand-loom.

Homespun travelling dresses, of modest color and make, were really very pretty and appropriate; but some had the bad taste to try to make them fine with red cards, flounces, velvet buttons, etc., which was a very unsuitable and incongruous way of trimming them. Some enthusiastic country ladies spun and wove, with their own hands, full suits of clothing for themselves; and a famous present for soldiers was a pair of gloves, or socks, made, from beginning to end, by the fair hands of the donor. Such gifts pleased the soldiers, and led us to believe that we were following in the footsteps of our revolutionary ancestresses, who, we had been told, were mighty at the spinning-wheel and knitting-needle. Those of us who were not inclined to industry, testified our "patriotism" with much outward show and parade. We had ball-dresses of white factory cloth, such as our negroes used to wear for under-clothing. By candle-light, it had very much the effect of white merino, and worn with neck-lace and bracelets of strung corn, and coiffure cotton balls, constituted an eminently Southern dress, which would make its wearer the star of any ball-room.

All this was well enough while the novelty lasted, but that wore off in a season, and when summer came, we found our homespun insufferably hot. Still, the blockade did not pinch us very hard: there were a few dry-goods left in the shops, and we pounced upon these with greedy fingers. There began to be, however, a marked change in our style of dress. Instead of kid gloves, we wore silk, or lace mitts; we had no fresh, new ribbons; our summer dresses were no longer trimmed with rich Valenciennes lace, and our hats and bonnets were those of the last season "done over." In a word, we began to grow seedy, and we felt it; but our Southern soldiers still swore that we looked prettier and dressed better than they had ever seen us, so we were consoled—while their dazzling uniforms gave that brilliancy to our ball-rooms which our apparel failed to supply.

In time, however, things began to grow desperate. There were no goods in the shops, save in a few old-fashioned *robes a lé,* double-skirts, and other marvelous prints, in huge patterns, which the skill of the best *modistes* could not render presentable. Buttons, needles, and pins began to fail. Imagine a dearth of pins in a lady's toilet box! Think of it, my fair reader, the next time you dress for a ball, and know what we Southern women endured! Laces, ribbons, flowers, and trimmings were out of the question. We could not even freshen an old dress with a new bow or a cambric ruffle, and every-body knows how much such little trappings assist and brighten the most indifferent toilet. We had to patch up something out of nothing—to make bricks without straw.

Happily, Fashion favored us, where Providence did not—that is, such fashions as came to us. We knew very little of the modes in the outer world. Now and then a Godey or a "Bon Ton" would find its way through the block-ade, and create a greater sensation than the last battle. If it were rumored that Annie or Julia had a book of fashion, there would be an instant rush of all womankind for miles around, to see it. I remember walking three miles once to see a number of the Lady's Book, only six months old; then learned that it had been lent out, and, after chasing it all over town, found it as last, so bethumbed and crumpled that one could scarcely tell a fashion-place from a model cottage. However, the vague rumors that reached us were all favor-able to patching. The blessed *Garibaldi* came in, which must have been invented expressly for poor blockaded mortals, whose skirts had outlasted their material bodies. Havoc was made of old merino shawls, sacks, silk aprons, scarfs, etc., and then we all appeared in waists of every conceivable shade and color, with skirts of every other conceivable shade and color.

The same fashion was continued through the summer in white spencers, which we wore with faded old skirts, whose bodies had gone the way of all human productions. There was great scarcity of material for making them, but we found an ingenious method for increasing the supply. Faded, worn-out muslins, which were too far gone to be worthy of a place, even in our dilapidated wardrobes, were boiled in lye so as to remove all the color, and then they were ready to be manufactured into white spencers. It is true, this material was very flimsy and rotten, but we had learned to take tender care of our clothing, and to make the frailest fabrics last. I have seen an organdy muslin dress worn five summers without washing, and crepe bonnets last three seasons.

The introduction of tight sleeves also favored us greatly, for it was very easy to cut our old ones down; but the greatest blessing of all was the fashion of trimming dress skirts round the bottom. It was so convenient to hide rags, or increase the length of a skirt, by putting a puff or flounce round it. This style of trimming was very highly appreciated, for we could use one old dress to puff and flounce another. Some of our ladies would have presented a grotesque appearance on Broadway or Chestnut Street, in a tricolored or tri-patched costume, with perhaps a crimson merino Garibaldi waist, a blue alpson skirt, and silk flounces. But, fortunately, we had no fashionable rivals to our shabbiness worse by comparison, and although painfully conscious that we were very, very rusty, we really did not know the full extent of our own *seedineur*. All were in the same condition, patched and pieced alike. Sometimes a blockade runner or a rich speculator would give his daughter a pair of gloves, a piece of ribbon, a dress, or, perchance, even a bonnet, of some of the dazzling new colors, which would drive the rest of us to frenzy for a little while, but such cases were too rare to give tone to the prevailing fashions. Piecing, and patching, and squeezing was the general rule, so that we who could not emulate those who caught glimpses beyond the blockade, consoled ourselves with the sight of each other, and with the comforting assurances of our soldiers, who stood it out manfully that they could not desire to see us better-dressed. I suppose the men really thought us very fine, for, in order to hide stains, and rents, and patches, we piled on trimmings to such a degree as to make our clothing extremely gay, and practice made us so skillful at patching, that we often did it very gracefully. If we wished to lengthen a skirt, instead of putting the trimming on in a straight row at the bottom, we could cut it in waves or festoons, slip the lower part down an inch or two, and put the trimming on so as to produce an effect, which was pretty enough, when we saw nothing better.

But to my dying day, no matter what the fashion may be, I can never look upon a skirt of one color and waist of another, or see the latter decorated with any solid trimming, without instantly suspecting a patch or a make-shift and I believe most Southern ladies have the same prejudice. We feel so guilty of such practices, that the most beautiful little jacket, or the most elegant lace flounces, even when worn by the daughter of a New York or Philadelphia merchant, who surely ought to be above suspicion of patching, only remind us of the scant patterns and covered flaws, of "Confederate times."

Occasionally, when very hard pushed, we would have two old dresses, of hopelessly incongruous colors, dyed black, and place them together into a new one. Sometimes the same dress was dyed two or three times, the hue being darkened as stains deepened, and it was not uncommon to see skirts that had been turned inside out, upside down, and hind part before. I well remember one faithful old jaconet, which, after submitting to various alterations as dress and petticoat, was finally, when too much worn for either, cut up and hemmed for pocket-handkerchiefs. All old linen served the same purpose, while our fine handkerchiefs were made of Swiss or mull muslin—the sleeves of worn-out spencers, or best parts of old petticoats trimmed with footing ruffles and transferred work. When the ruffles were fluted or crimped, they made a very pretty edging.

The prettiest trimming gotten up during these times for a dress skirt, was made of transfer work out from a piece of coarse, black Chantilly lace, and sewed on in medallions, with steel beads. The skirt was cut in scallops at the bottom to get rid of certain little snags and dingy places, with a medallion in each scallop. It was really beautiful, and did not appear to disadvantage among the novelties introduced at the end of the war.

Black silk was the favorite material for piecing out our old clothes, because it suited everything. Dresses of all colors and textures were eked out with flounces, puffs, cords, quillings, folds and ruches of black silk, and when that failed, as it very soon did, alpson and merino took its place. We had many things dyed black for the purpose of using them as trimmings. I wonder if there be a woman in the South who has not darned two or three dresses with streaks of black round the bottom. An old black silk skirt with nine flounces was a treasure in our family for nearly two years, and when that store was exhausted, we fell back upon the cover of a worn-out silk umbrella. The finest travelling dress I had during the war, was a brown alpaca turned wrong side out, upside down, and trimmed with quillings made of that same umbrella cover. I will venture to say that no umbrella ever served so many purposes or ever was so thoroughly used up before. The whalebones served to stiffen corsets and the waist of a homespun dress, and the handle was given to a wounded soldier for a walking-stick.

The waists of our dresses were no less patched up than the skirts. I have seen a tight sleeve pieced in sixteen places, and so ingeniously that one could not detect a single seam. It was done by means of puffs and quilling put on in points from the armhole to the elbow, so that the foundation of the sleeve could be cut out of very small pieces, the trimming hiding seams and covering deficiencies

I also remember a cavalry jacket that was pieced in *thirty-six* places with equal skill. Cavalry jackets were in high favor with us, for two reasons: first, because they answered the same purpose as the Garibaldi in helping out bodiless skirts, and secondly, because they were so military. We ladies were perfectly daft about gold lace and brass buttons, and would all but break our necks to get a jacket trimmed with them, thinking, I suppose, that they would be as bewitching on us as they were on the men. Sometimes a generous officer would despoil his sleeve of the admired Hungarian knot in order to gratify the whim of some fair one, and many a little brother has posted all day over a Sunday jacket robbed of its brass buttons to decorate the waist of a sister. Gold lace was so scarce, so dear, and so highly prized, that we would rip it from old, battle-worn uniforms, and rub it with soda, vinegar, alcohol (when we could get it), chalk, and ashes, in order to brighten it for further use, and sometimes its tarnished lustre would faintly revive.

Elaborate decorations were used on waists for the same purpose as on skirts, which has prejudiced me against much trimming as giving ground for a suspicion of patches. Strange to say, none of us were ashamed of the shams we practiced, for we had what Caleb Balderstone so ardently coveted —a good excuse. It was a blessed thing, having everybody in the same situation. We used to laugh together at our own devices, and give one another the benefit of our experience. She who was most skillfully patched up was admired for her ingenuity.

The only things that really mortified us, in spite of excuses and plenty of company in our misfortunes, were the horrible shoes and stockings we had to wear—stiff, shapeless, clumsy things, so different from the beautiful little French boots and sea island thread stockings to which we had been accustomed. Some women contracted an awkward, uneasy manner of walking from the constant effort to hide their lower extremities. All kinds of fancy stitches were invented, and Southern women became expert knitters, but the more fancifully they were made, the more vulgar did our course stockings look, as coarse finery always will. No Balmoral petticoats and looped-up dresses for us! If the mud were ankle deep, we dared not lift our skirts an inch for fear of revealing those frightful shoes and stockings. We all felt like peacocks who, it is said, are so ashamed of their ugly feet that if they happen to catch a glimpse of them, even when most proudly flaunting their gay feathers, will instantly drop all, and assume a humiliated, mortified air. We had no fine feathers to flaunt, but, such as they were, our ill-shod feet and gloveless hands were too bad for them. No lady feels herself wholly lost to good taste with neat shoes, gloves, and collar, nor well dressed without them. In fact, these little things are the real test of whether a lady knows how to dress.

We managed very well for collars, as small ones were worn, and linen lasts a long time, but the introduction of large cuffs staggered us for a while. We could not afford so much linen. Necessity, however, was the mother of invention in this case as in many others. We learned to make cuffs of white cotton shirting, which looked very well as long as no one else had linen to put them out of countenance.

Our heads fared little better than our feet. As bonnets grew larger they were pieced with ribbon or silk borders round the front, as our skirts were lengthened with puffs and flounces. We were ignorant of the reign of *waterfalls* till the blockade was raised, and went on increasing our *sky scraper* with great labor and difficulty.

Ribbons soon gave out, and all kinds of villainous substitutes appeared. Artificial flowers made of goose feathers became very fashionable, and were sold at enormous prices. They were not so ugly as one might suppose, especially when they did not have to stand a comparison with French flowers. Bonnets at last became almost an utter impossibility. I have known fashionable milliners pay one hundred and fifty dollars for an old velvet bonnet which was renovated and sold for five hundred. During the last year of the war, $1000 (Confederate money) was not considered an unreasonable price. Hats made of palmetto straw were very much worn, and were in as high favor as homespun dresses, because they were entirely Southern made. Veils, even of the coarsest *barège*, were very scarce and dear; seventy-five dollars was the price of a very ordinary one. Of course, many inventions were started by ladies desirous of preserving their complexions. I have seen veils made of the remains of a pink tarletan evening dress, dyed brown with walnut hulls, and they were a pretty good imitation of grenadine. An old *berège* dress was a treasure, and its inevitable fate was to be cut up for veils.

But it was in underclothing that we suffered most. When our linen wore out, as the best of linen will sometimes do, there was nothing to replace it but the coarse factory cloth manufactured at the South, which had heretofore been used only for clothing for the negroes. What Georgia girl has not a feeling recollection of *Macon Mills*? In vain we corded, stitched, and trimmed with white ruffles, it was coarse and yellow still. No matter what there was outside, we could not help felling ill dressed in those coarse underclothes. If any one had a nice dress, she felt like a whited sepulchre—very fair without, but yellow homespun and cotton yarn within.

Evening dresses were unheard of towards the close of the war: even brides, unless they were the daughters of quartermasters or blockade-runners, never aspired higher than Suisse muslin, and many contented themselves with humbler fabrics. I saw the waist to one wedding dress made out of the flounces of an old tarletan skirt. They were sewed together and drawn at the seams, so as to make one of the pretty puffed waists so much in fashion two or three years ago.

Any kind of simple muslin dress, and even thick, dark skirts with white muslin spencers, figured in elegant ball-rooms without seeming out of place. As many things may pass muster by candle-light which can not stand the glare of day, it was comparatively easy to dress for evening. I have seen ladies look very well in old silk petticoats trimmed with black lace or white tarletan ruches. Of course all things are by comparison, and what looked very fine in those days would be intolerable now. Our style of dressing degenerated so gradually that we could scarcely perceive the change from one season to another, and did not fully appreciate our own destitution till the blockade was raised, and we compared ourselves with the rest of the world.

The pretty fashion of frizzing the hair was introduced at the beginning of the war, and many of us adopted it, both on account of its beauty, and because hair-pins and braids were not to be bought. It was impossible to obtain false curls, so we cropped off our own hair, and made free use of curl-papers and irons. Imagine our consternation, fair reader, when rats, and mice, and waterfalls, came in, and caught us with short hair. The war did not trouble us much as to evening head-dresses, for our land teems with myriads of beautiful flowers, fairer than any ever displayed in the shop windows of Demorest or Olympe, and it was not in the power of man to blockade Nature.

Neither was it possible entirely to blockade Fashion. *Godey, Madame Demorest,* and *French Leslie* would find their way to places where the most daring raider would never venture. Whenever a bold soldier "crossed the lines," he was sure to bring back a book of fashions as the most acceptable present to his lady. We toiled, we struggled, we contrived, and generally managed to come in at the fag-end of every new fashion. I have heard more than one *pater familias,* when importuned for a piece of ribbon or a yard of muslin, costing from sixty to one hundred dollars, groan out: "Oh if the Yankees would only blockade the fashions, I'd forgive them everything else!"

But women will dress so long as there is a particle of woman's nature left in them. I verily believe that when our mother Eve first pinned the fig-leaves around her, she took pleasure festooning them as gracefully as possible, and that she hailed the cost of skins as the advent of a new fashion.

We Southern women labored under peculiar difficulties during the war, for, strange as it may seem, never did we need dress more. Every little town was a military post, crowded with strangers—refugees, exiles, and fascinating officers—what man in brass buttons is not fascinating to woman's eyes? There was no end of balls, parties, picnics, *fêtes* of every description. I once heard a young belle, fresh from a circle of dazzling beaux, express pity for the poor girls who lived in stupid, peaceful countries, away from the "pomp and circumstance of war," and I think a good many of us held the same opinion, but that was before the horrors and devastations of war had fallen upon our own homes.

Think, then, of the temptation we were under to dress, while the power was denied us. We were compelled, by necessity, to spend so much time in plotting and planning and scheming for something to wear, that we had little time to think of anything else. A lady who had run the blockade was stared at as a natural curiosity, and her wardrobe made the subject of conversation for weeks afterward. The simple fact that new things were so much noticed, made us all desirous to have them.

This much experience has taught me—that the way to make a woman devote her whole soul to dress, is not to give her everything she needs, but to make it necessary for her to plan, and think, and study what to wear; how to "Gar suld claes amaist as weel's the new." And this we had to do for four long years. We never thought as much about dress in all the rest of our lives put together, as while the blockade was upon us, and I am sure some of us ever dressed so little. For my part, I spent three days and nights in meditating how to trim the only new dress I had, and a much longer time in thinking how to patch and alter old ones.

At least the struggle ended, the blockade was raised, and goods flowed in. Our eyes were dazzled with brilliant new colors, in comparison with which all we had ever seen before seemed faded and dull. Fabrics of marvelous texture, trimmings and ornaments of flashing brilliancy put to shame our poor old make-shifts. The rest of the world had taken a long stride during the four years that we had been going backwards. Were articles of woman's attire really more beautiful than they had ever been before, or did they only seem so to our starved Confederate eyes? Certainly, new goods and new fashions never had appeared so exquisite to us, nor our old rags so forlorn. We looked as if our clothes had been bought before the days of Noah. One might have mistaken us for fossil women, so faded and mouldy were we. Northern ladies came out a-blaze with finery, and some few of our own people, who had escaped the general shipwreck, arrayed themselves in "blue, and purple, and scarlet," but the rest of us could only look, long, and wonder. Our riches had taken themselves legs and walked away; our pockets were as empty as our wardrobes, so we had to turn from feasting our eyes in the shops, to rack our brains with thoughts of how to make ourselves presentable at home. But cheap substitutes and contrivances will never be permissible again as they were during the blockade. I suppose the only resources left us is to live in sublime poverty, like the Fauborge St. Germain, and turn up our noses at everything rich or fine as *parvenu*.

## Professions and Employments Open to Women
*by Elzey Hay*

SCOTT'S MONTHLY MAGAZINE, January 1869

The world acknowledges but one vocation for women. Taste, talent or necessity may often lead them into other pursuits, but they are felt to be out of their natural sphere when engaged in other business than the rearing of children and fulfillment of household duties. I do not, of course, mean to assert that the world actually discountenances the efforts of a woman to live by her own exertions in any honest calling which she may find it necessary to pursue; yet, there is an instinctive feeling that she is out of her natural element the moment she steps—whether by choice or necessity—beyond the pale of that tender, protecting care which shields her more favored sisters from rude collision with the world, and society feels that it has an equal right to pity her and condemn her husband. It is to be observed that the world usually takes it for granted that some man is to blame for every necessity which compels a woman to take up a profession and go to work on her own responsibility, and her husband or nearest male relations are sure to be made the scapegoat. Why don't Mr. A. take care of her? Isn't Mr. B. rich enough to help his cousin? I should think Mr. C. might give her a home. How can Mr. D. let his own niece go knocking about the world in that fashion, and he living in a great big house with only a wife and six children to support? Such are the comments of society upon every accession from its ranks to the band of professional women; and the fear of its idle criticism, no doubt, influences many a worthy man to forego the assistance he might receive from his wife and daughters, and makes many a timid woman hesitate to engage in an honest profession, lest her husband's character and reputation should suffer more than his finances would be benefited by her exertions. Many a poor wife will wear her life away in all kinds of domestic drudgery, when she might, by the lighter labor of giving music lessons, or coloring photographs, find means to relieve herself of harder work, and add greatly to the comfort of her household besides. Public opinion is always hard upon men who receive pecuniary assistance through the efforts of their wives or daughters, and the entrance of a woman upon any field of labor, outside of home duties, is usually the signal for a general assault upon her nearest male relative.

"My husband would work his fingers to the bone before he'd see *me* teaching school," says Mrs. Jenkins, complacently, as she sits over her work-basket and watches a troop of children pouring through the gate of her neighbor, Mrs. Jones, who has exchanged needle and thread, patches and buttons, for the more remunerative labors of the school room. Between the destructive knees and elbows of the little Jenkinses and the refractory buttons of their papa. Mrs. Jenkins probably has a much harder time of it than Mrs. Jones; yet she feels, somehow, that she occupies a position of advantage over the latter, and feels herself entitled to speak of her as "poor Mrs. Jones," with a half-pitying, half-patronizing air, as who should say "she has to work for a living. I don't; Mr. Jenkins takes better care of me than that;" and straightway all the Jenkins circle begin to think disparagingly of Jones a poor village doctor, perhaps, who has never been able to collect a cent on the numberless prescriptions made out for colic-stricken young Jenkinses.

But, after all, the prejudices of Mrs. Jenkins and her little world, however false and distorted in themselves, are the natural off shoot of a social system in which women are regarded as a sort of pet and plaything for the other sex. It is a principle of our modern civilization that women were not made for hand to hand conflict with the world, but to be cherished and cared for by those who were, and when one is forced by necessity, or led by inclination, to step beyond the place reserved for her sex, it is, perhaps, not unnatural that she should be regarded as an object of pity, or a target of criticism by those who remain within its sheltered precincts.

To return to our illustration. Mrs. Jenkins does possess this advantage over Mrs. Jones, that she is accountable to nobody but her husband if the buttons are not sewed on or the elbows not patched, while Mrs. Jones is amenable to the public for what transpires in her school-room. Mrs. Jenkins is sheltered by her husband from open contact with the world. Mrs. Jones has to face it in person. It cannot be denied that, in direct contact with the world, women are apt to lose something of that exquisite delicacy, that soft, shrinking dependence upon others which all civilized people, but especially we of the chivalrous South, consider so essential to the perfection of female character, or if they retain it, they are always liable to be imposed upon by the selfish and wounded by the vulgar. In either case there is much to regret, for while nothing can atone for the loss of feminine graces of character and feeling, yet timidity, ignorance of the world, even their tender-heartedness, and the charming incapacity of taking care of themselves which men find so attractive in young girls—that soft, confiding trustfulness which is one of the chief graces of women, all lay them open to be swindled and preyed upon. "But," I think I hear some chivalrous reader exclaim, "these very qualities are women's best protection—her weakness is her strength." And so it would be if the world at large were a knight-errant, going about to redress the wrongs of unprotected females, but here is a long *if*. The world is a very worthy old fellow, in his way, but rather too old for sentiment. Besides, he has a large family and too much business on his hands to spend much time, thought or money in Quixotic endeavors to relieve the fair; and the daintiest woman that happens to be thrown upon his mercy must take her chances along with the roughest vagabond that crosses her path.

One great difficulty in the way of professional women arises from the nature of the employments which are considered within the legitimate

scope of female efforts. Those countenanced by public opinion are never
such as lead to wealth or fame—never those in which success is attended
with the *eclat* that often crowns the efforts of successful men. A law student may be sustained through the weary intricacies of Blackstone by
visions of judicial honors, and even the dreary pages of theological dis-
cussion may be brightened by distant glimpses of satin and lawn, but
what glory is to crown the success of a milliner or school-mistress? Bread
to eat, clothes to wear, with possibly a modest competency upon which
to retire in old age, with a temper soured by petty cares—this is the most
a professional woman has to expect. I am aware that many fine things
may be said about the sustaining power of duty, the glory of woman's
moral influence, and all that, but the question at present is not of the
feelings that ought but to those which do most naturally influence the
human heart, and we all know that the prospect of honor, fame or riches
will sustain our exertions more effectually than an humble desire to "do
our duty in that state of life to which it has pleased God to call us." So far
from encouraging ambition, however, most of the professions in which
women are countenanced by public opinion are little trifling affairs, whose
success will not count much one way or another. The most a woman can
expect to do by her own exertions in any of the orthodox feminine vocations, such as sewing, teaching, &c., is to maintain her independence,
and perhaps earn a modest competency for herself. As to social advantages, a working woman is more apt to lose than to gain by her profession. Now, I do not wish to be understood as disparaging working women
or their vocations. Such a course would ill become one whose own countrywomen have given such noble proof of the grace with which genuine
ladies can descend from the most exalted stations in life to work at the
humblest callings; but, at the same time, no one can deny the fact that
the working women of any community do not constitute the leading
members of society. We may theorize as we please about the true basis of
social position, and lay down most equitable rules on the subject, but we
cannot make the world abide by them any more than we can alter the
fact that milliners, dress-makers, school-mistresses, &c., do not as a class,
compose the aristocracy of any community. However honorably a professional woman may sustain her social position it never receives *eclat*
from the profession. I grant that many a milliner may be superior to the
best of her customers, that the most injured of governesses may be far
more of a lady in feeling than her employers; that does not alter the fact
as to their actual position in the world, which certainly is not one of

advantage. At the same time, it would hardly be fair to accuse society of snubbishness because its highest honors are not generally accorded to people who have little or no time to devote to its requirements. Society is the only sphere outside the home where women are permitted to play a conspicuous part, and society requires leisure. One who is closely occupied in any kind of business has not time to visit or be visited, to entertain or be entertained, and as the highest successes of ordinary professional women are never attended with any very dazzling *eclat* to attract the public attention, it is natural that they should drop out of public society without anybody's knowing exactly why. There are certain purely masculine professions, such as the law, diplomacy, divinity, the army, &c., in which any very decided success will bring a man before the world in a blaze of glory; but the ordinary vocations of woman standing as they often do in square opposition to mental culture, and calling for no exercise of talent, give no occasion for brilliant results. School-teaching, the most intellectual of them, and I suppose the best, as it seems to be much in favor of reduced gentlewomen, is merely a sort of mental tread-mill, and its tendency is to contract and narrow the mind, by making it travel continually the same dull road over and over again. It calls for the exercise of no higher powers than a good stock of patience and various degrees of acquired knowledge.

But the nature of women's employments is not so much a matter of regret to the generality of those who have to engage in them as the narrow range of vocations open to the sex. While millions of men are making a comfortable living out of professions that are closed to women there is scarcely one of ours which is not equally open to them. Yet, while this unequal distribution of things places the workingwomen at a disadvantage, the difference is more than made up to the sex at large by the fact that men have to work for us, and if they possess advantages over us they use them for our good. This much must be said for the men, not one of them in a thousand is working for himself alone. Whatever goods he acquires, a man is always ready to share with some woman—if not with a wife, then, with a mother, a sister or daughter; so that I think it fair to say that, upon an average, at least one woman profits by the exertions of every man in the world. If it is hard for us to acquire wealth or fame for ourselves, we have the compensation of knowing that all men who gain either share them with some woman, and I think there are few of us but must acknowledge that we owe more to the efforts of a husband or a father than we could have gained in a lifetime by our own exertions, if the whole range of masculine employments were open to us. The present arrangement of things, it seems to me, goes to prove not that society is ready to impose upon women, but that it expects men to provide for them. Now, though this is a very pleasant arrangement for the generality of women, it is a little hard upon those few unfortunates who happen to be left out in the cold, and have to take care of themselves. Their situation is one that society does not seem to have contemplated, and hence the hand to hand struggle of woman with the world, will always be a very unequal, and consequently a very hard one.

There is one noble profession within the legitimate scope of female faculties, which public opinion has very unreasonably, it seems to me, closed against the better class of women: I allude to the stage. It is esteemed little short of madness, for a respectable woman to think of appearing on the boards, and many an honest man will suffer his daughter to starve on the pitiful salary of a country school mistress, or toil at the needle till her thread of life is stitched away, when as an actress, she might not only had a comparatively easy life, but won both riches and renown. Even the unambitious *role* of a second or third rate actress, seems to me far preferable to the wretched existence of a needle-woman or a country school mistress; and yet I have known women that might have rivaled Rachael or Ristori, who chose to earn a miserable pittance by selling embroidery or giving music lessons, rather than submit to what they consider the degradation of displaying their genius to the world. It is strange to think what histrionic talents are sometimes buried in the earth; and stranger still, how idle prejudice can deem it a disgrace to become the living embodiment of a poet's dream, to put life and action into the divine creations of Shakespeare and Goethe, or to give vocal utterance to the heavenly strains of Donizette and Bellini—honors of which the proudest might be proud. As to the morality of the stage, it must be confessed, that has sunk extremely low in these days of *Black Crook and White Fawns*—a circumstance hardly to be wondered at, since the effect of public prejudice is to banish respectable women and abandon the stage to such as are indifferent alike to public opinion and public decency. But that a profession whose business is to give life and reality to the conceptions of genius, is not essentially degrading in its influence, such characters as Mrs. Siddons, Mrs. Mowatt, Miss Bellamy, Garrick, Ristori and Jenny Lind, amply prove. As to the awful bugbear of appearing in public, it must be remembered that a good actress appears on the stage only in the character which she represents, and her personal life may be more retired than that of many a ball-room flirt. It is not Miss A., B. or C. who is fixing the attention of a crowded theatre, but Lady

Macbeth, Juliet or *Marguerite*. Herself, is the very last person that a good actress ever presents to her audience.

It must be remembered, too, that the mere fact of appearing in public, is a very small matter; our manner of appearing there is the thing to be considered. While no one will contend that public life is the sphere of action for which women are peculiarly fitted, yet this is no argument that they should not emerge from obscurity when there are good reasons for so doing. No person whatever, man or woman, has any right to claim the attention of the world, unless he can show it something worth attending to. Publicity is a thing which must justify itself, or it becomes impertinent notoriety. Retirement is not intrinsically more proper for women than for men, but the business and pursuits of men oftener justify publicity. A mere vulgar love of notoriety is as ugly in one sex as in the other. The criminal folly of Herostratus would not have been more culpable in a woman—or, to draw an illustration from our time, the female half of a certain ridiculous couple who contrived a few years since, to gain a transient newspaper notoriety by going up in a balloon to be married among the clouds—was not a whit more absurd than her whiskered partner. The main difference between the sexes with regard to their manner of living, is that women's employments so seldom call for the abandonment of private life, that the chances are, one is wrong in bringing herself prominently before the world. While the occupation of men place them so openly and naturally in contact with it, that the odds are small, but their position, whatever that may be, will justify itself. Yet, as I have said before, when circumstances do warrant a woman in appearing conspicuously before the public, she is no more out of her proper element than one of the other sex. Mrs. Siddons was no more out of place when standing before the curtain to receive the thunders of applause which were the just meed of her glorious performances, than were Garrick and Sheridan, in a like situation. It is always the circumstances, not the mere fact of a woman's appearance before the world that must justify or condemn her. Queen Victoria may, with perfect propriety, read a speech at the opening of Parliament, but a very different comment would be passed upon the conduct of any of my fair countrywomen who should attempt the same at the opening of Congress. The wife of a certain gallant Confederate General, compromised nothing of feminine dignity when she rushed through the streets of Winchester, regardless of Yankee shot and shell, striving to rally her husband's flying columns, but I could not say as much for any of my gentle readers who should play the same part in a street riot. Again, to multiply examples, no one feels that Queen

Elizabeth transcended the bounds of womanly duty, when she rode through the British lines at Tilbury, and encouraged her troops in that admirable speech, which has never been surpassed by any patriotic oration, before or since; but it does not therefore follow that any of my female readers would make an equally dignified appearance, if she should present herself the next time General Grant reviews his troops, and commence a patriotic address to the United States army. It may be objected by some, that the example of Queen Elizabeth is a very *mal a propos* to the present case, as she was a women of strong and masculine temper; but after all, I question whether she was not more conspicuous for feminine follies than masculine vices. Her love of dress was proverbial—her coquettries unrivalled in the annals of flirtation, her vanity the plaything of all around her. It is true, she was somewhat addicted to cursing and swearing, and would box the ears of offending courtiers now and then, but these practices, far from being fostered by the exalted position she occupied, seem rather to have been faults of the age in which she lived, and were restrained rather than encouraged by her public station. Had she been the daughter of a private gentleman, she would no doubt have tried the same exploits, with double vigor, upon less illustrious victims.

What has been said about the legitimate appearance of women in public, will not, I hope, be construed into a defense of what may be termed the school of female radicalism, advocated by Mr. J. S. Mill and his followers. Because some women may, under certain extraordinary circumstances, leave the retirement which is their natural and appropriate sphere is no reason why others should force themselves into political assemblies, join their acclamations with those of a thousand rowdies, and send their bonnets into the air along with the hats of clowns and rogues, as is the fashion with certain representatives of the modern "Woman's Rights" school. These advocates of what they term their rights are the real authors of all women's wrongs. By their unreasonable and unwomanly conduct, they have prejudiced the world against even the legitimate appearance of woman in public, and pointed the shaft of ridicule against efforts which often merit better treatment. In contending for political rights, they would give up social privileges which are more than worth them all. It is unnecessary here to make a question of woman's capacity for the exercise of political freedom. To judge from the acts of a certain Congress, which has for a long time presided over the destinies of a great nation, one would hardly think it possible for women to exhibit greater incapacity for government than men sometimes do: —but that is neither here nor there— the question may be settled on more convincing grounds. Women have their own part to play in the economy of creation, for which they are especially adapted by Providence, as are the other sex for theirs; and any attempt to make them fill the place of men, would be as unreasonable as to expect a railway locomotive to do duty for an ocean steamer. The Saturday Review very justly remarks that you cannot make men of women, nor women of men, and any attempt to establish the one for the other, will end in degradation of both. The higher a woman rises in those qualities which make woman truly admirable, the further is she removed from any touch of the distinctive characteristics of the other sex, and vice versa. A masculine woman, an effeminate man, are equally terms of reproach and scorn.

But aside from these considerations, women would lose far more than they could gain by acquisition of those rights which Mr. Mill and his adherents are so eager to confer upon the sex. In our present position, we enjoy privileges and immunities that would never be accorded to demagogues and politicians. Men would never lavish those delicate attentions, those tender cares, that respect and deference which they now regard as due the very name of woman, to creatures whom they had seen strutting around the polls on election days, jostled by roughs and blackguards. It is now our privilege to take precedence over men, in all that concerns our real comfort. The best accommodations in all public places are reserved for our use; we occupy the best rooms at hotels, the best seats in theatres, the best berths on steamers. It is our privilege to sit when men have to stand, to ride when they have to walk, to stay comfortably at home when they are exposed to the hardships and dangers of war—and shall we exchange such privileges as these for the miserable right to lounge about street corners, and talk slang in bar rooms? It is our privilege to enjoy comforts which it is men's business to provide, our privilege to claim the protection of strong arms and brave hearts, where it is the duty of men to struggle and overcome. Who would forego all these for the poor right of claiming one thirty-millionth part of a share in the government of a nation—a right which the lowest blackguard among all those thirty million people possesses in an equal degree with you—a right that will not even pay a dress-maker's bill, or buy a new bonnet, and which rather lays you open to insult, than protects you from it—a right which is often used to wrong others as to protect the possessor—a right which the best of men often scorn to assert, and which the basest hold so low that they will buy or sell it for a drink of mean whisky! No, no, give us women's privileges, and we will do without the rights; rights which would degrade our sex, without elevating the government of our country. Whether circumstances may sometimes justify women in appearing conspicuously before the world, an ambition to figure in republican politics is not one of them. In other countries, women may be sovereigns with honor and dignity, but they cannot, without degradation, be numbered among the "sovereign people" of a republic.

There seems to be something essentially vulgarizing in the influence of republican institutions upon society, as any one must acknowledge who has observed their effect upon the manners of the ladies of our republican courts. There is something too *prononcee*, too independent, about them, to suit very refined tastes. They are not all positively course and unfeminine, but there is about the best of them, an excess of ease, so to speak, which is not exactly consistent with our notions of perfect feminine grace. They have the air of being used to be stared at, and not minding it—nay, some of them seem rather to like it. Now, I would have a woman, while she is perfectly easy and graceful under the ordeal of being stared at, look, at the same time, as if she would rather not be so, if she could help it. Madame de Staël has hit the right thing exactly, in describing the appearance of Corinne, when she was crowned at the capital. "Son attitude sur le char était noble et modeste; on apercevait bien qu'elle était contente d'etre admiree, mais un sentiment de timidite se melait a sa joie, et semblait demandee grace pour son triomphe." Now, it is the want of this timidity, this "seeming to ask pardon for their triumphs," which detracts so much from the charms of the class referred to.[5] Some of them even go beyond the mere absence of positive refinement, and acquire a sort of swaggering, demagogue manner that savors strongly of election days and country politics. If the demoralizing influence of republican politics is so perceptible upon women who are brought in contact with them only through the medium of their husbands and fathers, what might we not fear, if they should ever take an active part and appear in person on the arena of political excitement!

But to return from this digression. There is one of the higher professions which seems to be common ground between the sexes, but even here, in the field of literary labor, men have decidedly the advantage. To those of mediocre powers, the lower walks of literature, such as corresponding and reporting for newspapers, are open, but as women have no facilities for acquiring the information necessary for such undertakings, their literary performances must always be of an ambitious character, in which failure is certain, except to persons of real genius, though it must be confessed, that literary aspirations are by no means confined to these last. Women of the present day have a perfect mania for book writing. As an English reviewer declares, no woman seems to think her education complete, till she has sent a manuscript novel or poem to the editor of some leading periodical. The great mistake of these aspirants is, that instead of testing their powers first on a modest essay, or a simply story for children, they plunge headlong into a three volume novel, and, of course, break down at the very start. Little as ordinary readers may realize the fact, novel writing is the very highest branch of prose literature, and ranks next to dramatic and epic composition, in its demands upon the creative faculties. There is not one person in a thousand likely to succeed in such an undertaking, and, hence, the reason why so many female aspirants for literary honors make ridiculous failures, and bring contempt upon the efforts of the sex. The mere suspicion of female authorship will prejudice many people against a book, before they know anything else about it—a prejudice for which the folly of pretenders who aim at what is above their powers, must be held responsible, and which only an established reputation like that of Charlotte Bronte or the author of Adam Bede is sufficient to overcome. It is this prejudice which leads so many female authors to veil their first efforts under masculine names, as the only chance to get fair play—a practice which has the sanction of such remarkable precedents as Currer Bell, George Elliott, and George Sand.

Public opinion as to the merits of ordinary female writers, is pretty generally divided between two classes—those who take it for granted that anything penned by women is sheer nonsense, and those undiscriminating literary prigs, whose blind veneration for everything in print, leads them to entertain a mighty respect for the intellect of any country miss who has sent a copy of verses to the nearest village newspaper. Even a really clever female writer must, at certain periods of her career, run the gauntlet of both classes of critics, and before she can vindicate her claim to the respect of the one, run the risk of being made ridiculous by the exaggerated and undiscriminating applause of the other. There are some people, such as country critics and professors in female colleges, who think the mere fact of having written a book, is enough to cover its author with immortal glory—no matter whether the book be Milton's Paradise Lost, or one of Miss Braddon's novels —it is all one to them. The silent contempt of people; who won't read your productions, is really less annoying than the stupid veneration of those who, if they read, can not understand them, for the former is at least a negative and unaggressive sort or injury, while the latter becomes a positive wrong by making one seem a pretender, in spite of oneself. Suppose for instance, my fair reader, that you have been induced, for some better reason than a mere desire to see your name flourishing in the papers, to write and publish a book. It may be that you are conscious of having written a very poor book—a mean story, perchance of which you are heartily ashamed, and which you were only induced to publish, because you were sorely in want of funds, and the editor of some fifth-rate magazine, with a large circulation among journeymen laborers and servant girls, offered a good prize for your performance. It may be that you are particularly anxious to keep the secret of your authorship, and to mention it in your presence is like talking of the gallows to a man whose father has been hung. The idea of having written that silly story (you have grown a good deal abler since it was published) hangs over you like a night-mare, and you are never allowed to forget it. Go wherever you will, you are heralded as the lady that has written a book. You are invited to visit some friends in a distant part of the country, where neither you nor your writings have ever been heard of before, and where you fondly hope to keep the latter in the background, so that you may, for once escape the necessity of figuring as a blue-stocking. But, unluckily, some injudicious friend at home, with worse taste than intentions, happens to have an acquaintance in the place to which you are going, and thinking to do you a great service, sits down and writes of your projected visit to his town, informing him, at the same time, that you are a lady of remarkable literary attainments, and once had a story published in the "Weekly Repository of Moral Reading." This person spreads what he has learned from your *maladroit ami*, and when you arrive at your destination you find yourself already known as the lady that has "written a book of not less than three hundred pages." You go to a ball the night after your arrival, and soon become uncomfortably conscious that everybody is watching you, and that some of the company are quietly expecting a little amusement at your expense. The men all stand off, afraid to approach you, thinking they would have to talk about books and metaphysics to so learned a lady—and we all know that men don't go to balls to talk metaphysics, any more than ladies go there to talk to each other. You stand toying with your fan, and feel so foolish that it would be hard to make your situation more uncomfortable; yet this is done by some one in the company who pretends to a great deal of *savoir faire*, and who brings up a person with formidable red whiskers— probably the editor of the village newspaper, or president of some female college, and introduces you to him by your *nom de plume*, as the author of "Florabel, the Lost Maiden of Elfindale." Everybody looks very complacent at this stroke of policy, and feeling satisfied that the right thing has at last been done, in bringing two such congenial spirits together, you are left to the mercy of your companion, who, having posted himself for the occasion, quotes newspaper poetry and extracts from your own productions till you wish yourself a man that you might pull his nose. Finally, when he bids you good-night, as the assembly is breaking up, and you begin to hope that your troubles are over for that evening, he caps the climax of your woes by asking you, in a loud voice, so as to be overheard by everybody in the house, to write some poetry for his paper! You feel the more inclined to resent this injury, because you know it never enters his head to think of paying for your productions: he takes it for granted that the glory of appearing in the Bumpkinsville Gazette ought to be sufficient remuneration for your labors. Next day he comes to bore you for two hours and calls again in the afternoon to take you out driving. Everybody turns to look as you pass through the village, and when you meet the sarcastic Miss MacBee, riding with the fastidious Mr. MacDee, you cannot help perceiving that they appear highly amused as they pass you, and that they are going to say something satirical as soon as you are out of sight. Even here your troubles do not end. In the next issue of the Bumpkinsville Gazette there will appear an editorial notice of the "gifted young authoress now sojourning in our city," or, worse still, in the poet's corner some doggerel lines to Miss ——, signed by the red whiskered editor's initials, and you may consider yourself happy if he does not take it into his head to make love to you.

Nor are country editors and female college professors the only persecutors you have to encounter. Some day, when you feel particularly inclined to be indolent, there comes a delegation from Miss Aspasia William's select school, to inform you that the young ladies are going to have a May party next week, and you are expected to write speeches in verse, of a hundred lines each, for the May Queen, Flora, and four personified seasons. Then comes Miss Cecelia Dunn, with a request that you will write acrostics on the names of twelve favorite authors in her album. You are constantly annoyed by pert school misses for comic or sentimental compositions on subjects of their own choosing, to be read as their own productions at public examinations, while some fond mamma makes the modest request that you will teach her daughter to write poetry. In short, the annoyances entailed by a small literary reputation are incalculable, though these are counterbalanced if one succeeds in the profession by greater and equally numerous advantages.

The great beauty of anonymous writing is to protect one against bores and the other annoyances of a small reputation, till one can claim the advantages of a great one. Under all circumstances, it is wisest to feel one's ground first, before advancing boldly upon it, and for a timid or reserved person there is nothing like a pseudonym, which throws a veil over one's identity, and stands like a tower of defense to shield one's private life from the invasions of public curiosity. If by the public were meant merely that vague assembly of individuals which makes up the world at large, one would care very little about it, save in so far as one's interest was concerned in pleasing its taste, but each one of us has a little world of his own, bounded by the circle of his personal acquaintance, and it is the criticism of this public that literary novices dread. Within this circle there is always some one individual who, to young female writers in particular, is the embodiment of public opinion. One could not write a line without wondering what this person would think of it, if the blessed anonymous did not come to one's aid. Safe behind this shield the most timid writer may express himself with boldness and independence. This I take to be the only legitimate use of anonymous writing. An honorable man or woman will never use a fictitious name as a mask for the utterance of things to which he ought to be either afraid or ashamed to fix his own.

Though there are trials and difficulties attending even the most honorable professions in which women can engage, this is no argument against their entering the lists with resolution and perseverance, when occasion demands it. Home and society are the legitimate and natural spheres of woman, but where fate has denied one the cherished privilege of being taken care of herself. We have all known women who, without a stiver of their own in the world, continued somehow, by dint of sponging and a certain sort of graceful imposition upon their friends, to fare as well as the richest and grandest in the land. No one can tell how they manage it, but like the lilies of the field, they toil not, neither do they spin, yet Solomon, in all his glory, was not arrayed like one of these. And the very women who lead this sort of existence are the ones that feel most complacently the superiority of their position in society over that of their less fortunate sisters who have to work for a living, while, in reality, they are far less respectable than the honest servant girl, who eats her brown bread and owes no man a "thank 'ee" for it. The most despised profession in which a woman can engage, if it be but that of a kitchen scullion, is more respectable by far than a position of cringing dependence, or even a magnificent sponging upon those to whose protection she has no special claim. Independence is not particularly to be desired for a woman, if she has those to whom she can legitimately look for support and protection; but even then it is often better to help by a little honest labor for one's own than to hang a dead weight upon the hands of an aged father or an invalid husband, and lead a starvling, beggarly life at home, for the poor grandeur of not having it said that one is obliged to work for a living.

# Southland Writers
## *Miss Fanny Andrews (Elzey Hay)*

*Ida Raymond,* Southland Writers *(Philadelphia: Claxton, Remsen, and Haffelfinger, 1870): 512–19*

This record of "Southland Writers" would be incomplete without mention of a young lady, the daughter of an able legal gentleman of Washington, Georgia, and herself born and educated in the State, who has, since the close of the war, been a frequent contributor to the periodical literature of the country, under the pseudonym of "Elzey Hay." Until recently, "Elzey Hay" was "Elzey Hay" merely.

Miss Andrews believes that "the great beauty of anonymous writing is to protect one against bores and the other annoyances of a small reputation, till one can claim the advantages of a great one."

Her identity was published to the world without her knowledge, and she feels diffident in appearing among "Southland Writers" with that mask which separated her from the public thrown aside.

As she expresses the matter in a recent article, we prefer to use her words:

> Under all circumstances, it is wisest to feel one's ground first, before advancing boldly upon it, and for a timid or reserved person there is nothing like a pseudonym, which throws a veil over one's identity and stands like a tower of defense to shield one's private life from the invasions of public curiosity. If by the public were meant merely that vague assembly of individuals which makes up the world at large, one would care very little about it, save in so far as one's interest was concerned in pleasing its taste; but each one of us has a little world of his own, bounded by the circle of his personal acquaintance, and it is the criticism of this public that literary novices dread. Within this circle there is always some one individual who, to young female

writers in particular, is the embodiment of public opinion. One could not write a line without wondering what this person would think of it, if the blessed anonymous did not come to one's aid. Safe behind this shield the most timid writer may express himself with boldness and independence.

From my first acquaintance with the articles of "Elzey Hay," I felt the identity of such a sparkling, piquant writer could not long remain concealed.

Sometimes I am almost tempted to call her the "Southern Fanny Fern,"[6] but "Elzey" is a woman, and "Fanny" a bloomer, perhaps! Both excel in a peculiar style—so bright, witty, caustic; but the wit of "Elzey Hay" is as keen as a Damascus blade and as polished. Fanny Fern's wit reminds one of a dull, spiteful, little penknife. The former "holds the mirror up to nature;" the latter caricatures it. The one laughs merrily and good-naturedly at the faults and follies of mankind; the other sneers at them. "Elzey Hay" is a great favorite with her own sex; Fanny Fern is not. In one, we recognize the champion of *the* sex, in the other a "Woman's Rights lecturer." But both are a terror to the "lords of creation." They deal stinging blows to domestic tyrants, would-be exquisites, and pretense generally; the small weaknesses and foibles of the "lords of creation" are not dealt with tenderly. Satire is a powerful weapon in cutting off the excrescencies[7] of society. Juvenal and Pope and Thackeray effected some good in their day. So will "Elzey Hay." "Elzey Hay" has been a frequent contributor to Godey's "Lady's Book" and "Scott's Magazine" (Atlanta), "Dress under Difficulties" a paper concerning the "fashions in Dixie during the war," which appeared in Godey's "Lady's Book," for July, 1866, is "Elzey Hay's" most widely read article.

Her first début as a writer was in the "New York World," shortly after the close of the war, in an article entitled "A Romance of Robbery," exposing some infamous proceedings of the Bureauites in a village in Georgia. She assumed the character of a Federal officer in this instance. She has also been correspondent for other New York papers under "masculine signatures." We venture to predict that, if she lives, Miss Andrews will be widely known, and "sparkling Elzey Hay" will be as familiar as a household word in the homes of our land. A book that will "live" is what we have a right to expect from "Elzey Hay."

Her home is in the charming town of Washington, where Miss Andrews is one of the attractions, entertaining with her delightful conversations, for she converses as well as she writes.

The selections we make give only a slight idea of her talents.

## A Plea For Red Hair
*By A Red Haired Woman*

There has always existed all unconquerable, and it seems to me unreason-able prejudice against red hair among the nations of Northern Europe and America. In vain do physiognomists, phrenologists, physiologists, or any other ologists, declare that the pure old Saxon family, distinguished by red heads and freckled faces, is highest in the scale of human existence, being farthest removed from the woolly heads and black faces of the African or lowest race; the world positively refuses to admire red heads and freckled faces, or to regard them as marks of either physical or intellectual superi-ority. In vain are nymphs, fairies, angels, and the good little children in Sunday-school books, always pictured with sunny tresses; the world is so perverse that it scorns in real life what it pronounces enchanting in books and pictures. Now this inconsistency is the main cause of quarrel that we red-heads have against the rest of the world. Little does it advantage us that our hair is thought bewitching on the angels in picture-books, while it is sneered at on our own heads in drawing-rooms. Willingly would we resign the ideal glories of sylphs and angels to our dark-haired sisters, if we could in return share some of the substantial glories they enjoy in real life. The world is too inconsistent: while our *crowning* feature seems to be acknowledged as the highest type of ideal beauty, it is at the same time regarded as a trait of positive ugliness in real life. No painter ever made a black-haired angel. Men's ideas of celestial beauty seem to be inseparable from the sunny ringlets that dance round azure eyes like golden clouds floating over the blue canopy of heaven. I challenge any of my readers to name a single poet or painter who has ventured to represent angel or glorified spirit with black hair. Even the pictures and images of our Savior—with reverence I speak it—are generally represented with some shade of yellow hair, and surely all that relates to Him must come up to our highest ideas of perfect loveliness. If red hair were really such a bad thing, why should the inhabitants of heaven be always painted with it? Who would think of representing even the lowest of the angels with a red nose? And yet in real life red heads meet with little more favor than red noses.

Poets are as friendly to red hair as painters. Milton describes his Adam and Eve—

> *"The loveliest pair*
> *That ever since in love's embraces met;*
> *Adam, the godliest man of men since born*
> *His sons: the fairest of her daughters, Eve"*

—both as red-haired.

> *"His fair large front, and eyes sublime, declared*
> *Absolute rule: and hyacinthine locks*
> *Round from his parted forelock wanly hung*
> *Clustering, but not beneath his shoulders broad;*
> *She, as a veil, down to the slender waist*
> *Her unadorned golden tresses wore."*

Milton's admirers will doubtless be shocked at the idea of a red-headed Adam and Eve, and consider the accusation a slander on the poet; but substitute the epithet auburn, golden, or *hyacinthine,* and nobody's taste is offended. Poets always take care to observe this nice distinction, and their readers are satisfied, few ever stopping to consider that *auburn* is only a polite name for one kind of very red hair. The difference is simply this: What is golden or auburn hair on a pretty woman, is blazing red on an ugly one; and people are apt to like or dislike it, according as they see it with pretty faces or plain ones. After gazing at a portrait of the beautiful Queen of Scots, one is enraptured with auburn ringlets; after beholding a picture of her ill-favored rival, Elizabeth; one is equally out of humor with *carroty hair.* The force of prejudice in this matter is strikingly illustrated in the case of two sisters—the one very pretty, the other very plain, who once spent some time in the house where I was boarding. Though the hair of both was precisely the same color, that of the younger, or handsome one, was always called *auburn* the other red. A lady one day had the kindness— some people are very fond of making such pleasant little remarks—to tell the ugly one that her hair was not near so pretty a color as that of her sister. The person addressed made no reply but, when the polite lady had departed, told me that she was wearing frizettes made of her pretty sister's curls, which had been cut off during an attack of fever.

On first thoughts, it may seem strange that red hair is nowhere held in such contempt as it is among those races of whom it is most characteristic;

but this results from the general disposition of mankind to depreciate what they have, and overrate what they do not possess. In France, Spain, Italy, the nations of Southern Europe, nothing is so much admired, as the most fiery red hair—called by a more poetical name, of course; while a dark browned Mexican, whose stiff wiry locks bear greater resemblance to the tail of a black horse than anything else in nature, will all but fall down and worship the beauty of any happy possessor of sunflower tresses. "Coma Bella, Coma Blanca," are the pleasing sounds which greet the ear of a red-headed woman on landing in Mexico, as she finds herself surrounded by an admiring group of natives; doubly pleasing by contrast to the less flattering remarks which she has been accustomed to from Americans or English-men. Châteaubriand seems to have found it impossible to reconcile his ideas of the beautiful and poetical with the presence of sable tresses, for he describes the hair of his Indian heroine, Atala, as a *golden* cloud floating before the eyes of her lover!

If poets and painters are the friend, of red hair, novelists are its mortal foes. It is the business of these latter to make the ideal approach the real, and their highest excellence consists in making the one so like the other one can scarcely tell them apart. They take advantage of the prevailing prejudice against red hair to paint their worst characters with it. Tittle-Titmouse and Uriah Heep are a perpetual slander upon red-headed people. The character usually ascribed to these last, and with much truth, is entirely out of keeping with that ascribed by the great romancers to their villains. Red-haired people are generally high-tempered, impulsive, warm hearted; and, though it may not become a red-headed woman to say so, I do not think I have ever known one to be either a fool or a coward. Such characteristics are entirely at variance with the low sneaking craftiness of Uriah, or the sottish imbecility of Titmouse. It always seemed to me that the latter ought to have been drawn with a certain pale, sickly shade of sandy hair, which looks as if it might once have been red, but had got faded, like piece of bad calico, from constant using. Uriah, on the other hand, should have stiff straight, puritanical locks, with a dark, sallow complexion, and green eyes. There are some people who look as if they had lain in the grave until they had become mouldy, and then risen to wander about the world without ever getting dry or warm again. Uriah Heep belongs to this class, and should have nothing about him so warm and bright as a sunny head.

One reason for the common dislike of red hair may be found in the fact that it is often accompanied by a red or freckled face, neither of which is exactly consistent with our ideas of the most refined and delicate beauty. But is it not unfair to lay the faults of the face and complexion upon the hair? Nobody objects to their black hair because it sometimes accompanies a dark, muddy complexion, and upon the whole, I think brunettes oftener have bad complexions than blondes. After all, there are as many pretty faces framed in gold as in jet. There are three golden threads from the head of Lucretia Borgia preserved in the British Museum on account of their rare beauty. It is said that Cleopatra had red hair; the beautiful Mary of Scotland certainly had it, and the present Empress of France is crowned with something which is cousin—german to it; and this seems to be the secret of the present triumph of blondes. Whenever a reigning beauty happens to be crowned with the obnoxious color, prejudice dies out for a time and light hair becomes the fashion, as at present. Brunettes are in despair, and red-headed women have their revenge. Modes are invented, such as frizzing and crimping, which do not at all become raven tresses, but render golden locks bewitching. There are started all manner of devices for giving dark hair a tinge. Gilt and silver powders are used without stint, while some devoted worshippers of fashion submit to the ordeal of lying with their hair in dye for thirty-six hours, and then run the risk of making it blue, green, or purple, as did their worthy prototype, Tittlebat Titmouse, in his famous attempt at the reverse and more common operation.

But these wayward freaks of fashion never last long. So soon as the belle, whose beauty in spite of red hair cheated people into the belief that she was beautiful because of it, becomes *passé* or out of fashion, and some sable-tressed rival succeeds to her triumphs, the old prejudice revives. The pretty names of auburn, golden, sunny are dropped, and red hair falls into such disrepute that any charity schoolboy will fly to arms if the odious epithet is applied to his pate. Men and women are unconscious of the power there is in a pretty face; they are influenced by it involuntarily. Many an ugly fashion gains ground just because pretty women will look so pretty in spite of it, that others are deluded into the belief that the fashion is itself graceful and becoming. Thus it is with red hair; some of the reigning belles of Europe having been supplied with it by nature, and making a virtue of necessity, have brought it in fashion. Let the rest of us make the most of the triumph they have won, and pray that a dark-haired empress may not ascend the throne of France till we are too gray to care what our hair was in the beginning. The ascendancy we enjoy at present cannot endure forever, that is certain for though the world may submit to the dictates of fashion for a season, she has a spite against red hair at the bottom, and will make war on it to the end of time. When eternity begins, as it seems pretty generally conceded that angels have—well, I won't offend the reader by saying *red* hair, but certainly something very like it, if poets and painters are to be credited—it is to be hoped that our triumph may then prove more lasting.

## Paper-Collar Gentility

"Ward's patent reversible, perspiration-proof paper collar, warranted by the chemicals used in its composition, to equal in polish the finest linen finish to rival in durability the best," etc., etc.

What a commentary on the age in which we live! What a catalogue of shams and vulgarities! "Fine linen finish," a sham upon raw material, "reversible," a slander on personal neatness; "perspiration-proof," an insult to friendly soap and water, the only honest means that nature has provided for making a man thoroughly "perspiration-proof." The present has often been called an age of shams, and who can question the justice of the accusation, when we see a "patent, reversible," many-sided sham boldly asserting itself as such, and obtaining public favor through the very hollowness of its pretensions?

Considered merely in themselves without reference to their usual accompaniments, paper collars are comparatively small affairs, scarcely worth singling out for special reprehension, from among the greater shams to which the age is addicted, but they are significant of much beyond themselves. They are the outward and visible signs of in inward and by no means *spirituelle* state of things, which is not *chic*, as the Parisians say. They are suggestive of a small shopkeeper, second-rate boarding-house state of society, where frowsy young ladies in pink ribbons sing sickly ballads to amorous dry-goods clerks, and ogle, at the sentimental parts, some slender swain in shining paper collar and soiled kid-gloves. They are suggestive of plated forks and printed cards of invitation; of bad cigars and cheap perfumery; of suspiciously large and showy brooches, stuck into not always the most immaculate of shirt-bosoms;—and worse than all, they are suggestive of a mind to save washing-bills; of a desire to keep up the "outward and visible signs" of decency without the "inward and spiritual grace;" of a white-sepulcher style of toilet, content to be all rottenness and corruption within, if it is beautiful enough without; of a class of men who can stay three weeks from home on a box of paper collars. Think of a man's going to spend Christmas at a country house, with his baggage in his pocket; think of his deliberately turning the soiled side of a "patent reversible *perspiration-proof*" in toward his skin; what liberties may we not suspect him of taking with the invisible and unmentionable parts of his toilet? Imagination shrinks from exploring farther the recesses of such a whited sepulchre.

Paper collars are typical of a class of men as well as a state of society. A cast-off "patent reversible perspiration-proof" gives as clear an insight into the habits and manners of the wearer, as the comparative anatomist can obtain from a tooth or a bone of any other animal. The individual distin-guished by the "Professor at the Breakfast Table" as the *Kohinoor* is a per-fect specimen of the paper-collar class, and I am as well satisfied that he wore a "patent reversible perspiration-proof," enameled and embossed on both sides, as if the "Professor" had taken special care to inform us of the fact. The man of thorough paper-collar breeding is essentially one of the "fellers." He always has very sleek, greasy hair, carefully curled, and perfumed with cinnamon or bergamot, and is much addicted to light kid-gloves always a little soiled. He wears a huge seal ring on his little finger, (his nails are never clean,) and a miraculous brooch, with perhaps studs to match, in his shirt-bosom. From his vest-pocket dangles a bulky chain, with a quantity of big seals, secret-society badges, etc., at one end, and possibly, a watch at the other. His coat and pants are in the latest fashion, his boots are glossy as a mirror, but who shall dare to say what is under them.

His habits vary slightly in different localities, but not enough to destroy the unity of the species. North of the Potomac, he talks through his nose, and says, "I calc'late;" farther South, he drawls his vowels, puts his knife into his mouth when he eats, and tries to talk literary on magazine stories and Miss Evans's novels. As to business pursuits, the Northern type of the *genus paper-collaris* is usually a merchant's clerk, or a small tradesman in the dry-good line; the Southern, a country beau, who puts on a clean shirt every Sunday to go "sparking" among the girls. The species is chiefly indigenous to large commercial towns, and always flourishes best where laundresses' fees are highest. It is very widely diffused, however, and exists, with slight variations, under all vicissitudes of civilization and nationality, and individuals may readily be detected, even when the most prominent mark of the species is wanting. Circumstances may have placed certain individuals beyond the reach of paper-collar influences, but they have paper collar souls, all the same as though they carried the outward badge of the species round their necks.

There is a class below, as well as one above, paper collars—an honest, humble, hard-working class, in homespun shirts, without collars—a class perfectly free from vulgarity because perfectly free from pretension. The two extremes of society are, perhaps, the only classes entirely free from vulgarity, in the proper acceptation of the word. The one, because it pretends to nothing it is not, the other, because it pretends to nothing at all. In Europe the peasantry are treated with more familiarity by the aristocracy than the *bourgeoisie*; and of all the lower strata of American society, the least vulgar, because the least assuming, are, or rather *were*, the negroes of the South. The ignorance and simplicity of these people kept them below pretension, and therefore above vulgarity. The idea of a respectable old "Uncle," as old "Uncles" were once, in a paper-collar, is as preposterous as the thought of General Lee or Wade Hampton[8] in the same guise. Extremes often meet, and in many respects the lowest stratum of society is less removed from the highest than are the intermediate, or paper-collar classes. The only difference between the homespun-shirt man and the paper-collar man is the difference between a good piece of stout brown wrapping-paper and the bill of a broken bank. The one is good for all it pretends to; the other is good for nothing at all.

# Notes

## Preface

1. Col. Garnett Andrews, Fanny Andrews's brother, was mayor of Chattanooga in the early 1890s.

2. Eliza Frances Andrews, *Wartime Journal of a Georgia Girl: 1864–1865* (New York: D. Appleton, 1908) (hereafter cited as *Wartime Journal*). An edition of the journal with an introduction by Spencer Bidwell King appeared in 1960 (Macon, Ga.: Ardivan Press). A 1997 edition was published by the University of Nebraska Press with an introduction by Jean V. Berlin.

3. Mary Boykin Chesnut, *A Diary from Dixie*, ed. Ben Ames Williams (Boston: Houghton Mifflin Co., 1949).

4. Maude Annulet Andrews, Fanny's niece, the daughter of her brother Henry and her sister-in-law Cora.

5. Mattie Morgan was the sister of Fanny's sister-in-law Cora Morgan Andrews, the wife of Fanny's brother Henry. For a comprehensive description and analysis of the changing place of women in the nineteenth-century South from the antebellum era through Reconstruction, see Laura Edwards, *Scarlett Doesn't Live Here Anymore: Southern Women of the Civil War Era* (Urbana: Univ. of Illinois Press, 2000).

6. Andrews, a classical scholar, was referring to Macedonian King Philip. Philip, the father of Alexander the Great, was noted for his devotion to strong drink.

7. Drew Gilpin Faust, *Mothers of Invention: Women of the Slaveholding South in the American Civil War* (New York: Vintage Books, 1996), 255–57. Faust argues that the defeat of the Confederacy left many southern women with doubts about their own abilities and with reservations about the competence of their men.

8. Spencer Bidwell King, ed., *Wartime Journal* (Macon, Georgia: Ardivan Press, 1960), vi.

9. Bell Irvin Wiley, *Confederate Women* (New York: Barnes and Noble, 1975), xii.

10. The landmark U. S. Supreme Court decision, *Brown v. Topeka Board of Education* (1954), ruled legal separation (de jure) of the races in public education unconstitutional.

11. Anne Firor Scott, *Making the Invisible Woman Visible* (Urbana: Univ. of Illinois Press, 1984), 313–22.

12. Edward T. James, Janet James, and Paul S. Boyer, eds., *Notable American Women, 1607–1950*, 3 vols. (Cambridge: Harvard Univ. Press, Belknap Press, 1971).

13. Scott, *Making the Invisible Woman Visible*, 317.


# Introduction

1. Anne Firor Scott, *The Southern Lady: From Pedestal to Politics, 1830–1930* (Chicago: Univ. of Chicago Press, 1970). See also LeeAnn Whites, "'Stand by Your Man': The Ladies Memorial Association and the Reconstruction of Southern White Manhood," in *Women of the American South: A Multicultural Reader*, ed. Christie Anne Farnham (New York: New York Univ. Press, 1996).

2. Christie Anne Farnham, *The Education of the Southern Belle: Higher Education and Student Socialization in the Antebellum South* (New York: New York Univ. Press, 1994).

3. Children of Judge Garnett Andrews and Annulet Ball Andrews: Ann Corinthia "Cora" Andrews, 1829–1909; John Frederick "Fred" Andrews, 1830–1890; James Garnett Andrews, 1832–1834; Henry Frances Andrews, 1834–1892; James Garnett Andrews, 1837–1903; Eliza Frances "Fanny" Andrews, 1840–1931; Texas Willamette "Metta" Andrews, 1845–1925; Daniel Marshall "Marsh" Andrews, 1853–1917.

4. The old house that Fanny identified in her diary as "Tuscan Hall" (see the diary entry for Aug. 29, 1870) is referred to in some sources as "The Timothy Ball Home."

5. John Andrews's will names "older son Marcus," "son John," "son Garnett," "son James," and "son Daniel." The document also names daughters Sarah, Elizabeth, and Emily. The will stipulated that with the exception of "one Negro girl Fannie" that was to be given to John's granddaughter, Mary Ann Daniel, at the time of her marriage or when she became eighteen, "my negroes shall remain on the plantation and kept together under the direction of my executors" (Andrews Family Papers, Lupton Library Special Collections, Univ. of Tennessee at Chattanooga).

6. *Chronicles of Wilkes County*, 260, 275.

7. *Wartime Journal*, 2.

8. Several of the Andrews' servants were still alive and living near Haywood in the early 1900s, supported by the youngest Andrews daughter, Metta.

9. Christie Anne Farnham's comprehensive analysis of the antebellum education provided to women of the southern elite indicates that the science education was virtually equal to that of men. However, in a 1920s newspaper interview, Fanny recalled that her education in the sciences was meager.

10. Washington, Georgia, during Fanny's youth could have been a primary model for Christie Farnham's comprehensive description and analysis of the education available to the children of the South's antebellum aristocracy. See Farnham, *Education of the Southern Belle.*

11. Robert Willingham Jr., *No Jubilee: The Story of Wilkes* (Washington, Ga.: Wilkes Publishing, 1976), 88–89. See also *The Story of Washington–Wilkes,* by the Works Progress Administration, Writers' Project (Athens: Univ. of Georgia Press, 1941).

12. "Georgia Woman Wins International Honor," *Atlanta Journal,* Mar. 28, 1926.

13. The education of antebellum southern women of the upper class, according to modern scholars, was often of high quality. However, the role for which the antebellum woman was educated was tightly defined and limited, according to the standards of the late twentieth through early twenty-first centuries. Farnham argues that young women of Frances Andrews's social rank were educated to be showpieces of the aristocracy. For the young women of the upper class, education was a sign that they were worthy of male protection, admiration, and chivalrous attention. See *Education of the Southern Belle,* 3, 28–29.

14. Judge Andrews's antebellum fear echoes in the twentieth-century observation of historian Peter Kolchin. Writing in 1993, Kolchin commented in his work *American Slavery: 1619–1877,* "Ironically, by going to war for the preservation of slavery, they (Southern planters and politicians) took the only action that could foreseeably have led to its speedy and complete abolition" (198–99).

15. *Wartime Journal,* 176–77.

16. Ibid.

17. Betsy Trotwood is a character from Charles Dickens's *David Copperfield.*

18. The scrapbook now rests among the Garnett Andrews Papers, Southern Historical Collection, Univ. of North Carolina at Chapel Hill.

19. The articles are included in the final section.

20. *Wartime Journal*, 386.

21. Ibid., 2.

22. Fanny's views expressed in her anti-suffrage newspaper articles reflected the popular nineteenth-century cultural metaphor of "separate spheres." According to the metaphor, a white woman's place was one of benevolence centered in the home. For a review of the place of the metaphor in the development of a feminine identity in the South, see Farnham's *Education of the Southern Belle*.

23. Garnett Andrews Papers, folio 1839, box 2.

24. Diary entry preceding July 15, 1871. Drew Faust argues that defeat-generated reservations about the competency of southern men created within many women of the post-war South a hesitancy to rely on men for support and survival. See Faust, *Mothers of Invention*, 256.

25. *Wartime Journal*, 95 (entry for Feb. 16, 1865).

26. Eliza Frances Andrews [Elzey Hay, pseud.], *A Family Secret* (Philadelphia: J. B. Lippincott, 1876) (hereafter cited as *Family Secret*).

27. The *Washington Gazette*, Friday, Nov. 10, 1876, reprinted excerpts from the *St. Louis Republican*, the *Albany (New York) Journal*, the *Pittsburgh Commercial*, the *Baltimore Bulletin*, the *Newark (New Jersey) Advertiser*, the *Philadelphia Enquirer*, and the *New York Evening Post*, among others. The *Washington Gazette*, Friday, Nov. 17, 1876, carried a lengthy front-page review from the *Macon Telegraph and Messenger*.

28. *Wartime Journal*, 178.

29. Mary Bondurant Warren, ed., *Chronicles of Wilkes County, Georgia* (Heritage Papers, Danielsville, Ga., 1978), 384–85.

30. Decades after Cousin Eliza's death, the history upon which she had worked for a number of years was transcribed and edited by Mary Bondurant Warren. Warren's work was published in 1978 as the *Chronicles of Wilkes County, Georgia, from Washington's Newspapers: 1889–1898*.

31. Eliza Frances Andrews [Elzey Hay, pseud.], *A Mere Adventurer* (Philadelphia: J. B. Lippincott, 1879) (hereafter cited as *Mere Adventurer*); *Prince Hal; or, The Romance of a Rich Young Man* (Philadelphia: J. B. Lippincott, 1882).

32. Ida Raymond's *Southland Writers* review of Andrews's writing is part of the last unit of this book.

33. Barbara Reitt, "Eliza Frances Andrews," *Dictionary of Georgia Biography*, vol. 1 (Athens: Univ. of Georgia Press, 1983). The text of Fanny's article is included in the final section of this work.

34. *Family Secret*, 74–75.

35. Ibid., 75.

36. Letter to Garnett Andrews, Garnett Andrews Papers.

37. *Wartime Journal*, 78. The horrors of Andersonville in the South were echoed in the North in U.S. prisoner-of-war camps like Fort Delaware. (Thomas Ware, "'Equal in the Presence of Death': The Curious Absence of Grave Markers in the Finn's Point National Cemetery," paper presented at the annual convention of American Culture, San Diego, California, Apr. 3, 1999).

38. *Family Secret*, 118.

39. *Wartime Journal*, 372–73.

40. Ibid., 57–63.

41. For a review and analysis of the changing social structure of the post-emancipation South, see Laura Edwards's *Gendered Strife and Confusion: The Political Culture of Reconstruction* (Urbana: Univ. of Illinois Press, 1997).

42. *Family Secret*, 128.

43. Diary entry preceding entry for July 15, 1871.

44. *Family Secret*, 128.

45. Diary entry preceding July 15, 1871.

46. Germaine de Staël (1766–1817) was a French-Swiss woman of letters. The Paris salon of Madame de Staël was a powerful political and cultural center until 1803. Her opposition to Napoleon I resulted in her exile to an estate on Lake Geneva. Her principal work, *On Germany* (1810), influenced European thought on German Romanticism. Other works included a sociological study of literature, novels, and a memoir. Mme. de Staël is credited with capturing the intellectual and artistic frustrations of women of her age in the classic *Corinne, ou l'Italie*. Frances Andrews refers several times in her writings to the life and strength of de Staël.

47. *Family Secret*, 128–29.

48. Scott, *Southern Lady*, 132

49. The fear of disease apparently hung constantly over the family of Colonel Andrews during the time in Yazoo City. Years later, the colonel's son, also named Garnett, wrote that the family left Yazoo for Chattanooga, ". . . on account of the health of my Mother and myself and two other children. He (Col. Andrews) had lost two children from Malaria and Pneumonia." ". . . At the various times that we had yellow fever in that county, my Father would take his family to my Mother's old home up in Virginia where we refugeed, but one year we drove thru the country and could not get any further than French Camp, some where between Koskiusko and Clarkesdale, when my brother, Champe, was taken with a bad attack of swamp fever and we had to stay there all Summer, could not get out of the state" (Letter to Mrs. Albert Bridgers, Dec. 9, 1936. Andrews Family Papers).

50. Charlotte A. Ford, "Eliza Frances Andrews, Practical Botanist, 1840–1931," *Georgia Historical Quarterly* 70, no. 1 (spring 1986): 65–66.

51. See, for example, the *Augusta Chronicle,* Jan. 13, 20, and 27, 1884; Feb. 10 and 17, 1884; Mar. 3, 10, 17, 24, and 30, 1884; and other Friday editions through June 1884.

52. *Popular Science Monthly* 28 (1886): 779–81.

53. For a chronological bibliography of Fanny's botanical publications, see Ford, "Eliza Frances Andrews, Practical Botanist," 79.

54. E. F. Andrews, *Botany All the Year Round* (New York: American Book Co., 1903).

55. A copy of the 1895 tour brochure is in the private collection of David Harris, Washington, Georgia.

56. *A Practical Course in Botany* (New York: American Book Co., 1911).

57. Ford, "Eliza Frances Andrews, Practical Botanist," 63–79.

58. Eliza Frances Andrews, "Remarkable Behavior of a Veteran White Oak," *Torreya* 26 (1926): 54–55.

59. *Wartime Journal,* 13–14.

60. The other two Americans were Presidents Woodrow Wilson and Theodore Roosevelt.

61. Garnett B. Andrews to Elizabeth Harris, Aug. 5, 1932, Floyd County Library archives, Rome, Georgia.

62. *Wartime Journal,* 13–14.

63. Fanny's brother-in-law Troup Butler was the husband of Fanny's older sister, Cora. The Butlers owned a plantation in southwest Georgia.

64. *Wartime Journal,* 93. Andrews's knowledge or image of the South's lower class, the "crackers," of the mid-nineteenth century is evidenced clearly in her novel *A Family Secret.*

65. Jean Berlin, introduction to *The Wartime Journal of a Georgia Girl,* by Eliza Frances Andrews (Lincoln: Univ. of Nebraska Press, 1997), ix.

66. *Wartime Journal,* 2

67. *Montgomery Advertiser,* Apr. 1911, 16.

# 1870

1. Possibly Capt. Francis M. Kelley (1831–1885). The graves of Capt. Kelley and his wife Sara are only a few yards from the Andrews family plot in Washington's Resthaven cemetery.

2. Fanny mentions the Reverend Mr. Henry Allen Tupper, Washington's Baptist minister, several times in the *Wartime Journal of a Georgia Girl.* For example, in her entry for May 7, 1865, she wrote: "I went to the Baptist

church and heard a good sermon from Mr. Tupper on the text: 'For now we live by faith, and not by sight'" (225).

Fanny also tells of problems and frustrations visited upon Kate Tupper and "Old Mrs. Tupper" by federal troops, in her *Wartime Journal* entry for July 21, 1865 (303). Mr. Tupper is described in the same entry as refusing to read from his pulpit a notice issued by occupation authorities concerning the marriages of "negro couples" (345).

3. The Reverend Mr. J. Knowles.

4. Possibly Charles Stuart Vedder, 1826–1919.

5. Mortimer Ward was the son of Fanny's cousin Elizabeth "Lilla" Littell Ward and Richmond Ward.

6. The four-acre Clinton Park at Broad Street and Clinton Avenue was laid out in 1850. The park in the late twentieth and early twenty-first centuries is the focal point of the Lincoln Park Historic District. Around the park are brownstone mansions built, for the most part, in the mid-nineteenth century by Newark's elite.

7. Joree is another name for the Towhee, a member of the Finch family (*The Audubon Society Encyclopedia of North American Birds* [New York: Alfred Knopf, 1980], 352, 562).

8. Richmond Ward was the founder of R. Ward & Company, a large Newark manufacturer of patent and enameled leather. Ward died in 1872, two years after Fanny's and Metta's visit. After Ward's death, the name of the company was changed to Reynolds & Wood. See William Ford, *The Industrial Interests of Newark, N.J.* (New York: Van Arsdale, 1874), 31–32.

9. A "wen" is a cyst usually created by a blocked sebaceous gland.

10. Fanny's spelling of Clark's last name varies from place to place in the diary. The correct spelling is "Clark" without a final *e*.

11. Julia Bruen Ward, the wife of Fanny's cousin Lilla's son, Mortimer.

12. A piazza is a verandah or porch. Before the widespread use of air-conditioning, piazzas or verandahs were a part of virtually all homes in the South. Family evenings and entertainments, especially during the summer months, often occurred on the ubiquitous architectural feature of the southern house.

13. According to some genealogical records, the first husband of cousin Lilla's mother's mother was a Nathanial (in some records "Nethaniel") Seabury. Lilla's mother was Matilda Ball Littell. Matilda's mother (Lilla's grandmother) was Sarah Ross. Why Fanny Andrews would say that her cousin Lilla has the blood of the Seaburys in her veins is not clear from the records available. However, Nathanial Seabury may have been an offspring of the first man to be ordained an Episcopal bishop in the

United States. Fanny's brother Garnett also recognized the Seabury link to the Andrews family in naming his third son—Champ Seabury Andrews. Fanny named the father of the heroine of her first novel, *A Family Secret*, Mortimer Seabury. Fanny's fictional Seabury was a descendant of a "respectable English country gentleman" and a southern aristocratic woman fallen on hard times.

14. In his introduction to the 1960 edition of the *Wartime Journal of a Georgia Girl*, historian Spencer King mentions the southern humor reflected in the attitudes and writings of the diary: "A sense of humor, perhaps as much as anything else, saved the South from collapsing completely after its traumatic experience of war and postwar desolation. Fanny Andrews symbolized that trait . . ." (xiv).

15. At one time more than two-dozen servants worked in the Andrews family home. However, the outcome of the war forced a severe reduction in their number. Fanny wrote in her journal on April 23, 1865 (*Wartime Journal*, 375) that because of the family's financial problems, the number of household workers had been reduced from 25 to 5.

16. Montrose was one of the city's premier residential neighborhoods at the time of Fanny's visit to Newark. By the end of the century, the area was home to a number of prominent families. (*The Oranges and their Leading Business Men* [Newark: Mercantile Publishing, 1890]), 58.

17. Construction began on Newark's original Trinity Episcopal Church building in 1733. According to tradition, the site for the church was granted by Newark in the town's Training Place (Military Park). "The Church of the Park" was issued a charter in 1746. A year later the charter was suspended; however, in 1748 King George II granted the current charter. The church building was completed in 1746. It was destroyed by fire in 1804, and rebuilt and refurbished in 1810. The church became the Cathedral for the Newark Diocese in 1942. In 1966 the church was united with St. Philip's Episcopal Church and, since 1992, has been known as Trinity and St. Philip's Cathedral.

18. George A. Clark (1824–1873) was a native of Paisley, Scotland. George and his brother William were major figures in the development of the cotton thread industry in the United States. Clark died on February 13, 1873, three years after meeting Fanny Andrews. The brothers made their fortunes in the manufacture of cotton sewing thread. The huge Clark factory was built during the Civil War and was destroyed by fire more than 130 years later in 1998. At one time the factory employed a thousand workers. The same year of Fanny's Newark visit, 1870, William Clark completed construction of a grand new home at 346 Mount Prospect Avenue.

Referred to in the nineteenth century as "the Clark Mansion," the structure is now known as the North Ward Center. The Prospect Avenue mansion contains 28 rooms, and it was considered one of the most handsome
homes in the country at the turn of the nineteenth century. The cost of
the home in 1870 was $200,000. See William H. Shaw, *History of Essex and
Hudson Counties, New Jersey,* Vol. I (Philadelphia, Everts and Peck, 1884,
611-13.

19. Fanny's brother Frederick, "Fred," attempted several businesses
after the Civil War. Apparently none of his ventures was successful.

20. Grace Church was thirty-three years old and the building itself
was twenty-three when visited in 1870 by Fanny and Metta Andrews.
The cornerstone of the present building at Broad and Elm Streets was laid
in 1847. The church architecture is brown freestone in the early English
style of the thirteenth century. The building seats about seven hundred
worshippers.

21. Fanny's reference is to Jesus' parable of Dives and Lazarus—a rich
man and a beggar. According to the story told in Luke 16:19–31, during
life, Lazarus lay before the gates of Dives, "desiring to be fed with the
crumbs which fell from the rich man's table." Both the rich man and
Lazarus died, and after their deaths, it was Dives who pleaded from the tor-
ments of Hell for Lazarus to dip a finger in water to touch Dives's dry
tongue. The point of the parable, as Fanny well knew, was that people pass
their lives, daily, within sight and sound of one another, but in different
worlds; and as was the message of several of Jesus' parables, there will be a
reversal in time: the first will be last and the last will be first.

22. The record is not clear on whether the Hobbs who accompanied
the Andrews sisters to Newark and to whom Fanny refers several times in
the 1870–72 diary, and the Captain Richard Hobbs referred to several
times in the *Wartime Journal* are the same man. Circumstantial evidence
indicates the two may well be the same. One photograph in Metta's photo
album is of a one-armed older man labeled "Hobbs." Fanny and the Captain Richard Hobbs mentioned several times in the *Wartime Journal* apparently had a friendly and playful relationship during the last months of the
war (see pp. 74, 82, 85, 94, 95, 97, and 99). Fanny also mentioned in the
*Wartime Journal* on p. 294 a "Mr. Hobbs" of Albany as being a conduit for
letters to the family from Fanny's older sister, Cora. According to the Ros-
ter of Confederate Soldiers, 1st Lt. Richard Hobbs (born 1825) was an
officer in the Dougherty Guards, Company K, 51st Regiment of the Georgia Volunteer Infantry of the Army of Northern Virginia. Albany is
located in Dougherty County. According to the record, Lt. Hobbs was

elected captain on March 22, 1862. Capt. Hobbs was wounded in the left shoulder at South Mountain, Maryland, and his arm amputated. In 1870 Capt. Hobbs would have been forty-five years of age—an old man, certainly, to women of Fanny's and Metta's ages.

23. During the period of this diary (1870–72), Fanny's work was appearing in print under the pen name of "Elzey Hay." Shortly after the war, in 1866, her article entitled "Dress Under Difficulties; or, Passages from the Blockade Experience of Rebel Women" was published in *Godey's Lady's Book and Magazine*. Several other publications followed, and in 1871, the year after Fanny's visit to the Wards, the true identity of "Elzey Hay" was made public in Raymond's *Southland Writers*. During this time Fanny kept a scrapbook of her published work. However, she failed to indicate with the clippings from which newspapers or on what date the clipped articles appeared. The scrapbook is now a part of the Garnett Andrews Papers.

24. Lubins extract was a 19th century perfume.

25. Fanny's letters home echoed the discomfort with "Old Mr. Ward" expressed in her diary. Fanny's sister-in-law Rosalie copied to her husband, Garnett, in August 1870, comments in a letter from Fanny that Mr. Ward was frightening. Rosalie's letter now rests in the Andrews folio of the Southern Historical Collection (Univ. of North Carolina, Chapel Hill).

26. Perhaps they attended Newark's "New Presbyterian Church" located across Broad Street.

27. The House of Prayer (Episcopal) has been located in the 300 block of Broad Street since 1849. The cornerstone of the church building was set on November 28, 1849, and opening services were conducted a year later, November 26, 1850. In 1861 the church added a brick parochial school; and in 1870, the same year that Frances and Metta Andrews visited their Newark cousins, the church dedicated a new organ.

28. Union general Ben Butler commanded the occupation of New Orleans during the Civil War. He was known as "Beast Butler" throughout the South because of his ruthless and corrupt occupation policies.

29. Fanny was so unimpressed with the "little prig," that she shared the evening's experience in a letter home to the family. Her sister-in-law Rosalie quoted Fanny's description of the incident in a letter to her husband, Fanny's brother Garnett. (Garnett Andrews Papers).

30. The Bruens were family of Mortimer Ward's wife, Julia. Fanny used the Bruen family name in *A Family Secret*. Fanny's fictional Bruens were pictured as a family of the southern planter class. The Bruen name also appears in eighteenth-century Ball family genealogical records.

31. Experience Ball (1797–1882). Her father, Timothy Ball (1758–1828), was a brother of Dr. Stephen Ball, Fanny's great-grandfather. Timothy and Stephen were children of Ezekiel Ball (1721–1804).

32. Hannah Ball died in 1858, about twelve years before Fanny's Newark visit.

33. Fanny writes the nickname as "Peri." Other sources give "Peeny."

34. Caleb Camp (1790–1872).

35. In her first novel, *A Family Secret*, a project on which she was working during the period of the 1870–72 diary, Fanny made good on the promise to soften her condemnation of Yankees. She uses a detachment of Yankee soldiers led by a sympathetic officer to rescue her two Confederate heroes, Audley Malvern and George Dalton, from a band of bushwhackers and brigands during the novel's climax; and in the novel's conclusion Fanny marries one of her characters—a southern belle of the old aristocracy, Claude Harfleur—to the Yankee officer Schuyler.

36. Eagle Rock Reservation remains open to the public. The reservation is located in West Orange (Essex County), south of modern Route 506 and east of Route 577 west of Montclair. The park is popular with hikers, horseback riders, and bird watchers. See Michael P. Brown, *New Jersey Parks, Forests and Natural Areas: A Guide* (New Brunswick, N.J.: Rutgers Univ. Press, 1992), 63.

37. Llewellyn Park was initially developed by New York druggist Llewellyn Haskell in 1855. The original residential park covered almost eight hundred acres. Thomas A. Edison, among a number of other prominent New Jersey businessmen of the late nineteenth century, maintained a residence in the park. (*Oranges and their Leading Business Men*, 24–25).

38. According to an 1866 *New York Times* article cited by Douglas Keister, "It is the ambition of every New Yorker to live on Fifth Ave., take his airing in the [Central] Park, and to sleep with his fathers in Green-Wood" (Keister, *Going Out in Style: The Architecture of Eternity* [New York: Facts on File, 1997], 38).

39. The young girl who lay beneath was the focus of a tragedy well known in the mid-nineteenth century, and the monument under which she lay was of her own design. The girl, Charlotte Canda (1828–45), was the daughter of French parents who ran a finishing school in New York City. When she was sixteen, Charlotte sketched a funerary monument for her aunt. Charlotte's sketch for the aunt's tomb was used less than a year later to build the sculpture that now covers her own grave, when, on Charlotte's seventeenth birthday, she was killed in a carriage accident. In

the center of the monument is a statue of Charlotte in the party dress she wore the night of her death (Keister, 100).

40. Called by some the father of modern journalism, James Gordon Bennett was the publisher of the *New York Herald* during the mid-nineteenth century. Bennett was a major player in the development of "penny press" journalism in the United States. In 1866 Bennett turned over the newspaper to his son, James Gordon Bennett Jr. (1841–1918). In addition to running the *Herald,* the younger Bennett was a noted New York yachtsman and society figure of the Gilded Age.

41. Stoke Poges is the site of the English churchyard where tradition holds that eighteenth-century poet Thomas Gray found the setting for his "Elegy Written in a Country Church Yard."

42. Fanny's body today rests in Washington's Resthaven cemetery. A large granite obelisk stands in the center of the Andrews family plot to one side of her grave. The obelisk is inscribed on one side with her name, on another side with the name of her brother Garnett, and on its third side with the name of Garnett's wife, Rosalie. Only a small stone with the initials "E. F. A." marks Fanny's actual grave.

43. New York City's Beach Pneumatic Subway opened in February 1870, about five months before Fanny's and Metta's visit. The railway stretched from the corner of Warren Street and Broadway to Murray Street. The line was New York City's first subway. Passengers rode in a car pushed by pneumatic pressure created by a large fan located at the Broadway end of the tunnel. When the car reached the end of the line, the driver would ring a bell to signal fan operators to reverse the device, and the car would then be "sucked" back to the Warren Street Station. The subway operated for only a few years, and the 312-foot tunnel was converted sometime in 1873 into a storage shed that was later abandoned. The tunnel was rediscovered during the 1912 construction of the BMT Broadway subway line. See "First Subway Here Was Like a Popgun: Opened 80 Years Ago, It Shot Its Car, Full of Passengers, With Compressed Air," *New York Times* (Feb. 25, 1950), 19.

44. Fanny refers to Cousin Lilla's companion, Miss Gardner, several times as the "lynx."

45. Bishop James Roosevelt Bayley (1814–77) was a prominent Roman Catholic clergyman of the mid-nineteenth century. Bayley is credited with leading the expansion of the Catholic Church in Newark (*The Bishops of Newark: 1853–1978* [South Orange, N.J.: Seton Hall Univ., 1978], 7–21). The ecumenical council to which Fanny refers was the meeting of church leaders now known as Vatican Council I, the 1869–70

meeting called by Pope Pius IX at which the doctrine of papal infallibility was promulgated.

46. Possibly the Asbury–South Market Street Methodist Church, which was organized in 1860. In 1907 the property was sold and the proceeds were used to upgrade another Newark Methodist church.

47. During the years surrounding Fanny's and Metta's visit to their "Yankee kin," Long Branch, New Jersey, was a premier summer resort for the elite of the Northeast. Among the Long Branch residents and visitors during the mid to late 1800s were General Winfield Scott, Edwin Booth, George Pullman, Jim Fisk, Diamond Jim Brady, Lillian Russell, and Union generals Phillip Sheridan and George Meade. Ten years after Fanny's visit to Newark, in 1881, then President James Garfield was brought from Washington to a Long Branch home, Francklyn Cottage, after being shot. Garfield died on September 19, 1881 (Paul Sniffen, *Long Branch* [Dover, N.H.: Arcadia, 1996]).

48. Tuscan Hall is the historic home of the New Jersey Ball family. Fanny's great-great-grandfather, Ezekiel Ball, built the mansion in the 1700s. Ezekiel's son Stephen, the revolutionary war surgeon, was the father of Fanny's grandfather Frederick.

49. Cora Rose was Fanny's older sister, the wife of Troup Butler; and Aunt Cornelia was the youngest sister of Fanny's mother.

50. Probably Sophia: "my dear old mammy—Sophia by name . . . so superior, and as genuine a 'lady' as I ever knew . . ." (see p. 294 in the *Wartime Journal*).

51. Georgia's Reconstruction governor, Republican Rufus Bullock. Bullock's administration was marked by controversy. He hurriedly resigned in 1871, leaving the state to avoid prosecution on charges of corruption. Judge Andrews's Washington neighbor Robert Toombs led the prosecution efforts.

52. Guipure lace is of a heavy and large patterned style.

53. The adventures of Fanny and Metta in their escape from Sherman's invaders are chronicled in Fanny's *Wartime Journal.*

54. Stereoscopes were a popular form of parlour entertainment during the late nineteenth century. See the Robert Dennis Collection of Stereoscopic Views, Photography Collection, Miriam and Ira D. Wallach Division of Art, Prints, and Photographs, New York Public Library (http://digital.nypl.org/stereoviews/).

55. The words "are a horrid vulgar minded race and" are marked through in the original.

56. "The truth is, Yankees have not a spark of genuine hospitality about them" is marked out in the original.

57. Passage marked through in original.

58. According to Wilkes County historian Robert "Skeet" Willingham, the depot riot described by Fanny was known as the "Affray at the Depot." The "affray" was a gun battle between rowdy gangs of whites and blacks that gathered to meet a train arriving with Republican candidates. One group of the rowdies came to show support for the candidates. The other group came to heckle. During the confusion, shots were fired and several men were hit by the gunfire. One of those wounded was William Harris, a black man, who died an hour or so later. The *Washington Gazette* reported that Harris was "looked upon as dissentious and troublesome."

59. William Henry Toombs (1851–1917) was a nephew of Robert Toombs (1810–85). Robert Toombs was former secretary of state for the Confederacy and an outspoken antebellum politician. The elder Toombs was a friend but a political opponent of Fanny's father. The Toombs family numbered among the planter aristocracy of pre-war Georgia. Robert Toombs maintained a lucrative legal practice in Washington, and he owned a large plantation in southwest Georgia. According to Fanny's wartime diary (entries for May 11 and July 30, 1865), within ten weeks of General Toombs's escape from the federals, the Toombs family was twice "turned out" of its home by the occupation army (243, 357). Fanny does not tell how long the Toombses were refugees. The term "Unreconstructed Rebel" may well have been designed to describe Robert Toombs. In the years after the Civil War he consistently refused to take the oath of allegiance to the United States, and he was thus barred from voting or holding public office. Nevertheless, Toombs remained a political power for the rest of his life. He wrote the 1875 Constitution of the State of Georgia, which remained law until it was replaced in 1945. The Toombs family home is now a museum maintained by the state.

60. C. E. "Charlie" Irvin (1844–1916) was mentioned by Andrews in her "explanatory" notes written after the turn of the century to accompany her *Wartime Journal:* "The Irvin Artillery, so frequently alluded to, was the first military company organized in the county, and contained the flower of the youth of the village. It was named for a prominent citizen of the town, father of the unreconstructible 'Charley' mentioned later, and an uncle of the unwitting Maria, whose innocent remark gave such umbrage to my father's belligerent daughter" (180). Charlie Irvin's father, Isaiah Tucker Irvin, was for many years a law partner of Judge Andrews. Isaiah Irvin served as Wilkes County state representative from 1851 until his death in 1860. Irvin was speaker of the Georgia House of Representatives from 1859 until the steamboat accident in which he died off the coast of Galveston,

Texas. Following Irvin's death, Judge Andrews was elected to replace him in the state legislature. Charlie's grandson, Charles Edgar Irvin, was for many years a librarian of the Mary Willis Memorial Library in Washington. He retired in 1989 as assistant director and head of technical services.

61. Dudley M. DuBose (1834–83) was elected to the congress in 1871. The DuBose family, the Toombses, and the Irvins are mentioned by Andrews a number of times in her *Wartime Journal*. Dudley was a cousin of Robert Toombs's wife, and he married the daughter of General and Mrs. Toombs, Sallie. Sallie is the Mrs. DuBose referred to in the *Wartime Journal* on pp. 243 and 357. James Rembert DuBose was the brother of General Toombs's wife, and it was around and in the James DuBose home that Union negro troops were camped during May 1865: "While Gen. Stacy's men were camped out at the mineral spring, he made his headquarters at Mrs. James DuBose's house, and permitted his negro troops to have the freedom of the premises, even after Mrs. DuBose had appealed to him for protection" (235).

62. Henry Thomas Slaton (1834–1918) was elected to office in the 1871 state election. Slaton owned a gristmill about ten miles southwest of Washington, Georgia.

63. William Harris was one of the men killed in the riot at the Washington railroad station.

64. According to Wilkes County historian Robert "Skeet" Willingham, Canaan was properly known in the years just after the Civil War as Wylieville, and it was a center of Radical activity. The area in the late twentieth century is the Whitehall area of Washington, Georgia.

65. Henry Francis Andrews (1834–92) is described by Fanny in the *Wartime Journal* as "the hottest" rebel of her family. During the Civil War Henry served as a surgeon in several Georgia units of the Confederate army. It was Henry who provided the cloth for the rebel flag sewn secretly by Fanny and her older sister, Cora. John Frederick Andrews (1830–90) served the Confederacy in several Georgia artillery units. He was promoted near the end of the war to major.

66. John T. Erwin, Captain, Company G., 61st Regiment, Georgia Volunteers, "The Hill Wilkes County Guards," CSA.

# 1871

1. Fanny uses the same allusion, "the play of Hamlet, with the title left out," in her 1908 introduction to the *Wartime Journal* (8–9).

2. Alexander H. Stephens, former vice president of the Confederate States. Stephens was a native of Wilkes County. The arrest by federal troops of Alexander "Little Aleck" Stephens was described in the *Wartime*

*Journal* entry for May 11, 1865 (242). Stephens was elected in 1873 to serve in the United States House of Representatives. He held the seat until 1882. Stephens left his House seat when elected to be the governor of Georgia. Several Stephens letters to Fanny's brother Garnett may be found in the Garnett Andrews Papers. Stephens died in office in 1883.

3. The garden of the Waddeys is mentioned by Fanny in her wartime journal (July 21, 1864) as being the place where "Ben Jones shot a negro the other night, for stealing . . . and it is a miracle that he escaped being put in jail. Fortunately the negro wasn't hurt" (340–41).

4. Although she spelled Wynn without a final *e* in the journal, Fanny may have been referring to Samuel W. Wynne (1815–82). His son, Samuel W. Wynne Jr., was a Civil War veteran. Both men lived in Washington during the 1870s and both are buried in Washington's Resthaven Cemetery. Sam Wynne Jr. is listed in one source as Samuel Moss Wynn. Mary Wynn and the "Wynns" are mentioned several times in Fanny's *Wartime Journal* (see pp. 189, 295, 300, and 308).

5. Fanny identified Lilly Legriel as a "school friend" in her diary entry for February 5, 1864, in the *Wartime Journal* (84).

6. If the "old Hobbs" mentioned several times by Fanny in this diary is the same Captain Hobbs of the *Wartime Journal*, Fanny's attitude and opinion of the fellow changed considerably in the years separating the two diaries. The photograph of "Hobbs" in Metta's album may be the man Metta was trying to decide what to do about. The album today is in a private collection in Washington, Georgia.

7. Belle Nash is mentioned in the *Wartime Journal* on June 27, 1865: "I went to see Belle Nash after dinner, before going to the bank to dance with the children. She invited me to go driving with her, but I declined, and walked to the bank with Jim Bryan, who spied me as I was leaving the Randolph house . . ." (312).

8. Mr. Hunter was the Episcopal priest for the Washington, Georgia, parish church. Hunter lived in Augusta and regularly came to Washington to conduct services.

Dr. J. J. Robertson was the cashier of the bank. The bank went out of business during the Civil War, but the Robertson family continued to live in the old bank building. It was in this building that Jefferson Davis signed the last official document of the Confederate States of America. Fanny described the bank building in her 1908 notes that accompany the *Wartime Journal:* "Two rooms on the lower floor were used for business purposes, while the rest of the building was occupied as a residence by the cashier. On the outbreak of the war the bank went out of business, but Dr. J. J. Robertson, who was cashier at the time, continued to occupy the building in the interest of the stockholders. Mrs. Robertson, like everybody else in the village at that time, had received into her house a number of refugees and other strangers, whom the collapse of the Confederacy had stranded there. Its original name clung to the building long after it ceased to have anything to do with finance, and hence the frequent allusions to 'the bank' in the diary" (175–76).

9. Lettie Pope was Fanny's cousin, the daughter of Aunt Cornelia.

10. The "Navy Hunters" were Captain and Mrs. Thomas T. Hunter who lived at the "Anchorage" just south of Washington, Georgia. Capt. Hunter was married to Harriet DuBose. He had been married to a daughter of Alexander Pope, Anne Pope, who died in 1867.

11. Julian Edings did not die from the childhood illness. He lived until 1945.

12. Rosalie Champe Andrews (1868–71), the daughter of Fanny's brother Garnett and sister-in-law Rosalie Beirne. Rose died in Yazoo, Mississippi, and was originally buried there. Her body was moved in 1872 to the Andrews family plot in Washington.

13. Mattie Morgan was the sister of Cora Morgan, the wife of Fanny's brother, Henry. The Morgans are described as Andrews houseguests in the *Wartime Journal*, and Eddie (Ed) Morgan is mentioned several times in the earlier journal (see pp. 91, 324, 334, 335, 355, 357, and 370). From the text of a letter written by Fanny to Garnett in 1902, it is apparent that the Andrews and the Morgan families were linked by the long love affair between Henry and Cora (Garnett Andrews Papers).

14. This may be Cornelia J. Slaton (1842–76).

15. Henry Thomas Slaton (1834–1918).

16. Maude Andrews, Fanny's niece, grew up to be a journalist and a novelist. She was a columnist for a number of years for the *Atlanta Constitution* (Mary Bondurant Warren, *Chronicles of Wilkes County, Georgia, from Washington's Newspapers: 1889–1898* [Heritage Papers, Danielsville, Ga., 1978], 207, 229, 381). Maude used the pen name of "Annulet Andrews." She married Josiah K. Ohl, and moved from Georgia to New York. She died in 1943 and is buried in Bronxville, New York, far from her native Washington.

17. According to Wilkes County records, Annie Maxwell married Wylie Walton on November 24, 1875, several years after the visit to the Dunwoodys mentioned in Fanny's diary.

18. Audley Malvern, Julia Malvern, and George Dalton are characters that eventually appear in Fanny Andrews's first novel, *A Family Secret*.

The novel apparently provided Fanny with an escape from the day-to-day life she describes in her diary. Her novel reflects a picture of the southern aristocracy of the 1860s that comes from first person experience. Julia and

George are torn apart by the ravages of the war. Julia's family loses its fortune, and her father dies as a consequence. Julia and her mother are left to depend on their own resources and the goodwill of friends for survival. In some ways the fictional plight of Julia Malvern echoes the real situation of Fanny Andrews.

19. The Fred mentioned here is probably Frederick Ball Pope, Aunt Cornelia's son born in 1854. This Fred later married Mary Wynn, the daughter of Samuel W. Wynn.

20. Probably cousin Eliza Andrews Bowen.

21. Belle Nash is mentioned in both of Fanny's journals.

22. Lettie and Lucy were probably Lettie and Lucy Pope, the daughters of Fanny's Aunt Cornelia.

23. The farewell was not lasting. Fanny's literary creations—Audley Malvern, Ruth Harfleur, Uncle Bruen, and George Dalton—were presented to the public about four years later with the 1876 publication of *A Family Secret.*

24. Cousin Eliza Bowen. During the early 1870s "Cousin Liza" was living away from Washington attempting to support herself as a teacher. Bowen apparently lived and taught for several years in Atlanta, then moved to Paris, Kentucky, before returning permanently to Washington.

25. A portion of the path that reached from Haywood to the seminary may still exist in Washington, preserved as a public walkway and park not too far from the town square.

26. Fanny mentions cousin Robert Ball in her wartime diary in the entry for April 25, 1865: "Our whirlwind of a cousin, Robert Ball, has made his appearance, but is hurrying on to New Orleans and says he has but one day to spend with us" (185). Apparently no evidence remains of what the "awful memory" may have been.

27. Fanny uses a country tournament as a major plot device in her novel *Family Secret.* During her novel's tournament, one of the principal characters is accused of being a Yankee spy, and another character, Claude Harfleur, is crowned Queen of Love and Beauty (96–101).

28. *My Schools and Schoolmasters,* by Hugh Miller (Boston: Gould and Lincoln, 1854), was a popular memoir of the mid-nineteenth century.

29. The Sand Hills is a section of Augusta, Georgia, in which the Church of the Good Shepherd is located.

30. Fanny's older sister, Cora (Mrs. Troup Butler).

31. Several years later, in 1878, Fred Pope was the business manager of the *Washington Gazette.* At the same time, Fanny's younger brother, Dr. Henry F. Andrews, was listed on the mast of the paper as the editor.

32. Mattie was the sister of Henry's wife, Cora. What eventually became of Mattie Morgan is not known from the existent historical record.

33. The nature of "Fred's case" is not made clear in Fanny's diary, and the historical records are neither clear nor specific. However, a letter written in August 1869 to Garnett Andrews by his wife, Rosalie, hints that Fred too was dealing with an alcohol problem: " . . . Sister told father, Fred was threatened with delirium tremens . . . Father did not speak a word but the tears came" (Garnett Andrews Papers). Fred Andrews did attempt a number of jobs after returning to Washington from the Confederate army, including, for a time, editing the *Washington Gazette*.

Fred's frustrations are apparent in a letter he wrote to his older brother about eighteen months before Fanny's 1871 diary entry. Fred wrote to Garnett on May 4, 1870: "I'm litterally [sic] doing nothing.—Editing Gazette amounts to nothing—and have tried everywhere for employment. Next year if nothing turns up I shall buy a mule and go to work on the place around home. Dr. Sale is cultivating it this year or I would be at it now" (Garnett Andrews Papers). There exists evidence that Fred was the editor of the paper in name, but that Fanny did much of the actual editing. Rosalie wrote to Garnett that "Fanny will not be able to edit the paper any longer on account of her eyes which are hurting very badly" (Rosalie Andrews to Garnett Andrews, Aug. 20, 1869, Garnett Andrews Papers).

Fred never married. He died on December 31, 1890, and was buried beside his mother in Washington's Resthaven cemetery.

34. "Old Mr. Morgan"—George W. Morgan, the father of Cora, Henry Andrews's wife.

# 1872

1. Cousin Will Pope was the stepson of Aunt Cornelia. Cornelia was the third wife of Alexander Pope. Will was the son of the elder Pope and his second wife, Sarah Joyner Barnett.

2. Acts 9:36–39.

3. Judge Andrews died the next year (1873) and was buried beside his wife in Washington's Resthaven Cemetery. The story on which Fanny was working became her first published novel, *A Family Secret*.

4. Dr. Bolling A. Pope was the stepson of Aunt Cornelia.

5. Benjamin Micoon Sr. (Micoon spelled with two *o*'s) was identified in 1898 by Mrs. T. M. Green (Metta Andrews) as a Georgia businessman who, in the 1870s, apparently controlled a company in which Fanny's

cousin, Eliza Andrews Bowen, invested and lost her entire inheritance (*Chronicles of Wilkes County, Georgia*, 385–86).

## Articles

1. Fanny commented in her wartime journal in the entry for August 9, 1865, about submitting the piece to a northern publication: "I have sent my account of the bank robbery to try its fate with the 'New York World.' In a private letter to the editor, I explained that I wrote as if I were a Yankee sojourning at the South, in order to make some of the hard things it was necessary to say in telling the truth, as little unpalatable as possible to a Northern public. What a humiliation! But it gave me the satisfaction of hitting a few hard knocks that I could not have ventured in any other way. I could say: 'We have been guilty of' so and so, where it would not do to say: 'You have been guilty.'" (*Wartime Journal*, 368-69).

2. The "Loyal League" was known also as the "Union League." The organization was formed originally during the Civil War in the North to inspire loyalty to the Union. During Reconstruction, the league spread to the South to support Republican and Radical policies among the newly enfranchised blacks. Between 1865 and 1877 the league became a major Republican propaganda and organizational instrument among the emancipated slaves. Southern whites countered the league by organizing their own, often-secret organizations, such as the Ku Klux Klan and the "Red Shirts." Fanny had little use for the Klan, although her brother Garnett may have been an early Klan organizer. After 1865 Fanny said that the Klan had been taken over by a lower class—"low-downers," as she described them in an 1865 *New York World* article (Jan. 9, 1866).

3. Georgia's Confederate governor Joseph Brown was elected to office before the Civil War and was strongly pro-slavery. He was an outspoken supporter of states' rights and a Democrat. After the South's defeat, Brown angered many Georgians by becoming a Radical Reconstruction Republican and urging the South's adoption of Radical terms. Brown suffered his only electoral defeat in his 1868 run for the United States Senate. When Republicans lost power in Georgia, Brown returned to the Democratic Party, and in his later years was known as Georgia's political boss. He was eventually elected to three terms in the U.S. Senate, serving from 1880 until 1891.

4. Pennsylvania congressman Thaddeus Stevens was perhaps the most outspoken of the Radical Republicans during Reconstruction. He advocated the confiscation of southern plantations by the government and the distribution of the land to freed slaves.

5. The quote as used by Andrews contains a grammatical error and is not complete. The complete, corrected quotation is "Son attitude sur le char était noble et modeste: on apercevait bien qu'elle était contente d'être admirée; mais un sentiment de timidité se mêlait à sa joie et semblait demander grâce pour son triomphe; . . ." (Germaine de Staël, *Corinne ou l'Italie*, ed. Mmes. Necker de Saussure and Sainte-Beuve [Paris: Garnier, n.d], 22). The English translation is, "Her attitude on the chariot was noble and modest; she was noticeably pleased to be admired, but a feeling of timidity was mingled with her joy, and seemed to ask pardon for her triumph."

The quote is from Mme. de Staël's novel *Corinne ou l'Italie* (1807). Like Andrews, Germaine de Staël was a strong advocate of women's rights and wanted recognition of their creative talents. The political overtones of her novels antagonized Napoleon, who exiled her from Paris. As the title suggests, she compares the discrimination against women in France with the more liberal attitudes toward them in Italy. Her heroine, Corinne, was a woman of intellect as well as strong emotions. In this passage, Corinne—the most famous poet in Italy—is being crowned in a ceremony in Rome. De Staël's views regarding France were not popular with Napoleon's imperial ambitions (Felicia Sturzer, professor of Eighteenth-Century French Literature, Univ. of Tennessee at Chattanooga. See also Sarah Maza, "Women's Voices in Literature and Art," in *A New History of French Literature*, ed. Denis Hollier [Cambridge: Harvard Univ. Press, 1989], 625–26).

6. Fanny Fern was the pseudonym of Maine native Sara Payson Wells Parton (1811–72), one of the most popular American female writers of the nineteenth century. Her work appeared in a number of newspapers, and she authored several books. The merit of Parton's work now is not due so much to its literary style as to its portrayal of the popular tastes of the mid-nineteenth century.

7. "Excrescencies": product or effect.

8. Wade Hampton (1818–1902) was a hero of the Confederacy and a South Carolina patriot. Before the war he owned several large plantations and hundreds of slaves. He served in the South Carolina legislature in the years leading up to secession. During the war he organized and supported "Hampton's Legion." After the southern defeat, Hampton supported President Andrew Johnson's program for Reconstruction, and he was an outspoken opponent of the Radical Republicans. Hampton served as governor of South Carolina from 1872 until 1891. His departure from office in 1891 is cited by some as the end of rule in the South by the genteel aristocracy.

# Bibliography

Andrews, Eliza Frances [Elzey Hay, pseud.]. *A Family Secret.* Philadelphia: J. B. Lippincott, 1876.

———. *A Mere Adventurer.* Philadelphia: J. B. Lippincott, 1879.

———. *Prince Hal; or, The Romance of a Rich Young Man.* Philadelphia: J. B. Lippincott, 1882.

———. *Botany All the Year Round.* New York: American Book Company, 1903.

———. *A Practical Course in Botany.* New York: American Book Company, 1911.

———. "Remarkable Behavior of a Veteran White Oak," *Torreya* 26 (1926): 54–55.

Andrews Family Papers. MSS004. Lupton Library Special Collections, Univ. of Tennessee at Chattanooga.

Andrews, Garnett. *Papers.* Folio 1839. Southern Historical Collection. Univ. of North Carolina, Chapel Hill.

Andrews, Garnett. *Reminiscences of an Old Georgia Lawyer.* Atlanta: Franklin Steam Printing, 1870.

Berlin, Jean V. Introduction. *The Wartime Journal of a Georgia Girl: 1864–1865,* by Eliza Frances Andrews (1908). Lincoln: Univ. of Nebraska Press, 1997.

Bernhard, Virginia, Betty Brandon, Elizabeth Fox-Genovese, and Theda Perdue, eds. *Southern Women: Histories and Identities.* Columbia: Univ. of Missouri Press, 1992.

Bowen, Eliza A. *The Story of Wilkes County, Georgia.* Ed. Mary Bondurant Warren. Baltimore: Genealogical Publishing, 1997.

Chesnut, Mary Boykin. *A Diary from Dixie.* Ed. Ben Ames Williams. Boston: Houghton Mifflin Co., 1949.

*Dictionary of Georgia Biography.* Vol. 1. Athens: Univ. of Georgia Press, 1983.

Dillman, Caroline Matheny. *Southern Women.* New York: Hemisphere, 1988.

Edwards, Laura F. *Gendered Strife and Reconstruction: The Political Culture of Reconstruction.* Urbana: Univ. of Illinois Press, 1997.

Edwards, Laura F. *Scarlett Doesn't Live Here Anymore: Southern Women in the Civil War Era.* Urbana: Univ. of Illinois Press, 2000.

Farnham, Christie Anne. *The Education of the Southern Belle: Higher Education in the Antebellum South.* New York: New York Univ. Press, 1994.

————, ed. *Women of the American South: A Multicultural Reader.* New York: New York Univ. Press, 1997.

Faust, Drew Gilpin, *Mothers of Invention: Women of the Slaveholding South in the American Civil War.* Chapel Hill: Univ. of North Carolina Press, 1996.

Ford, Charlotte A. "Eliza Frances Andrews (Elzey Hay): Reporter 1865–1920." Paper presented at the Symposium on the Nineteenth Century, the Civil War, and Free Expression, Univ. of Tennessee at Chattanooga, Nov. 3, 2000.

————. "Eliza Frances Andrews, Practical Botanist, 1840–1931." *Georgia Historical Quarterly* 70, no. 1 (spring 1986): 63–79.

Ford, William. *The Industrial Interests of Newark, N.J.* New York: Van Arsdale, 1874.

Foster, Gaines M. *Ghosts of the Confederacy: Defeat, the Lost Cause, and the Emergence of the New South.* New York: Oxford Univ. Press, 1987.

Hawks, Joanne V., and Sheila L. Skemp. *Sex, Race, and the Role of Women in the South.* Jackson: Univ. Press of Mississippi, 1983.

James, Edward T., Janet James, and Paul S. Boyer, eds. *Notable American Women, 1607–1950.* 3 vols. Cambridge: Harvard Univ. Press, Belknap Press, 1971.

Keister, Douglas. *Going Out in Style: The Architecture of Eternity.* New York: Facts on File, 1997.

King, Spencer Bidwell. Introduction. *The Wartime Journal of a Georgia Girl* by Eliza Frances Andrews (1908). Macon, Ga.: Ardivan Press, 1960.

Kolchin, Peter. *American Slavery: 1619–1877.* New York: Hill and Wang, 1993.

Massey, Mary Elizabeth. *Bonnet Brigades.* New York: Alfred Knopf, 1966.

Miller, Hugh. *My Schools and Schoolmasters; or, the Story of My Education.* Boston: Gould and Lincoln, 1854.

Newsome, Parks Smythe. "An Historical and Editorial Study of the *Washington (Ga.) News-Reporter*." Master's thesis, Univ. of Georgia, 1966.

*The Oranges and their Leading Businessmen.* Newark: Mercantile Publishing, 1890.

Rable, George C. *But There Was No Peace: The Role of Violence in the Politics of Reconstruction.* Athens: Univ. of Georgia Press, 1984.

————. *Civil Wars: Women and the Crisis of Southern Nationalism.* Urbana: Univ. of Illinois Press, 1989.

Raymond, Ida. "Miss Fanny Andrews." In *Southland Writers: Biographical and Critical Sketches of the Living Female Writers of the South*, 512–19. Philadelphia: Claxton, Remsen and Haffelfinger, 1870.

Reitt, Barbara. "Eliza Frances Andrews," *Dictionary of Georgia Biography*, vol. I. Athens: Univ. of Georgia Press, 1983.

Saggus, Charles Danforth. *Agrarian Arcadia: Anglo-Virginian Planters of Wilkes County, Georgia in the 1850s.* Washington, Ga.: Mary Willis Memorial Library, 1996.

Scott, Anne Firor. *Making the Invisible Woman Visible.* Urbana: Univ. of Illinois Press, 1984.

———. *The Southern Lady: From Pedestal to Politics, 1830–1930.* Chicago: Univ. of Chicago Press, 1970.

Simkins, Francis Butler, and James W. Patton. *The Women of the Confederacy.* Richmond, Va.: Garrett and Massie, 1936.

Sims, Anastatia. *The Power of Femininity in the New South.* Columbia: Univ. of South Carolina Press, 1997.

Sniffen, Paul. *Long Branch.* Dover, N.H.: Arcadia, 1996.

Ware, Thomas. "'Equal in the Presence of Death': The Serious Absence of Grave Markers in the Finn's Point National Cemetery," paper presented at the annual convention of American Culture, San Diego, Calif., Apr. 3, 1999.

Warren, Mary Bondurant, ed. *Chronicles of Wilkes County, Georgia, from Washington's Newspapers, 1889–1898.* Danielsville, Ga.: Heritage Papers, 1978.

Whites, LeeAnn. "'Stand by Your Man': The Ladies Memorial Association and the Reconstruction of Southern White Manhood," *in Women of the American South: A Multicultural Reader,* ed. Christie Farnham New York: New York Univ. Press, 1996.

Wiley, Bell Irvin. *Confederate Women.* New York: Barnes and Noble, 1975.

Wilkes, LeeAnn. *The Civil War as a Crisis in Gender: Augusta, Georgia, 1860–1890.* Athens: Univ. of Georgia Press, 1995.

Willingham, Robert M., Jr. *No Jubilee: The Story of Confederate Wilkes.* Washington, Ga.: Wilkes Publishing, 1976.

Works Projects Administration, Writers' Program. *The Story of Washington–Wilkes.* Athens: Univ. of Georgia Press: 1941.

# Index

Abbeville, Ga., 62, 64
abolitionist, xl
Abraham, Captain Lot, 63
Acquia Creek, Va., 33
Adam Bede, 94
Adams, Corlyn, xviii
Agricultural Society, 47
Alabama Department of Agriculture, xl
Albany, Ga., 31, 68, 69, 70
Albany, N.Y., 21, 22, 23
Alexander, Frances, xviii
Alexander, General E. P., 65
Alston, Col., 39
Anderson, Mrs. (bonnet maker), 28
Andersonville, xxvi, xxxiii, xxxiv
Andrews, Annulet Ball, xix, xx, xxi, xxii, xxx, xxxii, xxxiii, xxxvii, xl, xliv, 32, 42, 43, 44, 45, 46, 47, 48, 49, 50, 51, 52, 53, 54, 55, 56, 57, 58, 59
Andrews, Champ, xii
Andrews, Col. Garnett, xi, xxv, xxvi, xxxiii, xxxvii, xli, xliv, 9, 36, 50, 59
Andrews, Cora. See Butler, Cora Andrews
Andrews, Cora Morgan, 50, 51, 52, 59
Andrews, Daniel Marshal, xxv, xl, xli, xliv, 47, 50, 54
Andrews, Dr. Henry, xxiv, xxv, xxx, xliv, 34, 50, 51, 59
Andrews, Fred. See Andrews, Major Frederick
Andrews, Garnett (great nephew), xli

Andrews, Garnett, Jr. (nephew), xiii, xli
Andrews, John, xxi
Andrews, Judge Garnett, xx, xxi, xxii, xxiv, xxv, xxx, xxxiii, xxxv, xxxvii, xl, 26, 28, 31, 34, 35, 36, 41, 42, 43, 44, 45, 46, 47, 49, 50, 52, 55, 56, 58, 59
Andrews, Major Frederick, xxv, xliv, 43, 47, 51, 54
Andrews, Margaret, xli
Andrews, Maude. See Ohl, Maude Andrews
Andrews, Metta. See Green, Metta Andrews
Andrews, Oliver, xii
Andrews, Rose (Little Rose), xxxvii, 59
Andrews, Sara Martha, xxi
Angier, 42
Antiquarian, xxvi
Army of Northwestern Virginia, xxv
Arnolds, Mrs., 38
Atala (literary heroine), 102
Atlanta, Ga., xxv, xxx, xxxviii, 28, 35, 42
Augusta, Ga., xxx, 33, 40, 64
*Augusta* (Georgia) *Chronicle,* xxxvii
Aunt Cornelia. See Pope, Cornelia Ball

Baal, xxviii
Balderstone, Caleb, 80
Ball, Corinthia, xxi
Ball, Cornelia. See Pope, Cornelia Ball

Ball, Doric Seabury, xxi
Ball, Dr. Stephen, xx
Ball, Experience. *See* Camp, Experience Ball
Ball, Frederick (grandfather), xx, xxi, xliv
Ball, Frederick (uncle), xxi
Ball, Hannah. *See* Meade, Hannah Ball
Ball, Ionic, xxi
Ball, Robert Jamison, 48, 49
Ball, Tuscan, xxi
Barnett, Annie, 50
Barnetts, 36
Beckwith, Bishop, 50
beggar, xliii, 7, 8, 10
Bell, Currer, 94
Bellini, 89
Bennett, James Gordon, 15
Berlin, Jean, xli, xlii
Bibbe County, Ga., 69
Black Crook and White Fawns, 89
Bloomfield, N.J., 10
Bolling, cousin, 59
Bon Ton, 77
Booth's Theatre, 21
*Botany All the Year Round,* xxxix
"Botany as a Recreation for Invalids," xxxviii
Bowen, Dr. Isaac, xxx
Bowen, Eliza, xxvi, xxviii, xxx, xxxi, xliv, 49
Bowen, Sara Martha Andrews, xxx
Bowery, 16
British Museum, 103
Broad St. Church, Presbyterian, 30
Broad Street, xliv, 2
Broadway, 10, 11, 12, 21, 78
Bronte, Charlotte, 94
Brooklyn, N.Y., 15, 21
Brougham, Miss (of Florida), 21
Brown, Joe, 71
Browne, Miss (of Carolina), 21
Bruen, George, 20, 30

Bruen, Leonard, 9, 30
Bruen, Leone, 30
Bruen, Mr. and Mrs. George, 26
Bruens, 13, 20
Buffalo, N.Y., 23, 24, 25
Bullock, Gov., 28, 42
Burnet, Nancy, 13
Butler, General Benjamin "Beast," 13
Butler, Cora Andrews (Fanny's older sister), xxiv, xxv, xl, 28, 50, 56, 60
Butler, Troup, xxv, xlii

Camp, Experience Ball, 13
Camp, Mr., 13
Campbell, Duncan, xxi
Canada, 23, 35
Canada, museum, 24
Canda, Charlotte (gravesite), 15, 16
Cannan, 34
carpetbaggers, 14
Cataract House, 22
Catholic cathedral, 17
Catskill Mountains, 25
Central Park, 11, 14
Centre St. Depot, 26
*Century,* xxxix
Chambers St. ferry, 26
Chapel Hill, N.C., xvii
Charleston, S.C., xi, xliv, 1, 2, 28
Charleston wharf, 2
Charlotte, N.C., 33, 62
Charlotte and Columbia route, 33
Châteaubriand, 23, 102
Chattanooga, Tenn., xxxvii, xli
Chautauqua, xxxix
*Chautauquan,* xxxix
Chenault, Dionysius, 66
Chenault, John, 66
Chenault, Miss, 67
Chenault family, 65, 66
Chesnut, Mary Boykin, xiii
chivalry, xiv
Church of the Good Shepherd at the Sand Hills, 50

Civil War, xii, xiii, xvi, xix, xxii, xxiii, xxvii, xl

Clark, George, xliv, 9, 15, 16, 26, 27, 28, 29, 30, 31

Clark, William, xliv

Clark Spool Thread Company, xliv, 4, 29

Clarke, George. *See* Clark, George

Clay County, Ga., 69

Cleopatra, 103

Colley, Mrs., 47

colored vote, 70

Columbus, Ga., 50

Confederate, xi, xii, xvi, xx, xxiv, xxv, xxvi, xxxiii, xxxiv, xxxvi, 24; eyes, 84; flag, 48; General, wife of, 90; money, 81; times, 79; treasury, 62; women, xi

*Confederate Women*, xvi

Continental Hotel, 25

Corinne (literary heroine), 93

cotton planting, xii, 29

Courtland Street, 26

cousin, Bolling, 59; Fred. *See* Pope, Fred; Hannah. *See* Meade, Hannah Ball; Henry. *See* Slaton, Henry; Hetty. *See* Robinson, Hetty; Julia. *See* Ward, Julia Bruen; Lettie. *See* Pope, Lettie; Lilla. *See* Ward, Lillian Littell; Liza. *See* Bowen, Eliza; Lucy. *See* Pope, Lucy; Morty. *See* Ward, Mortimer; Nancy. *See* Burnet, Nancy; Peri. *See* Camp, Experience Ball; Robert. *See* Ball, Robert Jamison; Sarah. *See* Littell, Sarah; Southern, 6; Thom. *See* Pope, Thom; Will. *See* Pope, Will

cracker, xlii

Cretan Minotaur, xxvii

Cuffee, 71, 72, 74

Dallas, Tex., xxxix

Dalton, George, xxxii, xxxiv, 41, 46

Danburg, Wilkes County, Ga., 65

Davie, Doris, xvi

Davis, Jefferson, xii, xxv, xxvi

Davis, Mrs. Jefferson, 66

Dayton, Col., 67

de Staël, Mme., xxxvi, 93

dead line, xxxiv

Delavan House, 22

Delmonicos, 21

Democrat, 27

Democratic candidates, 34

Democrats, 27, 29, 71

*Detroit Free Press*, xxx

Dinah, 72, 74

Donizette, 89

Dorcas, 57

dual-gender, xvi

DuBose family, xxii

DuBose, General Dudley, 34, 36, 38

Dunwoody's, 40

Dutch Reformed, 18

Eagle Rock, 14

Ecumenical Council, 17

Edings, baby, 39

Edings, Julian, 37

Edings, Mr., 40

Edingses, 40

Edwards, Capt., 36

Elbert and Hart, 41

Ellington, Mrs., 55, 56, 57

Elliott, George, 94

Elzey, General Arnold, xxvi

Elzey, Mrs. Arnold, 59

Elzey, Touch, xxvi, 59

emancipated slaves, xxvii

entitles, 71

Episcopalian, 2, 12, 17, 18, 37

Erie R. R., 25

Erwin, Captain John T., 34

Fanny Fern, 99

Farnham, Christie Anne, xx

father. *See* Andrews, Judge Garnett

Faust, Drew, xv
Fifth Avenue, 10, 13, 15, 21
Florida, xxxviii, xxxix, 21, 50
Ford, Charlotte, xviii
Ford, Dr. of Augusta, xi, 1
Fort Sumter, 1
*Forum*, xxxix
Fourteenth Street, 10
Four-thousand, The, xxii, xxxiv
France, 15, 102, 103
Francis, Captain, xi, 1, 2, 25
Frankfort, xxxix
*French Leslie*, 82
Fulton Street, 28

Ganch's Restaurant, 10
Garden Club of Rome, Ga., xl
Gardner, Miss, 4, 9, 11, 12, 17
*Garibaldi*, 77, 78, 80
Garrick, 89, 90
Garthwaites, 13
Genoa, xxxix
Georgia: Abbeville, 62, 64; Albany, 31,
    68, 69, 70; Atlanta, xxx, xxxviii,
    28, 35, 42; Augusta, xxx, 33, 40,
    64; Bibbe County, 69; Clay County,
    69; Columbus, 50; crackers, 9; Dan-
    burg, 65; Hart County, 37; Macon,
    xxxix, 69; Regulars, xxv; Rome, xl,
    xli; Savannah, xx, xxi, xxv, 64;
    Smyrna, 39; Sumter County, 69;
    Tallulah Falls, 23; Washington,
    xvii, xviii, xxi, xxii, xxiv, xxv, xxvi,
    xxx, xxxviii, xxxix, xliii, xliv, 33,
    36, 61, 62, 63, 64, 65, 67, 98, 99;
    Wilkes County, xviii
Georgia Teachers Association, xxxviii
Gidell, 37
Gift, Belle (of Albany), 31
Gnoguchamna, N.Y., 25
Goat Island, 23
*Godey's Lady's Book*, xv, xxvii, 74, 77,
    82, 99

Goethe, 89
Goode, Nancy, xxi
Goode, Richard, xxi
Grace Church, 9
Grant, Gen. Ulysses S., xii, 91
Great Pacific R.R., 49
Greeley, Horace, 30
Green, Metta Andrews, xxii, xxiv,
    xxv, xxxi, xxxviii, xliv, 1, 5, 6, 8,
    9, 11, 12, 14, 17, 18, 22, 28, 30,
    34, 35, 36, 39, 40, 42, 43, 45, 46,
    47, 49, 50, 51, 52, 53, 54, 59
Green, Theodrick, xxii, xxxviii
Greens Grove, xxii
Greenwood Cemetery, 15, 16
Groton Reservoir, 11, 21

Hamlet, 35
Hampton (family name), 28
Hampton, Wade, 106
Hanson, Mrs. Ellen, 21
Harfleur, Claude, 46
Harfleur, Nettie, xxxii, xxxiii
Harfleur, Ruth, xxxii, xxxiii, xxxvi, 46
Harris, William, 34
Hart County, Ga., 37
Hatteras, 1
Hay, Dr. Gilbert, xxii
Hay, Elzey, xv, xxvi, xxvii, 74, 84, 98,
    99
Haywood, xxii, xxiii, xxiv, xxv, xxvi,
    xxxviii, 3, 12, 19, 38
Herostratus, 90
Hicks, Mr. (editor), 10
Hively, Virginia R., xvi
Hobbs, xliv, 10, 11, 15, 21, 22, 25, 36
Hoboken, N.Y., 26
Hogue, Mrs., 48
homespun, 76, 77, 80, 81, 82, 106
House of Prayer, 12, 18
Howell, 30
Howell, Lizzie, 26, 27, 28
Howells, Mr. and Mrs., 26

Hoxey, Elza, xxi
Hudson River, xxxv, 21, 22
Huguenot Church of Charleston,
    S.C., 2
Hunter, Mrs., 36, 37, 40
Hunter, Rev., 36, 50
Hunter children, 37
Hunters, 36

International Academy of Literature
    and Science, xl
Irish, 29, 30
Irish woman, 8
Irvin, Charles, 34
Irvin family, xxii
Italy, xl, xli, 102

Jackson, Gen. H. R., xxv
Jenning's linen sheet, 31
Jersey City, N.J., 2, 26
Jones, Mary Lou, xvi
Juliet, 90
Juvenal, 99

Keene, Mr. (of Augusta), 9
King, Spencer Bidwell, xv
King of the Terrors, 53
Knickerbocker family, 11
Knowles, xi, 1, 2
Know-nothing, xx
*Kohinoor*, 105
Ku Klux Klan, 33, 34

lace, 17, 28; black, 82; black thread,
    30; Brussels point, 5; Chantilly, 79;
    exquisite, 27; flounces, 79; gold,
    80; llama, 38; mitts, 77; point, 3, 9,
    12, 28, 30, 31; print, 38; shawl, 16;
    Valenciennes, 3, 77; Venice point,
    xxxv; white, 39
LaGrange College, xxiv
Lake Erie, 2, 4
Lazarus (at the gate of Dives), 10

*Ledger*, 10
Lee, General Robert E., xii, 20, 106
Legriel, Lilla, 35, 37
*Les Miserables*, 50
Leslie, Mr., 13
Lincoln court, 45
Lind, Jenny, 89
Littell, Elizabeth Ball, xliv
Littell, Hobart, xliv
Littell, Matilda Ball, xliv, 19
Littell, Sarah, 9, 33
Little Miss Mag. *See* Andrews,
    Margaret
Liverpool, xxxix
Llewellyn Park, 14
Long Branch, N.J., 18
Lord Wodenhouse, 23
lords of creation, xxxi, 68, 73, 99
Loyal League, 68, 72
Lubin's extracts, 11
Lucretia Borgia, 103
Lumpkin, 59

Macbeth, Lady, 90
Macon, Ga., xxxix, 69
Macon & Brunswick and Atlantic &
    Gulf R.R., 49
Macon Mills, 82
Macys, 9
*Madame Demorest*, 82
Madison Square, xxxv
Magna Carta, 35
Major-General Bagpipe, Mrs., xxxv
Malvern, Audley, xxxii, xxxiv, xxxv,
    41, 45
Malvern, Julia, xxxii, xxxv, xxxvi, 41
mammy, 74, 76
Manhattan (steamship), 2, 21
manufacturers, rich, xii, 29
*Marguerite*, 90
Market Street Methodist Church, 17
Marriage, xxx, 36
Marxian theory, xl

Mary of Scotland, 103
Maston, 64
Mattox, Mrs., 43
Maxwell, Annie, 40
Meade, Hannah Ball, 13
Memphis, Tenn., xii
Mercer family, xxii
Mexican, 102
Mexico, xl, 102
Micon, Ben, 59
Middleville, N.J., 19
Mill, John Stuart, 91, 92
Millbank prison, 74
Miller, Ella, 30
Miller, Hugh, 50
Miller, Joe, 41
Miller girls, 3
Miller home, 13
Millers, 30
Milton, 94, 101
Mississippi: farmlands, xxxvii; law
    practice, xxxvii; lawyers, xxxvii;
    legislature, xxxvii; plantation,
    xxxvii; Yazoo City, xxxvii, xxxviii
Montclair, N.J., 10
Montgomery, Ala., xl, 60
Montrose, N.J., 8
Moree, Mrs., 66
Morgan, Cora. *See* Andrews, Cora
    Morgan
Morgan, Mattie, xiii, xix, xxxvi, 37,
    40, 50, 51
Morgan, Mr., 43, 51, 59
mother. *See* Andrews, Annulet Ball
Moultrie, 1
Mowatt, Mrs., 89
Mt. Enon, xlii
Muller, Mrs., 37
*My Schools and Masters*, 50

Nash, Belle, 36
negro, xxvii, xxviii, xxix, xxxiii, 1, 5,
    34, 66, 67, 71, 73, 74; clothing, 82;

emancipation, 30; fondness for
    noise, 68; language, 70; marksmen,
    69; mob, 71; with gun, 69
negroes, xxvii, xlii, 22, 29, 30, 33, 34,
    62, 66, 69, 70, 71, 72, 73, 76, 106
New England, xxviii
New England women, xxviii
New Hampshire, xxviii
New Haywood, xxii
New Jersey: Bloomfield, 10; early set-
    tlers, xx; Jersey City, 2, 26; Long
    Branch, 18; Middleville, 19; Mont-
    clair, 10; Montrose, 8; Newark, xi,
    xii, xv, xx, xxvii, xliii, xliv, 2, 5, 8,
    9, 12, 13, 14, 19, 21, 26, 28, 31,
    33; Orange, 8; Passaic, 3
New York, 22, 61, 68; Albany, 21,
    22, 23; Brooklyn, 15, 21; Buffalo,
    23, 24, 25; Gnoguchamna, 25;
    Hoboken, 26; Niagara Falls, 23,
    25; Rochester, 22, 23; shopping,
    30; shops, 9; Syracuse, 22, 23;
    visiting, 28
New York Central R.R., 22
New York City, xxxix, 21; beggars,
    xliii; boarding ship for, xliv; Cen-
    tral Park, 14; friends, delayed in,
    32; going to, 4; harbor, 2; Hobbs,
    visiting in, 10; merchant; 79; mer-
    chant, property of, 8; newspapers,
    99; rich man's tomb, 16; shopping,
    9, 11, 12; shopping alone, 12; tour-
    ing, 15; visiting, 15, 16, 21, 26, 30;
    winter things arrived from, 50
*New York Weekly*, 10, 28
*New York World*, xiv, xxvii, 25, 26, 61,
    68, 99
Newark, N.J., xi, xii, xv, xx, xxvii,
    xliii, xliv, 2, 5, 8, 9, 12, 13, 14, 19,
    21, 26, 28, 31, 33
Niagara, Canadian Falls, 23
Niagara Falls, 21, 22, 23, 25, 26, 44
Niagara River, 24

Norman, Sue, 47
Northern industrialism, xl
Northern manufacturing, xi
*Notable American Women*, xvi

Ohl, Maude Andrews, xiii, 40, 50
Orange, N.J., 8

Pacific Railroad, 70
Palisades, 22
Paradise Lost, 94
Paris made dress, 27
Paris *salons*, xxxv
Parmelie, Charley, 21
Passaic, N.J., 3
patriarchal, xv, xliii
Patten House, xli
Patton Seminary for Girls, xxxix
Peck, Mr., 13
pedestal, xiv, 15
Phelps, Mr., xi, 1, 2, 4, 10, 13, 30,
    31, 32
Philadelphia merchant, 79
piazzas, 4
Pine Wood, 68
Pneumatic Railway, 16, 21
policemen, 12
Pope, Cornelia Ball, 28, 36, 43, 52, 56
Pope, Fred, 50
Pope, General, 70
Pope, Lettie, 36, 43, 56
Pope, Lucy, 43, 48, 56
Pope, Thom, 43
Pope, Will, 57
*Popular Science Monthly*, xxxviii
Potomac, 32, 33, 105
*Practical Course in Botany*, xxxix
Presbyterian: Broad St. Church,
    30; church, 12; grim, 17; sermon,
    12, 17
Presbyterians, 36
Professor at the Breakfast Table, 105
Promulgation of Infallibility, 17

public decency, 89
public life, 90
public opinion, 85, 87, 89, 94, 97, 99

Queen Elizabeth, 91, 101
Queen of Scots, 101
Queen Victoria, 90

Radical, 5, 21, 29; awful, 26; doc-
    trines, 10; editor, 71; majority, 71;
    politicians, xxvii
Randolph, 28
Raymond, Ida, xxxi, 98
Reconstruction, xi, xv, xxvi, xxvii,
    xxxvii, xli, xliii
Reconstruction Act, 70
Reitt, Barbara, xxxi
Republican, 27
Republicans, xii; Radicals, 4, 10, 14,
    29, 30, 69, 71, 73; ticket, 68, 71,
    73; vote, 70
Resthaven Cemetery, xl
Rhine castles, 28
Rhine of America, 22
rich tradesman, 5
Richmond, Va., 33, 60, 64
Richmond Hosiery Company, xli
riot, 33, 34, 62, 90
Rip Van Winkle, 21
Ristori, 89
Robertsons, 36
Robinson, Hetty, 13
Rochester, N.Y., 22, 23
Romanism, 17
Romanists, 55
Rome, Ga., xl, xli

Salt Lake City, Utah, 49
San Francisco, Calif., 49
Sand, George, 94
Sandy Hook, 2
*Saturday Review*, 92´
Saunders, Wilkes, 39

Savannah, Ga., xx, xxi, xxv, 64
Savannah River, 64
Saxon, 100
Scott, Anne Firor, xvi, xix, xxxvii
Scott, little prig, 13
Scott, Walter, xi, 1, 4
*Scott's Monthly Magazine*, xxxii, 84, 99
Seabury, xx, xxi, 5
Seabury, Bishop Samuel, xx
Seminary, xxxviii, xxxix, 45, 47
Semmes, 28
separate-spheres, xv
Shakespeare, 89
Sheridan, 90
Sherman, General William T., xxv
Sherman's army, 30
shoppies, xii, 9, 18, 29
Siddons, Mrs., 89, 90
Simmons, Mr., of Atlanta, 35
Sixth Avenue, 9, 10, 11
Slaton, Cornelia, 38
Slaton, Frank, 38
Slaton, Henry, 34, 38, 39, 40
slave culture, xli
slaveholder, xl
slavery: African, xl; chattel, xl;
  wage, xl
slaves, former, 68
Smyrna, Ga., 39
soldiering, xii, 29
Southern: aristocracy, xi, xii, xv, xix,
  xxxiv, xliii; associates, 12; belle,
  xx; boards, 7; Confederacy, xv, xli;
  cousins, 6; culture, xvi, xxii; Judge,
  27, 28; manners, 6, 30; politics, 30;
  rivers, 22; schoolrooms, xliii; superiority, 18; sympathizers, 4; traveling companions, 8; ways, 6
*Southern Magazine*, 37
Southerner, good and tall, 12
Southerners, 14
*Southland Writers*, 98

Spain, 102
Spool Cotton Clarke. *See* Clark,
  George
spool thread, xii, 29
St. Germain, Fauborge, 84
St. John's Episcopal Church, Newark,
  25
St. Paul's Episcopal Church, Chat-
  tanooga, xli
Steamboat Daniel Drew, 21
Steedman, General, 67
Stephens, Alexander, 35
Stephens family, xxii
Stern Bros., 28
Stevens, Senator Thad, 73, 74
Stewart, Faith, xvi
Stewarts, 10, 21, 37
Stoke Poges, 16
Stratford-on-Avon, xxxix
street musicians, 7
suffrage, xxviii, xxix, 73
Sumner, Senator Charles, 74
Sumter, S.C., 1
Sumter County, Ga., 69
Sunday School, xlii
Syracuse, N.Y., 22, 23

Tallulah Falls, Ga., 23
Taylor, 64, 65
Taylors Restaurant, 12, 16
Tennessee River, xli
Terrys, 36
Thackeray, 17, 99
Thayer, Mrs., 9
"The Novel as a Work of Art," 37
Thomas, Judge, 41
Tilbury, 91
Tittle-Titmouse, 102
Tittlebat Titmouse, 103
Tombs, 16
Toombs, Robert, 63
Toombs, Willie, 34

Toombs family, xxii
Tower of London, 26
Trinity Church, 8, 17, 18
Trotwood, Betsy, xxvi
Tupper, Mrs., 60
Tupper, the Rev. Mr. Henry Allen, 1,
    52, 53, 57
Tuppers, 60
Tuscan Hall, xx, 19

Uncle Bruen, xxxii, 46
United Daughters of the Confederacy,
    xl, xli
Upper Suspension Bridge, 24
Uriah Heep, 102

vagabonds, 7
Valley Forge, xx
Van Antwerp, Mr. and Mrs., 14
Vedder, Dr. Charles Stuart, 2
Venice, xxxix
Virginia: banks, 64; colonists, xxi;
    family, 5; Winchester, 90
Virginia Springs, 36
Volkes, 8

Waddey home, 35
Wall Street, 16
Walthour, Bessie, 36
*War-time Journal,* xii, xiii, xiv, xv,
    xxxiii, xli, xlii, 1
Ward, Julia Bruen, 4, 8, 9, 11, 14, 20,
    21, 26, 32
Ward, Lillian Littell, xliv, 2, 3, 4, 5, 6,
    7, 9, 10, 11, 17, 18, 19, 21, 31, 32, 33
Ward, Mortimer, 2, 4, 6, 8, 9, 12, 26,
    28, 31, 32
Ward, Richmond, xliv, 4, 7, 11, 32
Wary, Mrs., 47
Washington, D.C., 33
Washington, Ga., xvii, xviii, xxi, xxii,
    xxiv, xxv, xxvi, xxx, xxxviii, xxxix,
    xliii, xliv, 33, 36, 61, 62, 63, 64,
    65, 67, 98, 99
Washington, General George, xx
Washington Academy, xxiii
Washington and Lee, xii
Washington Female Seminary, xxiii,
    xxxi, xxxvii, xxxviii
*Washington Gazette,* xxvi, xxviii, xxx,
    xxxviii, 10
Weed, Rector, 50
Weissinger, 64, 65
Wesleyan Female College, xxxix
*Westminster Review,* xxviii, 50
Wheeler and Wilson, 50
White House, xii
*Who's Who,* xl
Wild, General, 66, 67
Wiley, Bell Irvin, xvi
Wilkes County, Ga., xviii, xxiii, xxv,
    xxxi
Wilkes County Courthouse, xxi
Winchester, Va., 90
Woman's Rights, 91, 99
Wynn, Sam, xxxv, 36, 37, 40

*XIX Century,* 10

Yankee: in the aggregate, 14; beaus, 9;
    by birth, 37; blockade, 83; brogue,
    21; cousins, xi; d——d, xxxiv;
    decent, 14; fashion, 25; goods, 75;
    guard, 67; he-, 2; heaven, 13; hos-
    pitality, 2, 19, 32; housekeeping, 6,
    7; humor, 6; invading, xxvi; kin,
    xi, 3, 14; ladies and gentlemen, 6;
    lingo, 2, 5, 9; looks, 8; manufactur-
    ing, 8; money loving, 22; nation,
    15; nicest, 13; nose, 27; passengers,
    2; primness, 2; relatives, xvi; rich,
    4; scale, 7; schedules, 23; servants,
    14; sharp, 7; shoppy, 27; shot
    and shell, 90; society, 6, 8, 12;

Yankee (*continued*)
  soldier, 63; spy, xxxiv; swells, 13; tact, 31, 32; talk, 32; thankful not one, 31; trick, 12, 25; vulgar minded, 26; vulgarity, 32; Washington garrison, 33; way, 7; yacht victory, 2

Yankeedom, 23
Yankeeism, 9
Yankees, 14, 30, 33, 62, 63; good to us, 31; negroes better than, 22; have Niagara Falls, 23; and Rebels rejoicing, 67; respect for, 67
Yazoo City, Miss., xxxvii, xxxviii